Die
Hot
with a
Vengeance

Die Hot with a Vengeance

ESSAYS ON VANITY

Sable Yong

DEYST.

An Imprint of WILLIAM MORROW

DEYST.

HarperCollins books may be purchased for educational, business, or sales promotional use. For information, please email the Special Markets Department at SPsales@harpercollins.com.

FIRST EDITION

Design and illustrations by Jennifer Chung
Photographs on page v courtesy of the author

Library of Congress Cataloging-in-Publication Data has been applied for.

ISBN 978-0-06-323648-6

24 25 26 27 28 LBC 5 4 3 2 1

For her

Contents

Die
Hot
with a
Vengeance

To Be or Not to Be (Perceived)

Do you live in a body? Is your consciousness confined to an electrified meat sack propped up by a scaffolding of hardened calcium and muscle tension? Do you ever think about the shape of your head, the texture of the hair that grows out of it, the size of your torso, or the constant codependency of your thighs against one another and wonder, *What's the deal with all that?* Do you spend so much of your time trying to find your best angles, or changing your body in ways that some would consider altering "God's" plan?

Well, you're not alone! If you answered yes to any of the above questions, you most definitely live in a body. And let me tell you that I, and many others in our situation, are thinking about being incarcerated in these vulnerable, fleshy encasements nearly *all the time*. How it requires adequate nutrition, sleep, water, proper attire (environmentally and socially), and it's never quite right, even when it is functioning the way it's meant to. And the decor, *my God*, the decorating. It is a lifelong endeavor to be in a body.

This is the sort of thing I think about all the time, not only as a person in a body but as a member of the decorating committee: aka a beauty editor. I've held this position for many years, first entering the beauty blogosphere in the early days of the internet's personal essay era, writing about my head and face and what I was putting on them for any beauty publication that would have me. I kept at it until I made my way to one of the most illustrious media publishing houses in the world, Condé Nast, and nabbed a plum role as a beauty editor at *Allure* (the self-proclaimed "Beauty Authority"). Along with a team of other beauty professionals, I investigated, researched, experimented, and attempted to re-blueprint the blueprints for Beauty™ as I navigated its often confusing (if not very glamorous) and fickle constructs. And I made it to the top of the tower[*] in good timing too, considering how the beauty industry has become a juggernaut, valued at an unfathomable amount of money—over \$571 billion[†] globally in 2023. Beauty now even has its own seasons (holiday, festival, and awards), merchandising cultural events as quickly as they happen, and contributing 120 billion units of packaging waste per year.[‡] Even if you adamantly don't believe in beauty culture, it's not that simple; it's been integrated into our lives way before our original chromosomes paired up. It is everywhere, even if you don't see it—kind of like dust mites. Mostly what I mean is, beauty is embedded in the ways we are socialized to value people, so that makes it kind of a big issue. That someone like me, non-pedigreed, allergic to corporate work environments, and generally uncooperative, chose to enter this house of mirrors as a professional meant that I unwittingly took a detour into my own unexamined vanity, delusions and all—something I was never going to see from the outside. Understanding the back end of how the beauty industry works makes it a lot less intimidating, but it also dulls the glamour as well. In some ways, the least stressful way to engage with beauty requires a bit of dream-crushing (sorry). Like when you're a kid and you find

---

[*]   Of One World Trade, where the office was.
[†]   "Beauty & Personal Care," Statista, updated September 2023, https://www.statista.com/outlook/cmo/beauty-personal-care/worldwide#:~:text=Revenue%20in%20the%20Beauty%20%26%20Personal,(CAGR%202023%2D2027).
[‡]   Jennifer Okafor, "Environmental Impacts of Cosmetics & Beauty Products," Trvst, updated February 14, 2023, https://www.trvst.world/sustainable-living/environmental-impact-of-cosmetics/#:~:text=According%20to%20the%20latest%20reports,in%20landfills%20year%20after%20year.

out Santa isn't real (Christian or not, he's still a big figure dominating holiday culture). You can finally stop trying to wrap your head around how one old dude flies around the world in less than twenty-four hours and enters your house through the fireplace, which is most definitely sealed shut permanently. And then you can appreciate the effort your parents put in every year for you to have a magical Christmas (after being so pissed at them for lying to you for so long). Something like that.

When I was growing up, makeup and hair dye were forbidden fruit in my house. Naturally, this only made attaining them my number one objective, and my deep longing to participate in the glamour of beauty's self-making instilled a drive within myself to make it to the ugly-duckling-to-swan pipeline as hastily as possible. By the time my parental cosmetic embargo lifted, I had a lot of catching up to do! It's not like coming of age in the early 2000s was forgiving toward those who didn't fulfill all of beauty's feminine imperatives. Not that any of that stopped me; beauty was the Juliet to my Romeo (without the whole marriage-suicide thing in the end) and I obsessively pored over the beauty pages of every teen and women's magazines I could get my hands on (the internet wasn't as Pinteresting at that time in history). Analog as it was, beauty was very much so shoved down our throats—a much narrower kind of beauty than today's visions ("diversity" referred more to the abundance of ice cream flavors at Baskin-Robbins than to the faces you'd see in media). I pilfered the gift-with-purchase minis from my mom's department store makeup buys (a habit that would extend to certain beauty shelves themselves in my "rebellious" adolescence). My mom went from grounding me (more than once) for attempting to box dye my hair when I was a teenager to now texting me product requests for La Prairie, Shiseido, and Clé de Peau with regularity. I suppose if I had gotten it out of my system when I was younger, perhaps I wouldn't be such a beauty fiend as I am today, but who can say? Beauty always has been a symbol of self-expression to me—something I wasn't aware of back then, even if I would go to devious lengths to participate in it. My still-gelatinous prefrontal cortex understood that beauty was a way to freedom, even if I wasn't sure what that freedom was at the time. But I've gradually grown with that idea, redefining it again and again to shape the person I hoped to be.

Though it wasn't initially my career goal, becoming a beauty editor granted me an all-access backstage pass to every part of the beauty industry. It's the kind of career that grants you free neurotoxin injectables, $800 face creams and serums delivered to your door with the regularity and speed of Amazon Prime (also free), and as much Victoria's Secret Angel–looking balayage and hair extensions a human head can bear—but not so much in terms of livable wages and work-life balance. Imagine being sent on lavish trips to exotic locales, having a perpetually stocked home of designer fragrances, luxury beauty products, and expensive high-tech devices, and still feeling the need to financially negotiate between organic and generic produce at the grocery store (sorry to ruin the fantasy, but nothing is less glamorous than corporate budget cuts).

For everyone else *not* writing investigative stories about how beauty rumors like semen as an acne treatment get started or interviewing Juggalos about their makeup routines,[*] beauty can feel a lot more . . . prescriptive. Our collective anguish or annoyance with beauty is in its eternal expectation, something you're meant to strive for at all times—and all costs. For half the population, it's even come to define our value as people entirely. Before the digital age, it might've been easier to avoid the constant visuals and pressures, but the way people engage with beauty now has become a voyeuristic sport in and of itself. Influencers literally have careers built from their looks (they're like models if models . . . actually, a lot of them *are* models). The gorilla grip beauty has on us today is nothing short of pathological. We speed-

---

[*] I'm pretty sure that's still on YouTube somewhere.

jumped into a whole new digital age that's all but totally redefined our culture, as we're scrambling to understand it while keeping up with its continuous current. And as far as I can tell from my doom-scrolling scriptures, we're more concerned with our looks than ever.

Perhaps this wouldn't be so fraught if our bodies and faces weren't constantly subject to feedback from those around us about their shape and condition (and if our appearance wasn't conflated to represent our entire being and essence). But when it comes to bodies, it seems that every entity—your peers, family members, partners, colleagues, and corporate companies that like to pretend they're your friend—is incapable of letting people simply . . . exist as is. I'm sure many of you have noticed how beauty is suddenly everywhere, spawning new "trends" by the minute, and infiltrating every kind of way you can be in a body. Wellness, as it turns out, has not found us well.

I, for one, have spent so much of my early life feeling like a weirdo because I didn't look "right," and I didn't know how to correct it in a way that didn't feel totally humiliating and futile. It's a stupid way to live! Vanity's paradox is such that the effort we put into beauty often undermines its validity or merit—every makeover is one smear away from comedy or one botched surgery away from tragedy. Participating in today's beauty culture can feel like you're a politician avoiding a hot-button issue. Talking about beauty now is so full of contradictions it feels impossible to reconcile without shunning your own desires and pleasures—which are often far too complicated to extricate from beauty—or shunning beauty culture altogether. The demands to self-optimize at all costs and the growing pressures to resist beauty culture are reaching *West Side Story* levels of beef. But beauty doesn't solve Beauty™ when its standards and ideals remain as our North Star. It's a paradox that some are content to sit out and some can't get past. I have a personal investment in this because as time goes on, I'm not getting any less weird—the opposite, in fact. And I'd like to live well into my weirdness, rather than constantly contend with the labor of palatability just so I can, you know, be seen as a person deserving basic respect and human kindness. I would love it if we could untether our value as individuals from our appearances. Which brings us to where we are now.

This is not a self-help book or a guide in the traditional sense. There are plenty of books out there about how to improve your skin or get shiny hair (I've written a bunch of articles on the internet about those kinds of things). What I'm more interested in is how beauty and vanity can be meaningful for us now. How can we engage in beauty that isn't at odds with how we see ourselves, that prioritizes care and compassion, and celebrates our unique personhood rather than conforming to a hegemonic ideal? How can we parse through the cultural, social, and financial implications of feeding into these systems? What if, in doing that, we stopped thinking of beauty as a mandate and instead considered it an experience, a language of expression and self-exploration?

At its best, beauty culture is a way of communing with others, caring for yourself, and connecting how you want to be perceived and who you wish to signal to with your appearance. Having a pleasant experience with beauty is possible when you engage with it on your own terms, and hopefully, by the time you're done reading this book, the harmful cultural and social messages surrounding beauty will seem so much less relevant to your own definition of it. As Newton's secret seventh law states: a body in beauty stays in beauty until a greater force intervenes. The choices we are so generously given now (by the same oppressive models that previously narrowed them when that worked best for their bottom line) all tend to further the existing rationality, despite the modern sentiment of "doing it for yourself." How much can these choices free us from those overbearing standards we claim to reject when they are given by those same manipulative, dominating forces?

If there is "true beauty" to be found, it must be lived through. It cannot be sourced exclusively from an almighty algorithm of filtered, perfected, and decontextualized beauty images on social media (or more troubling, AI). Experience lends context and nuance to all the ways that beauty touches our lives. And my experiences have taught me that it isn't all a bummer (even though, as you'll read, some of them are very, very unpleasant). Beauty is just one way to reflect our inner selves outward as a means of creative communication. Our bodies are nothing if not robust, entertaining, funny, awkward, and often a vulnerable access point to connection—to ourselves and to others. Let's not throw the beauty out with the bathwater . . . or something like that. After all, the beauty you see around you is a reflection of the beauty within you.

Confessions of a Late Bloomer

I was born in the mid-eighties, when hair height was arguably at its highest, and spinning letters on a word-guessing game show was the most glamourous job in America. This was before you had to take your shoes off when going through security at the airport, before oats had been milked, and the only algorithms that mattered were the ones you manually programmed into your TI-84 calculator for algebra class.

Pop culture, fashion, and beauty news came directly from television and magazines. Whoever was on the cover of *People* magazine or starring in *Beverly Hills, 90210* and *Saved by the Bell* were a big part of determining who was Hot™ at the time. But there weren't many tabloids or fashion magazines around my house; the coffee table in our living room was mostly occupied by my dad's auto mechanic catalogs. My TV consumption was generally capped at one hour a day, which was usually spent on *The Simpsons* and after-school (or Saturday morning) cartoons. I watched a *lot* of cartoons. You may not assume that cartoons could have such an outsize influence on children, but they do. It doesn't matter how wacky or clearly unrealistic they are, they compounded one idea in my head more than any *People* magazine "Sexiest Person of the Year" issue could at the time: the power of beauty. As far as my (circa) six-year-old brain knew, beauty was a girl's superpower—it made everyone around her fall at her feet, or, at the very least, made their eyeballs pop out of their heads.

There was one cartoon character in particular who was the epitome, the uncontested queen, and the indelible face of beauty. She never fell for the flatterers and simps, she had a heart of gold, and was deeply in love with her paramour: a wrongly accused fugitive who adored her and made her laugh throughout all the trials and tribulations of escaping the law while uncovering the real villain—together, they were the Bonnie and Clyde of Toontown. During the most annoying parts of elementary school, any time kids would make fun of my name, or when I felt judged for looking and being *different* from what was being served through mainstream television and marketing, I looked to her as a beacon. What I wanted—what I thought would spare me the ridicule—was to change my name to *her* name.

Yes, I'm talking about Jessica Rabbit.

It's one thing to say you want to change your name to a cartoon character, and it's another to want to *be* that character, but to me at the time those two things were synonymous (these are the kinds of semantics that escape the grasp of a kindergartener). But what I really wanted was what Jessica Rabbit had: great hair and a jaw-dropping command over an entire room. I may not have understood the nuances or historical context of it at all, but I knew that her beauty gave her power. Who wouldn't want that? Beauty was the way to be desired, which was the way to attain that kind of power, and as I'd soon learn, beauty was the top priority for girls to spend their whole lives pursuing.

The things you watch as a kid have a profound impact on how you see the world, and every TV show or film had a hot girl character (mostly because every show or film centered around a straight dude with a horny character arc—hello, *Johnny Bravo*). There is no questioning of exaggerated femininity with cartoons. Lola Bunny from *Space Jam*, Roxanne from *A Goofy Movie*, and Holli Would in *Cool World*. The hot betta fish from *Fantasia*? Devastating beauty! The mean-girl mermaids in the Disney animated *Peter Pan* were the epitome of glamour to me. Even the antagonist of *Gremlins 2* was a hot girl gremlin with false lashes, extra-plush lips, and an animal-print bikini for some added villainous glamour.

The difference between cartoons and tabloids was the sheer exaggeration of femininity. The exaggeration of everything, really! Everything can be more dramatic or done-up in a cartoon. It becomes secondary influence, especially with the added intrigue that cartoons often gender animals to be feminized—or rather that anything and anyone can be run through the femininity wash to become undeniably and robustly gorgeous. Caricaturized femininity really drove home the sexualized beauty narrative in my developing little brain. Even when *To Wong Foo, Thanks for Everything! Julie Newmar* (I cannot believe they got to keep that movie title) was released in 1995, and I had no inkling of the concept of drag queens (I was literally nine), John Leguizamo's Chi-Chi Rodriguez taught me more about the impact of a flattering neckline and working a décolleté than in all the subsequent pages of *Vogue* I'd flip through later. It wasn't until the uncomfortable dress-up scene in *The Professional** (released in 1994, but I didn't get around to watching it until I was a freshman in high school), when a then-eleven-year-old Natalie Portman cooed "Happy Birthday" to Léon dressed as Marilyn Monroe with a face decorated (entirely too well for a child) in blue eyeshadow, black winged eyeliner, and red lipstick, that the theatrical portrayal of overly sexualized femininity on young girls tilted glamour into queasy territory for me.†

But those cartoon babes came off as powerful and dominant, and also sometimes violent and destructive—basically the gendered inverse of all the dude baddies in the movies. Holli Would in *Cool World* nearly destroyed multiple dimensions after using her beauty to manipulate men into aiding her ambitions.‡ When you illustrate beauty

---

* Or *Léon*, en français.
† Even though I understand that that is likely very normal behavior for any eleven-year-old girl (who grew up absorbing mainstream media) with a crush and no sense of what sexuality actually entails. When you're a kid, sexuality feels like the most grown-up thing, which makes it the most tantalizing concept to play at.
‡ The plot of *Cool World* is wacky, but Kim Basinger's performance is still to this day mesmerizingly camp.

through the clownish lens of animation, the violence and danger of it is removed of consequence and fatality. Eyeballs pop out of heads, jaws hit the floor, tongues drop from mouths and roll out like a red carpet, and yet the danger of desirability is never addressed, probably because it's mostly horny dudes drawing a male fantasy of the voyeurism they've always felt entitled to. The message (if you can even call it that) becomes a psychedelic overdose of oversexualization, often a racialized misogyny, and beauty standards concentrated into figures as unrealistic as the standards themselves. (Try explaining that to an eight-year-old who still thinks babies are delivered by storks.) Basically, the truth of beauty's reputation and value for women isn't flattened, so much as it is bluntly amplified in 2D—and without a healthy dose of cultural criticism, it's easy to absorb the messaging at face value. Thinking back on it now, my obsession with cartoons taught me that, yes, beauty is power, but also that being beautiful is an ideal life in and of itself.

Beauty felt out of range for me as a kid. I was Asian in a mostly all-white school, I had an unusual name, and I would sometimes bring "exotic" food for lunch.* I had no resilience for any sort of criticism, or micro- or macro-aggression. I viewed everything that was "different" about me as a potential target for criticism and ridicule, and beauty seemed like the most effective way to both inure myself against potential bullies and secure my own stakes in the social hierarchy of desirability that existed in my head then. (I mean, it's not that different to how many people use beauty today. Kids really do pick up on things quickly.)

My mom still remembers how I wanted to change my name when I was little. "You wanted to be named *Jessica*, HAH!" This was a hilarious

---

* All of which is apparently very cool now.

punch line to her. To be fair, having the name Sable in a school full of Jennifers, Amandas, Caitlins, and yeah, even a few Jessicas, was something that had to constantly be repeated and explained. That's a lot of emotional labor for a kid, you know? It's not like we were cognizant of social nuances like microaggressions then. Looking back on childhood photos now, I think, *What's the big deal? You were a kid, all kids looked like that, so what!* My awkwardness is palpable in old photos, but it's the kind of unsure, gangly self-carriage of youth that lots of kids pass through, sometimes a few times. It's not that I didn't have friends or wasn't well-liked, but I also remember being so much more focused on being likable than being myself.

The value of appearances was something I was steadily made aware of during childhood. I could not be introduced to an adult at the time without a comment being made about my appearance—they weren't mean, of course, it's not like a grown-up is going to diss a kid to their face—but still. Some kids lap up that kind of attention and some kids cringe and shrink from it, but all of them become dependent on it in some ways to gauge their standing in their community. I was the latter. It made me uncomfortable all the time ("she's just really shy") as something of mine that I wasn't entirely allowed to claim, for some not yet known reasons. I mean, observationally, on the grander scale of what I saw on television and who I was surrounded by (which is pretty much a kid's entire concept of the world), it seemed unsubstantiated. Meaning, I didn't see anyone who looked like me in a position of beauty. I was scrawny, had dark, thick, coarse hair, and eczema patches on my moon-shaped face—not exactly a Disney Princess in the making. I don't remember feeling entirely aggrieved about these particular traits at the time because I don't think I had the cognitive awareness to understand that I was allowed to dispute and even reject the notion of flaws at all. But knowing what I do now, my present self has become quite retrospectively protective of my inner child/past self; she was, after all, the one raw-dogging beauty culture's messaging without an ounce of critical thinking skills. Oof.

Beauty wasn't just a means to power, either. Pop culture has a funny way of championing a life devoid of nuance or context, giving plebes like me the idea that it's totally possible to be plucked from obscurity and thrown into a fantastical life adventure like saving the world, swapping places with a princess who looks just like you, or having a pop star alter ego. Look at the Olsen twins, or Anne Hathaway in *The Princess Diaries*, or the majority of the girl protagonists of the Disney Channel's original movies. My childhood actually had a similar if slightly less grandiose subplot to the plucked-from-obscurity model—one that did not outlast the consequences of real-world contextual limitations—but it's how I led a very short-lived career as a child model.

Before Instagram, the most glamorous thing that could happen to a girl was to be scouted by a modeling agent out in the wild. I was maybe six or seven at the time, riding the LIRR into the city with my mom and brother, and someone who worked at a modeling agency came up to my mother to tell her she had very adorable kids who could probably be successful child models or something. I'm pretty sure the agent was mostly focused on my brother, who was way more of a gregarious and expressive kid than I was. His head was the ideal adorable proportions, round and bowl-cut. I, on the other hand, was all cheeks, like a bean-bag chair in a dress. But two for one, why not, I guess. My mom had always worked in the fashion and garment production industry, and she knew her way around the modeling agency world a bit, so she knew they were legit and gave it a shot. My brother and I soon found our-selves in catalogs for Toys "R" Us, Kids "R" Us, Macy's, and Burlington Coat Factory—well, my brother was mostly booking the jobs, as he was much better at being cute on cue. He was the Gigi to my Bella. It was survival of the most precocious, and the kids who had full-time stage moms generally were always front and center. Our mom did not have time for all that because she had a job, but she did her due diligence to make sure we behaved on set.

As much as I wanted to be the very best child in the Macy's catalog, the stress of performing crushed my confidence as I was stuffed into outfits I felt so incredibly lame in. Even as a seven-year-old I knew no kid wanted to wear a floral tent dress with a frilly doily collar, or a sporty Adidas-looking soccer kit with matching terry cloth head- and wrist bands. It simply wasn't cool! And none of this was *me*. What baby me did not understand is that models do not choose their outfits and these shoots were not about me so much as they were about selling department store clothing. My displeasure at being sartorially misrepresented was visible. The hairstylist on set curled my Asian bob[*] into a "little lad who likes berries and cream" Shakespearean-page kind of coif, which I found extremely unflattering in my already vain opinion, and carelessly burned my head in the process. I yelped in pain, and he apologized, but the vibes were shot after that.

On the one hand, the fact I booked any jobs at all was endorsement that I belonged at least somewhat in that glitzy world. But the fact I didn't book way more was an indication that I was severely lacking in commercial viability, whatever that meant at the time. Beauty in the commercial sense is not just the right "look" but also the presence to embody it. The look is almost clinically pleasant—it's beauty in a nonthreatening and easily projectable way that simultaneously represents a generous baseline of our beauty standards while also reserving a certain amount of vacancy upon which whatever is being sold can be projected onto an inviting face. You start to disassociate from what you look like, depersonalizing and compartmentalizing your features into what is marketable and what could use some work to become more

---

[*] Every Asian kid who grew up in the early nineties knows what I'm talking about, but if you don't, just watch the show *PEN15*.

marketable. It's less about being a person than it is being a character who looks like a person. I may have had some real "picked last at gym" hurt feelings when I wasn't the star and started hearing more noes than yeses. It's hard not to take personally, especially at a really awkward, unformed age, even though the way these things were communicated was so clinically dry that you can't help but accept your failure as an inevitability. It also didn't help that I was not a natural-born performer and had a very low threshold for the stress of being perceived, which as a model is ostensibly what your value proposition is.

If you think kids absorb lots of messaging about performing beauty around that age, mimicking its performance that they see around them, imagine how the stakes rise when there's actual prizes involved (money, attention, heaps and heaps of validation and praise). It may feel like play but eventually it becomes second nature to understand how to perform for love, or what you think love is. That doesn't mean that child modeling wasn't the kind of experience that had a profound effect on my self-image and my ideas about what kind of life was ahead of me. If anything, it compounded my already emerging anxieties about what beauty is for, as I was being told in no uncertain terms all of the ways I did not possess those traits.

Like a lot of kids, I was desperate to grow up and get to the next level of maturation—the fun, sexy, glam, teen era. I prayed for menstruation and boobs until my boobs grew in enough to fill a training bra,[*] and then I got my period and realized that this was not worth having boobs. The miracle of becoming a woman is a bit like getting your driver's license—it sounds cool and promises freedom but mostly it's fraught, requires specialty insurance, and everyone just focuses on all the ways you can get killed. When you get to a certain age and your body starts getting long—and you, a young girl, start looking like a

---

* What a concept—a bra to train your boobs! What are we training our boobs to do??

young woman—that's when a modeling career can branch off into two directions. For the girls who get extra-long and remain thin, straight to runway. High fashion loves a youthful plank of a girl, the flatter the better. For the girls who grow to fulfill all of puberty's biological imperatives (they grow butts and b00bs), there's the commercial route (catalogs, TV commercials, ads). It's funny, with adult modeling your face can ostensibly remain as unique as it is made, but the body is subject to strict adherence to size regulations (aka being very thin). The modeling industry loves to celebrate unique features above the neck. I, however, stayed short *and* flat. My boobs never came in and my height topped out at just over five feet as my skull held fast to my baby fat. I'd never been so resentful of an overproduction of collagen as I was years eleven to sixteen. It was very "not a girl, not yet a woman"—but not a child, not yet a hot teen. And it also spelled the end of that so-called career path. "Come back in a few years and we'll see how you've grown," the ladies at the agency would say sweetly, in a cigarette-y, thick New York accent.

The dELiA*s, Mudd Jeans, Esprit, and Limited Too bookers wanted girls who looked like they were in Neutrogena ads, not *PEN15*. But not having to do all that anymore wasn't exactly devastating, especially when I remembered how anxious it all made me. And since most of my critiques weren't things I could really change (like my height and general babyish-ness), it was one of those "welp, whaddya gonna do?" kinds of losses. I was naive enough to give it a shot but not delusional enough to believe I was the kind of person who would excel at this. I'd see the girls who went on to really give modeling a go, and it was so clear to me that I was not . . . them. They got hot right after puberty, and I remained a slightly taller child. Modeling was something I'd only want to keep doing it if it was novel, easy, and most importantly, *glam*. Most of modeling is not glam at all. I mean, Giselle might say otherwise, but I'm sure she's had her days sitting for hours in hair and makeup with a fast-developing UTI, ahead of an all-night shoot.

The weird thing about being a professional child is that my world-view expanded just enough to form the kind of baby ego that told me that I was destined for bigger things, which can mean a lot of things to a kid who had serious inclinations to believe that the X-gene from *X-men* was real, and my entire life could potentially change once my mutant powers developed. Puberty was so much more disappointing when I finally came to accept that it would not be happening.

Instead, I attended public school where I made pretty good grades and wrote for the newspaper and had a ten p.m. curfew. I was still very self-conscious, insecure, and also possessed a constant undercurrent of disappointment in life at a pretty young age, all of which fed into the kind of demeanor that makes for a really charming teenager (not) or a nineteenth-century poet. By junior high, the part of my life in which I was a child model was mildly embarrassing to me; I didn't talk about it to anyone because I was pretty sure they would go, "Really? You??" And later on, of course, I developed other interests, and figured out the things I liked about myself, while still feeling like one day I would become *something* someday. I mean, think back to Jessica Rabbit—who knows what she was like before she was *the* Jessica Rabbit. What are the odds that she was a late bloomer too?

Sephora Good Time, Not a Long Time

The most frustrating thing about being a teenager is that you're a fully freethinking being who can easily spot the hypocrisy and bullshit within the systems you're made to live in but without the independent world experience to thoroughly process it, nor the legality to do anything about it even if you wanted to. Also, you think everything is about you. That hasn't really changed, as far as I've seen. Some people grow out of that angst and some people make it everyone else's problem. But now teenagers have way more distractions (and outlets) to express that angst. When I was an adolescent, we had eyeliner and dumbass local hijinks.

Smudgy, black eyeliner makes for an effective illustration for just how *over it all* you are. To me, there is no greater artistic truth than a teenage girl's handle on an eyeliner pencil. (Mind you, I grew up before liquid liner was a thing, and before there were makeup tutorials readily available online.) We worked with what we had, blackening our waterlines with ninety-nine-cent Wet n Wild eyeliners, smudging and smoking it out with Q-tips or our fingers. Did it look good? To us, at the time, yes. But that's only because edgy, black eyeliner was the epitome of angst, and angst was a very cool personality trait to express at the time, at least visually. *Feeling* cool and looking good are always synonymous, despite what onlookers may think, and as a teenager, anything that helps boost your confidence is a win.

The culture of my adolescence was very girl powered. The Spice Girls gave third-wave feminism a commercial voice and a look for mainstream youths—one that celebrated girl power without necessarily having to engage in any kind of political action required to attain it. (I wouldn't properly discover Riot grrrls until college.) Alternatively raunchy teen comedies and rom-coms were the basis of my cinematic diet. Their dramatic makeover mechanisms instilled a sense in me that all I needed to be hot was a popular senior to cut my hair into a flippy bob and to ditch my glasses. So being a girl felt like a mix of what was deemed popular by mainstream television and teen mags (colorful, fluffy, pink, and sparkly everything), and whatever was deemed cool by record label–planted alterative female musicians (smudgy black eyeliner, rubber bracelets, jean legs so wide they could smuggle candy strapped to your calves into movie theaters). Girls were encouraged to be whatever they wanted, with the caveat being always to make sure you're conventionally attractive when you do it. I was never really committed to one aesthetic, feeling too much like a poser for the alt crowd (my mom refused to buy me JNCOs) and not feminine enough for the girlie, preppy aesthetic (my mom also refused to buy me Abercrombie & Fitch . . . and she was right on both accounts). That much I was sure of, mostly because it appeared they're *only* letting hot girls into the "women getting ahead" club. It was in beta testing mode. Still kind of is.

The thing is, when you don't pick a side in high school, you become a floater, a person with no core group of friends who spends way too much time alone. I would spend full afternoons in the library, just hanging out by myself (do not get me wrong, I loved this). In the stacks, I'd pore over magazines. The library had all of them—*Marie Claire, Elle, Vogue, People, InStyle, Lucky*—bound in protective plastic binders. I studied these pages methodically; it was like my own research lab of how to be a girl. And when I had some pocket change, I could get subscriptions of my own. There was nothing I loved more than receiving the monthly teen and fashion magazines and dedicating a Friday night to poring over their pages, reading the beauty tips over and over to commit them to memory. I had subscriptions to *YM, Seventeen, Cosmo-*

Girl, Teen People, Teen Vogue, InStyle, Marie Claire, Elle, and *Allure*— some of them bought with cashed-in expiring airline miles my parents graciously allowed me to choose subscriptions from. But as much as I found comfort in these magazines, and genuinely loved them, trying to re-create any of those looks and editorial tips reminded me of two crucial things I didn't have: money and European features.

There was a slice of time when I was in high school, the age of Michelle Kwan's Olympic heyday and Lucy Liu's starring role in *Charlie's Angels,* when being Asian was kind of . . . trendy, for lack of better sentiment. More accurately, anything *aesthetically* Asian-looking was suddenly very on trend. Chinoiserie print satin dresses and little satin take-out box purses were all over dELiA*s catalogs and at the mall.* Dragon prints were emblazoned on Guess baby tees and chopsticks as hair accessories filled the Claire's shelves.

Finally, I thought, it was my time. At long last, I had an *edge.*

Unfortunately, imitation was by no means a form of flattery.

If you can believe it, when *I* wore the mandarin-collar satin tops, crane-embroidered flared pedal pushers, and dragon graphic tees, I did not get the kind of hype the non-Asian girls got when they did. Leaning into my ethnicity made me an even bigger target for regurgitated pop culture caricatures of Asians, complete with the kind of mockery and behavior that today leads to repeat cancellation. I changed it up, *quickly.* It made me even more invested in whatever lessons magazines had to offer me about mainstream beauty whether they were for me or not. They gave me something to look forward to as a refuge from the doldrums of late-bloomer-ism. I was downloading the blueprint for what I was to become once I emerged from my current chrysalis stage. It never occurred to me that glossy magazines were editorialized to be

---

* There was also an Abercrombie & Fitch faux-vintage graphic tee depicting a Chinese laundry with the slogan "Two Wongs Can Make It White," which took things a bit far to no one's chagrin but the small group of Asian Americans who made complaints to the company.

enticing and glamorous, to suspend the daily reality of cost, class, and appearance. Semantics were for basic, boring people—not me!

And, as it turns out, most of these magazines' beauty reportage wasn't for me either. No one who looked like me was involved, so I could only identify so much with them. Everything written was geared toward people with European features. Even the hair tips (especially the hair tips!). The few Asian models I saw in magazines all embodied a specific kind of exoticized East Asian beauty that emphasized pale skin, high cheekbones, waifish figures, almond-shaped eyes, and long swathes of straight, shiny black hair draped over their shoulders. Despite descending from not one, but two East Asian countries, that was not what I looked like at all. My skin was always slightly tan, my hair thick and bendy, my eyelids uneven, and again, that goddamn baby fat. My development into beautiful swan was taking a detour through Chicken Little. Not that it stopped me. But again, the other thing I didn't have: money.

For a lot of my youth, beauty felt like something secret I had to pilfer, bit by bit. For one, my parents wouldn't let me wear makeup. So I ripped out magazine spreads of makeup I liked and kept them in one of those plastic accordion file totes, a consolidated mood board that I'd reference when attempting to make frosted lipstick look like it does on Posh Spice on me.

This was also when Sephora just launched stateside, and the black-and-white Tim Burton-y gift-wrap–looking shop was an absolute *palace* to me. It was the best of department store makeup without the barrier of the counter in the way. You were invited to try things out by yourself, to touch things; you could totally help yourself to whatever. Which I did. I helped myself to Benefit lip glosses, Urban Decay glitter liners, bareMinerals loose powder eye shadows, Clinique Almost Lipsticks, Stila cream blush compacts, et cetera. What's a bored teen banned from makeup and filled with suburban ennui and a rebellious Avril Lavigne–fueled edge to do? I got good grades. I never got into substances. I did not call adults by their first names. I didn't have steady income (or any income, really) but I had the invincibility of youth and a casual disrespect for corporate authority. If I couldn't have beauty products, the next most glamorous thing to have was a secret.

If you believed daytime TV's obsession with out-of-control teens, shoplifting was considered the official gateway crime.[*] All my teen mags had these essay features of teens writing about how they got caught shoplifting and how it's not worth it and the great shame and regret they felt. I had the level of skill that only youthful arrogance abets and just enough disassociation to separate consequence from reality. Plus, sometimes forbidden fruit is made that much more tantalizing, isn't it? Nothing makes a kid want to do something more than telling them they can't. This amounted to having a stash of contraband cosmetics I'd take to school to wear and then shower off when I got home.

When the big makeup embargo of my adolescence slowly lifted around my seventeenth birthday, I was allowed color cosmetics—but only expressive, not corrective complexion products. My mom favored turquoise eyeliner or coral lipstick, while turning up her nose at any kind of complexion products that weren't skincare. She didn't get why people wore foundation[†] because it always looked so cakey and obvious to her, and its obviousness was off-putting in the way that seeing the seams or rips in one's stockings is unseemly. Plus, foundation largely sucked before the 2010s; it was goopy, never blended into skin well enough, and the shade ranges were pitiful.

Kids don't know how lucky they are today to have eyeshadow primer and fifty shades of foundation to find their match! The drugstores around me carried maybe five shades of orange-beige Maybelline Dream Matte Mousse pots, Great Lash in clear (come on, clear?!), stiff

---

[*] Which if you consider how most of the world's wealthiest people have all dabbled in a little tax fraud and loopholing, is technically putting me on the track to become a billionaire.
[†] My mom has always had perfect skin, so.

Wet n Wild eyeliner pencils that could give you a splinter if you didn't sharpen it right, and trashed Lip Smackers because someone always twisted them up in the tube and put them back on the shelf. I'd "buy" whatever drugstore-accessible beauty product a magazine said was good because I firmly believed that what magazines printed was unequivocally the truth. A lot of the makeup tips were written as though they were for people who weren't trying to solve anything with makeup (which, they probably were). I remember reading about all the ways you could use clear mascara: natural-looking lash enhancement, brow gel, taming flyaways, et cetera. *Clear mascara.* The only thing clear mascara is good for is disappearing wherever you put it in five minutes. I remember all the eye makeup tips for brown eyes involving vaguely derogatory descriptors of brown eyes and their inherent dullness (a lot of it involved purple eyeshadow and liner to "contrast" brown eyes' lightless luster). And I remember the face shape charts that depicted what haircuts would work for you. I bought a tin brick of Bag Balm[*] because Kristin Kreuk, an actress on the show *Smallville*, said in a magazine interview that it was always in her makeup bag. And I bought several tins of Smith's Rosebud Salve because for some reason every magazine said it was "the perfect, barely there pink tint" (valid if you're suffering from some blood-draining ailment). Lip balm fancier than ChapStick was very much a status item then. It was all about glossy tinted lips; nobody was lip-kitting at the time. Applying lip gloss at your locker was akin to the fan-waving flirting tactics of the Victorian era, if not a core bonding device of friendships between girls. Also, tinted lip goo was probably the most reliable cosmetic product because the quality of makeup sucked back then. Most of it was either chalky powder that never actually stuck to your skin or basically Vaseline with a bit of shimmery pigment that separated in its container after no time at all.

---

[*] A petroleum-based balm for dry lips and skin, also used to soothe cows' sore udders.

The irony is: Did I ever implement these beauty tips IRL? No, not really. And not just because I was a minor with a paltry allowance. As much as I thought being a hot teenage girl involved push-up bras, false lashes, and bold lipstick, the reality was that you were expected to be hot without looking like you put too much effort into it. In fact, wearing bold makeup had the opposite effect of looking like you were trying too hard and desperate for male attention—which, don't get me wrong, we all were, but we were also equally intimidated by what that attention would *entail*. Everything was about being "natural" and fresh-faced. I remember the word "fresh-faced" being thrown around a *lot* in those salad days.

I staked too much of my self-confidence on following what I thought was glam or cool (as teens do), based on whatever elicited the most external validation. I pretended I didn't care because it wasn't cool to be into your looks, even though everyone scrutinized the most minute detail of everyone's looks all the time. The predominant messaging from beauty was contextualized to the male gaze. That's how you'd know you were doing it well—when it "drove all the boys wild" or something to that effect.[*]

That tension informed a beauty-sex anxiety I (and lots of people who came of age in that era) internalized: the difference between wearing not enough makeup and too much makeup was invisibility versus being slut-shamed. The most damning thing you could do as a young girl growing up in that culture of hypersexualization was to engage in sexual behavior. The rise of jeans descended so scandalously low that a bikini wax was necessary to wear some of them. I don't know what the sweet spot was supposed to be with appearances—no one explained that. You just had to know. And by "know," I mean fit well enough into the kind of beauty standards placed on teen girls that

---

[*]   Making boys act goofy around you was the ultimate power move to a young girl. Still kind of is.

advertised sexual maturation without ever going so far as to suggest actual sex was being had. I was far from that ideal (still am, technically). I barely fit an A cup and had a generous helping of baby fat on my cheeks by high school graduation. "It's fine, you're a late bloomer," my mom would say, along with "You'll be thankful for that baby fat when you're older!" The virgin-whore complex was alive and well in the Y2K era, with beauty often the scapegoat and enabler. It's a far cry from today, when beauty has created its own artistic community where women share tips and tricks with other women (as they've always done) but on a much larger scale, to the point where the sexuality of it is eclipsed by its camaraderie and creativity.

I was so often told, "You don't need makeup, you're just a kid," as if the point of makeup is to look older, which we all know by our mid-twenties is absolutely not why women are socialized to wear makeup. I just wanted to express the little freak I was on the inside through makeup and hair color, and I wanted to do it on my own terms and be able to claim my own identity, which when you're a minor seems so out of your own control. That's probably why I started coloring my hair every color of the rainbow in my late twenties and well into my thirties and throwing every ornamental thing at my face for the sake of catching up on lost time.

Self-expression is something few people pull off with grace in the beginning. It takes a dedication to experimentation, shedding old scripts of what looks are acceptable and what aren't, and a lot of patience (especially when it comes to dramatic haircuts). Discovering your own identity for yourself and then figuring out what that looks like is a lifetime's work. Some people go their whole lives and never let themselves find out. And some people shoplift makeup until they can afford to buy their own. Beauty is a form of control as much as it is self-expression; it is a way to be independent, which is what I think most young people are so hungry for. Being *seen* for who you are (or want to be) is one of the key components of being a teenager.

Look, if you're thinking of having a kid—making a fully sentient person who is to be socialized into greater society—there's a real strong chance at one point they're going to want to do some stuff to their appearance: weird haircuts, clothes you think are dumb, makeup, hair color, piercings, all sorts of temporary and semipermanent cosmetic embellishment. Just let them do it (as long as it isn't harmful, obviously). They're going to do it anyway if they really want to. And not for nothing, but the consequences of one's own actions are lessons that teach themselves.[*]

Would I be as much of a vain little fiend as I am today had my parents let me dye my hair whatever Manic Panic I desired? I think the answer is probably yes. Maybe I would've have gotten a few of the rainbow hair colors out of my system sooner than my midthirties (and possibly curbed that shoplifting habit), but I absolutely still would've been entranced by beauty's transformative promises. There are endless ways to evolve at will, and you can always start over and over again. I have, several times over already. Magazines supplied me with the prototypes and the tips, music gave me the life force, and the mall gave me enough free makeup (whoops) to work with until the time came for me to finally bloom into the swan I was made to believe I would be one day.

---

[*] And your job as a parent is to take lots of pictures to show them later as an adult and go, "Remember when you bleached your hair in the sink and it turned orange?"

Smells Like Teen [Redacted]

"It's not a journey. Every journey ends, but we go on. The world turns and we turn with it. Plans disappear, dreams take over, but wherever I go, there you are: my luck; my fate; my fortune. Chanel No. 5, inevitable."

One evening at a gala, a woman in a green dress leaves a ballroom awards ceremony, sullenly walking through the lobby. Suddenly an arhythmic percussive beat is heard and she starts blinking to the beat. And then she starts contorting her face to the beat. And then she shimmies and struts throughout the halls as the beat expands into an Afro-Caribbean EDM song. She kicks, twirls, spins, and manically gesticulates throughout the hallway, spider-dancing on the mirrors, licking the face of a statue, shooting lasers from her fingers, and finally jumping through a giant floating eyeball on the steps on Lincoln Center.

An actress walks along a palm tree–lined street.

Cut to: a bedroom. "I love you—" a man says. She cuts him off, clutching her dress around her chest. "Prove it!"

Cut to: she's on a windy beach. She runs along a pier and jumps off into the water. She is running through a sunlit living room, being playfully chased by a man. They're embracing in slow motion in bed. They're embracing in the back of a bus. Now she's driving a pink convertible, spinning doughnuts on the pavement. The tire tread marks spell the word "love" in perfect cursive. We follow her on that palm tree street again. Suddenly, she abruptly spins around to face us, addressing us for the first time. "And you? What would you do for love?" she asks. She doesn't wait for an answer.

Now we're in a vast marble bathhouse. Several modelesque women languish about in sheer golden veils. One woman emerges from a deep, golden bath in slow motion. Now she's in a gilded, sequined gown, completely dry. So are the other women. They walk slowly in a geese-migration formation. A disembodied woman's voice sings a question: *Flashing . . . lights?* The woman mouths one word in slow motion: "J'adore."

If fragrance commercials written out sound like a deleted scene from *Zoolander*, they are just as bizarro in real life. I found myself on the set of one the summer after I graduated from college and was fucking around with on-screen background work for commercial and television productions around the city. Picking up extra gigs was a great way to idle around a two-block radius, eating craft services for the majority of an eight-to-twelve-hour day for a hundred taxable dollars.

Honestly, I cannot tell you what fragrance it was, but looking back on my very melodramatic LiveJournal entries from around this time, I only know it was for Prada. "Prada" needed bodies in Dumbo at five a.m. to portray people eating at a diner. I showed up along with a scant handful of other extras. We sat scattered across the bar and some booths, mostly with our backs to the camera, for several hours. Most of us were unable to see what was happening outside, where the big action shot of the commercial was taking place. I guess fake snow is a big to-do, and it involves cranes and stuff.

A handsome man stands at the bar and knocks back a mug of coffee before tossing his leather jacket over one shoulder and walking outside. A very attractive girl (the waitress, I think?) follows him out because he forgot something (??) or maybe just because he just smells so good, and she must, *must, MUST* do something about it. They unite on the street outside, where it immediately starts snowing even though no one has on proper outerwear, and they embrace . . . or something. Honestly, it's hard to recall the narrative because as Diner #4 or whoever, I was sat at the bar with my back to the window. From what I can understand, it was meant to be a brief vignette of hot people smelling each other and immediately kissing about it, in broad daylight, and in the middle of a traffic-heavy neighborhood. *We smelled the smell, and now we are in love.* Nothing sells fragrance like hot people in love.

When you're within the cinematic universe of fragrance, you must accept that you've been whisked away to a different multiverse world ruled by Big Perfume. Time slows down. Nobody can seem to keep their eyes open. Colors and lights are saturated. Everyone is kissing and caressing. Everyone is thin. Very fit men turn into very fit centaurs after swimming in the ocean with horses. Gravity's rules do not apply. You don't know what is going on. This is about perfume. But there are no actual perfume bottles around, nor is it being sprayed on anything, but I assure you, it is very much about perfume. Nobody seems to appear to be smelling anything, but we are to assume that whoever we are looking at smells incredible, and the ensuing action around them is in response to that very good smell. The wearer of this perfume becomes the main character of their own alternative dimension. These could easily be grad student films or the experimental video art of an interpretation of French New Wave.

Perfume commercials are meant to be . . . like that. I'm sure most of the creative team writing the treatments would call them "artistic" and "conceptual," and they are not wrong, but they always seem to omit "weird for weirdness's sake," which is perhaps the most inarguable assessment for the viewer. There is nothing that could happen in a perfume commercial outside the arsenal of "ways to sell perfume" that multimillion-dollar advertising firms would say no to. I imagine that it's every wealthy eccentric's dream to make a team of people they employ listen to their bizarre fever dream acid trip with great earnestness and turn it into *art*. Commercial art! And lest we not forget—at this point in the commercial, nobody's even smelled anything yet. Once you actually experience the fragrance, all that postured glitz and sexual artifice can be immediately undone by one errant, unwelcome spritz in the ladies' room or a department store aisle.

Like many people of American suburban origins in the late twentieth century, the mall was very much my initial immersion into the world of Perfume™. The main way to get into the mall was through department stores, and the entrances to department stores always dumped you straight into the beauty sector. Glamorous ladies would spray you with Givenchy* and Liz Claiborne as you walked past. Gigantic perfume bottles† (aka factices) decorated the counters as a beacon of glamour. You could not get to the mall without passing through the great hall of smells, so my brain has forever associated the smell of perfume with those leisurely, mall-trawling days—the precursor to my informal education on all things conspicuously consumable and class-expressive.

Designer perfume was the first gateway to luxury beauty to me. I don't think capital P perfume was as much of a thing when I was coming of age (mostly because there were fewer affordable options), but it was important to smell good—that much I knew. If you were going to wear a perfume, there was a very exclusive list of approved ones (as long as you weren't wearing the same scent as your best friend or those in your friend group), including Tommy Girl, Ralph Lauren Blue, GAP Heaven or GAP Dream, CK One—you know, anything fresh, airy, and *clean* smelling.

---

* This is how I discovered that it's pronounced *zhee-von-shee* and not phonetically, as I originally had been saying in my head: *Giv-en-chee* (hard g).
† I later learned that they are not filled with perfume, just perfume-looking water. Huge disappointment.

No one who knows me now would ever guess this about me, but in my most formative years, I had the clinical misfortune of being . . . the smelly kid. My associations with smells were born from a place of great anxiety and shame. A single swipe of Dove, Secret, or Degree under my pits would cause dramatic breakouts of cysts; one time, a mega-boss cyst required minor surgery to remove. It was a simple in-and-out excision at the dermatologist's office with the added humiliation of med students studying dermatological surgery gathering round my armpit to slice out a little sliver of hygienic resistance. I still have a tiny crescent of a scar in my left armpit from the stitches. I've never met anyone who has that same allergic reaction to deodorant as me, and when I mention this to people, they give me a horrified look like I just said I was born with thumbs for ears or something unimaginably uncommon. The number one reaction was "So what did you do??"

I smelled really bad. Like appallingly vile, *OKAY??*

What's a young, pubescent girl who's allergic to deodorant to do? Look, I'm not a chemophobic or anything—I'm a big supporter of benevolent chemicals—but you simply never know which chemicals are *out to get you*. It's been amply studied that the aluminum compounds in many deodorants and antiperspirants do not cause or contribute to breast cancer, so this admission is in no way some win for the smug "beauty causes cancer" crowd, but this is why we patch test, folks! The aluminum compounds that are the active ingredient in most conventional deodorants and antiperspirants work by blocking sweat glands, an effective way to stop moisture from building up in your pits and radiating its telltale odors. Unfortunately, though, aluminum did *not* work for me. Keep in mind that all this was before clean, green, all-natural products could be found in major drugstores. The only deodorant available was of the *un*natural variety . . . and that was very *un*fortunate for me.

Puberty is a very chaotic way to enter the world of adulthood, even without the odors (but also because of them). It's the time in a young person's life when the tooth fairy retires, passing the torch to the Puberty Fairy. The PF is a generous but rarely gratuitous entity—the girls get periods, boobs, acne; boys get tall(er), more vocally robust, acne. Everyone gets body odor, some more than others. What the Puberty Fairy declined to grant me in mammary glands it more than made up for in a rank, being-hunted-for-sport animalic bouquet that radiated throughout any room I occupied. The innocence of my childhood simply wafted away on the wavy stink lines emanating from my flat-chested little body, and I knew life would never be the same. Sigh.

Growing up is one part increase in mass, two parts horny, three parts drama. It's a grab bag of blood, sweat, and tears—sometimes all three if you're a girl with acne, overactive apocrine glands, and a penchant for overdramatizing minor inconveniences (aka moi). Most of this is generally manageable with Noxzema, a stick of Secret, and a bottle of Bath & Body Works body splash. But my nervous, sweaty armpits were nothing short of relentless for about two or three years. My allergy to deodorant and antiperspirant, coupled with my allergy to alcohol (I would discover that a few years later) made me fundamentally uncool.

I tried many things to mitigate the smell and also to avoid subjecting anybody to it. I tried science-ing my way around it. I learned that it was bacteria that caused odor, not the sweat itself, so I nicked as many handfuls of single-use alcohol wipes from the school nurses' office to swab my pits in between classes, or else I'd attempt to bathe my underarms in scented hand sanitizer in the girls bathroom. I liberally French-showered myself in whatever body splash I had around under my arms to counteract smell with smell. My last resort was also the most effective: I just stayed away from people. My friends' moms would be like, "Are you *okay*?" because they thought the stench was something indicating a profound medical unwellness. A handful of my schoolmates would sometimes loudly exclaim, "Yo, who *stinks*??"

in class. And a few of my more sociopathic peers would hiss at me in the halls, "Why don't you wear deodorant??" (As if I didn't try that!!) or make dramatic gestures, holding their noses and scrunching their faces when I passed by. That might've also been in response to the deluge of Bath & Body Works Cucumber Melon and Freesia body splash I'd spray on myself to mask any offending odors, which then created a confusing cloud of sweet and also repellent smells emanating from me. I spent a lot of time social distancing, years twelve to fifteen.

Eventually, I discovered Tom's of Maine, the first mainstream "natural" deodorant brand that eschewed aluminum salts in favor of a bunch of other stuff that instead of masking your body odor, transfigured it into something else both stale and tangy simultaneously—like a stinky expensive cheese (according to the tube, it was meant to be the scent of calendula). It wasn't great, but at least it was different odor, not so telltale BO. Its confusing stench offered a slight respite from that old familiar armpit aroma.

The economy-sized body splashes and mists were my first forays into personal scent, more out of desperation than personal enjoyment. They were an affordable and age-appropriate veil of sweet and fruity scents, plumes of girlhood that advertised feminine sweetness without the aroma of sexuality that we'd come to know from Perfume™.[*] Perfume offered something a tier above what body splash (or mist) and scented glittery roll-ons could at the time. For one, perfume came in glass bottles, which automatically made them fancier. Those glass bottles contained forbidden scents with their saturation dialed up to *radiate*, offering a range of concentrated aromas that strayed into spicy, sweet, daring territories distilled into complex bouquets of prescriptive femininity (or masculinity, pour les hommes). Really, it was all a sanitized interpretation of womanliness, pleasantly pulped into

---

[*] You can't really sexualize a scent, the same way you can't really gender a smell, but the fragrance industry does both, and how.

what I can only describe as "that perfume smell." It's all of them in one, bouncing off the marble floors and seeping into the surrounding sportswear and handbags of the fragrance aisle, a robotic garden that offered safety in beauty's most hygienically elegant aromas. Smelling nice wasn't only implicitly mandatory, there were several ways to do it that simultaneously signaled your class and taste levels. Subjectively, any scent could become sacred given its association, taking in the context and the company, but designer ones are best known mostly because they have the biggest marketing budgets. There is rarely ever a definitive moral authority on what scent is deemed "good" or "bad" the way other more visual forms of beauty tend to suffer from. And, conveniently, any perfume worn by someone you didn't like could also be labeled as cheap—even if it wasn't! But any scent worn by a culturally esteemed figure (like Rihanna) suddenly became the epitome of luxury and aspiration.

Our overall cultural obsession with fragrance is due in large part to self-elevation, away from our base, animal origins. We've been grossed out by body odor for centuries, our tolerance waning the more accessible hygiene became and the more products we can make for the purpose of personal hygiene. In ye olde days, only royalty could bathe daily, and the slightly less royals bathed only before special events and once their body odor became too powerful for whatever fragranced oils and powders could mask. Being smelly was for the poor masses; it was the literal stink of poverty. Any untamable condition of being in a body is an insult to civilization, and odor was the first telltale sign of one's access to regular bathing and therefore class.

But the *idea* of clean has come to surmount actual cleanliness. On a microscopic level, filth evades our most Lady Macbeth sensibilities of washing. And truthfully, as we've all learned in this current century's pandemic, apparently nobody's bothering to wash their hands in any effective manner anyway. But as long as they don't smell or appear unclean, no one complains. It's not filth we're opposed to, it's just the absence of soap, whose presence is usually confirmed by its fresh, sanitized scent.

And now that households in developed nations have at least one shower and/or bath and ample access to affordable personal care products, there is simply no excuse to be smelling any type of way other than what the creators of Ivory and Irish Spring have scented their bars of soap to be. Our collective understanding of what clean smells like is often labeled the likes of "mountain breeze," "spring rain," or in the case of certain male-coded brands, "swagger." None of these things actually smell like the things they say they smell like. If you did indeed smell like a mountain breeze (depending on the mountain), even that would be far too earthy and herbaceous to be considered civil by most Western noses.

Our hygiene neurosis has overcorrected to the point of no longer tolerating even normal and healthy bodily odors—particularly as it comes to one's nether regions, especially those that may emanate from female reproductive organs and cycles. Vaginas, unique as they are, all have their own individual musk (doesn't everyone?), which has suffered at the hands of marketing more than a few times in the mid-to-late twentieth century. After birth control usurped the function of douches as a form of primitive birth control and STI prevention, Big Douche had to come up with a new way to market a now redundant product. Obviously, they reverted to the usual low-hanging and effective route of shaming women's bodies. Any cocktail of water, vinegar, baking soda, or iodine solution came to provide the "freshness" and its implicit idealized sexuality that douching products advertised. And that's a big improvement from the early twentieth century, in which women would douche with Lysol (yes, the cleaning product) as a means of birth control. As we now know, douching is actually harmful to vaginas, upsetting the pH levels necessary to protect the vagina from harmful bacteria.* Vaginas (unlike armpits) are self-cleaning. They're supposed to smell like vaginas—not a summer's eve.

But the "clean" versus "cleanliness" adds a moral aspect to that. In the great celebrity showering debate of 2021, those who admitted to showering only when they deemed necessary caused a minor uproar from middle- and working-class Twitter users who deemed any amount of frequency less than at least once a day *grotesque*. It was an insult to wealth, and all its promises of separating one from the abject poverty of living in a body. How could someone so hot, rich, and famous (and with so many bathrooms in their house) tolerate the daily accumulation of filth from their extremely cushy lifestyles??†

Not showering every day was unfathomable to me until I was maybe twenty-one, when the whole body odor issue calmed down. Also, there were now more natural deodorant options on the market, some more effective than others. That didn't mean I was any less obsessed with smells, though. I was just able to enjoy them for what they were, without the desperate will to have them cover up my stench. Being that fragrance was the one thing I was never barred from in my youth, the way I was verboten to wear makeup or color my hair, my tastes in scent could evolve and grow, which they did. I understood the implicit perceptions of certain fragrance profiles. Green or aquatic scents like Prescriptives Calyx, Issey Miyake L'Eau d'Issey, or Davidoff Cool Water were always polished and fresh. Fruity scents like Victoria's Secret Pear Glacé, DKNY Be Delicious, and Nina Ricci Nina were girlie and fun. And the gourmands like Lolita Lempicka, Warm Vanilla Sugar, and Jessica Simpson's Dessert Beauty were bombasti-

---

* You know what does cause wacky vaginal odors? Harmful bacteria

† Lifestyles where one is rarely exposed to contaminants that require daily bathing, anyway. People who have everything also have the privilege of cosplaying as minimalists to reconnect to the simple life or something like that. Let them! They're not hurting anybody by not showering in their mansions. If anything, it's a great argument for water conservation.

cally and decadently indulgent—not for the shy or self-conscious.[*] I knew that *feminine* scents (the florals, musks, fruities) were some of the most effective tools of emotional manipulation. Of all the crude tools of seduction we had back then, scent was always the champion (still is!).

I was gifted a bottle of Chanel Chance in high school—a gift with purchase (the purchase made by my mother)—and that scent was a high-powered hose to my aromatic woes. It, along with my Cucumber Melon body splash and Victoria's Secret Dream Angel body mist, was in my arsenal against being anything other than the cute, nice-smelling girl I aspired to be. In my later teens, I wore Chanel Allure and Donna Karan Cashmere Mist—both made me feel very sophisticated and expensive. They were both a bit *lady* in ways that I very much was not, but wearing them made me feel like a better, more capable version of myself. Cashmere Mist, with its powdery enveloping bouquet of musky lily and jasmine, smelled as luxurious as its namesake material. It was subtler than the nectar-y, bright florals and sweet gourmands my friends wore, projecting a subdued, comforting aura, rather than anything *come hither*. Chanel Allure was the first fragrance I wore that inspired compliments—mostly from men—which imprinted on my mind as the scent of a desirability. I was starting to see what those perfume commercials were finally talking about! I mean, it's one thing to think someone smells good, but approaching a stranger to tell them that? Bold. Also, it was nice to finally be complimented for the way I smelled after years of the way I smelled being a great source of anxiety. Complimenting a person's fragrance or simply their very pleasant scent is one of the highest forms of flattery, I think. It's intimate by nature, seeing as proximity is required for the exchange to take place.

---

[*] In the early 2000s, these spicy, loud gourmands often gained the reputation of being the "slutty" scents, as anything that asserted one's femininity did at the time, at least in my social circles.

It's a moment of shared pleasure based on an appreciation of presence. Plus, there's a threat of romance in it.

Even today, one whiff of Lolita Lempicka takes me straight back to my one after-school job as a cater waiter at a country club; one of the other waitresses would absolutely douse herself in it because when she wore it she got more tips. And a whiff of Lancôme Trésor reminds me of passing by my mother's bureau in my parents' bedroom, picking up the bottle to sniff it and see how the sunlight shone through the diamond-shaped bottle like an amber crystal. Scents are powerful memory and emotional triggers mostly because of your internal real estate. Most sensory stimulation must first pass through the thalamus of your brain, but not smells! Smells are VIPs that get to waft straight to the olfactory bulb in your brain, which is in very cozy company with your amygdala and hippocampus—the emotional processors and memory Rolodex. Sense of smell is our most primal sense with the longest evolutionary history, which is easy enough to understand when you consider that we have at least a thousand types of olfactory receptors but only four types of light sensors and touch receptors. Smells are important to our biological imperatives and self-preservation. And now that those two things are amply covered by industrialization, we can create luxury perfumes made from aged tree fungus as well as Glade PlugIns, just for fun.

Once I discovered the spicy, heady aromas of oud, patchouli, and other earthly delights, the hold of sanitized freshness broke, and I was entranced by all things dark, woody, and aromatic. I think the dank earthiness of certain raw materials contained an echo of that animalic muskiness that used to repel me, but in the noses of talented perfumers, they became complex concoctions like the sweat of gods, no longer a forbidden fragrance. You know how some people think the smell of their lover's sweat is an aphrodisiac? It was like that, but obviously nicer than just sweat itself. It was everything I thought to be beautiful and filthy in one, creating a searing contradiction of spicy intimacy. Perfume was my own aphrodisiac, a way to become more acquainted with my own body odor as it intermingled with my Diptyques, Byredos, and even Old Spice. Instead of hiding it, I could dress it up in iris, musk, and vetiver. If deodorant was a harness for my body odor, perfume was my embellishment. I still think there's no better compliment than "you smell great," something I arrived at in a deficit. Maybe my anxiety about body odor made my sense of smell that much more sensitive, but after the hormonal turmoil of my adolescence, my sensory vigilance earned its own sense of reprieve. Perfume is one of beauty's most poetic expressions. You may not have a lot of control over the way you're perceived, but scent is one way to enhance your own presence, to be made memorable through sensory persona, and have I mentioned how nice it feels to be complimented on your fragrance? I spent so much of my younger years spooked by any whisper of an odor from me that any validation that not only am I *not* repulsing everyone around me, but instead beguiling and charming the noses off everyone I meet now, gives me a kind of satisfaction that feels like a form of olfactory justice for my inner child.

Once I discovered that fragrance is my mode of expression and communication, there would never be enough. There is no signature expression, the same way there is no signature, static mindset or emotion. It's a narrative that's constantly evolving. And it's always been my favorite way to connect with people. Everybody likes smells! Nobody really talks about it on account of smells being a contentious topic with too many hang-ups about hygiene and probably overstepping personal boundaries, but perfume is so much more than hygiene. It's an interactive form of beauty, one that exists beyond prescriptive ideals and instead communicates so much more about a person beyond the suggestion of their appearance. (Plus, your scent is one of the last experiential parts of your presence that can only be clocked IRL; you can't smell people in the metaverse, you know?)

But it's all a proposition. Of all the things fragrance might suggest to the world, the one thing you can rely on is that it's a surefire way to enjoy being with yourself. And it's a pleasantly silent invitation for others to enjoy you as well (or for those who don't share the same tastes as you to simply not bother). I've had ample experience being the smelly kid, so I know a lot about that. A halo of aroma has always followed me around—still does—and fortunately it's a scent of my choosing these days.

What's in My Bag (Really)?

You can learn a lot about a person by looking through their bag. Why go through the tedium of asking questions when you can get to know someone by stitching together a projection of their lifestyle, tastes, and proclivities based on a quick rummage through their personal effects?

That's the thinking behind every bag-spilling piece of content in every magazine. Except in the editorial context, the bag in question is the one that contains your most glamorous items only. The concept has expanded to full-on bathroom raids, examining the contents of one's medicine cabinet, what's kept on display on the vanity, and generally every aesthetically driven protocol a (very beautiful) person does. The beauty editorial WIMB (What's in My Bag) is a popular content format (generally to curate commerce links through a more personal lens). In the interest of "authenticity" however, if you were to conduct an interview with a very glam person—like me, for instance—and inspect their everyday bag, the contents inside might suggest a neurosis far more intimate than just lipstick and cigarettes.

WHAT'S IN MY BAG?

* **My wallet**, obviously. Can't leave the house without the thing that carries my ID, credit cards, various store membership cards (CVS, Walgreens, Sephora, Nordstrom, Macy's, IKEA), and even on some occasions, actual cash.
* **My keys.** Although in the winter I like to keep them in my jacket pocket because I have a weird paranoia about what if my purse gets stolen and then I can't get into my house.

It's the same reason I'd never have one of those wallet–phone case hybrids—if your phone gets swiped, there go all your credit cards and ID as well. You need to separate your valuables to make them more difficult to steal en masse. Like infinity stones, but without the weird glove.

* **An even smaller bag** containing a small mirror and my lip color choices for any given day—usually any variation of a tinted balm, a gloss, a matte balm, or a lipstick.

* Some really old scuffed-up **Band-Aids** waiting for a blister to mend.

* **Dusty hair ties** just in case I suddenly feel like braiding my hair into two pigtails on each side of my head.

* **Chinese herbal Po Chai Pills** I keep on hand in case of indigestion. I love to eat and if I'm leaving my house, there is a 90 percent chance it will involve food. I refuse to risk a bad time.

* **A Baggu reusable bag.** I never know when I'm going to pop by a grocery store or feel the impulse to buy a bunch of street produce.

* **Earplugs.** Really old, sticky ones with dust and fuzz all over them. And that's inside the case they live in. You never know when you're going to end up somewhere loud, like a concert or any intersection where a souped-up Honda Civic with IMAX theater levels of sub-woofer idles right beside you.

* **Old receipts.** Always ask for a receipt because you never know when you'll need a time-stamped alibi.

* **One flattened protein bar.** I originally picked it up at the grocery store as a backup snack for when I have early morning appointments (almost always for my hair color) and don't have (make) time for breakfast. It's a convenient, nutrient-adjacent food unit that will not require utensils,

preparation, or emit odors. Except I hate protein bars, so it remains squashed in the bottom of my bag, in the little inside zipper portion, probably waiting for the day I get trapped in an elevator for an unforeseen amount of time (at which time it will likely be a fossilized, inedible artifact).

* **Binaca breath spray.** This is also really old. So old the label is rubbed off entirely and I have completely forgotten its provenance, but I am pretty sure someone gave it to me so who *knows* how long it's been around. It makes me feel like a high school dweeb preparing for seven minutes in heaven every time I spray it in my mouth. Most of the time I miss my mouth and end up spraying my chin or somewhere around the side of my mouth and cheek, so my whole face smells minty. That's a hack, probably.

* **AirPods.** I love tuning out the sounds of catcallers and general bullshittery in the streets of New York (because there's a lot of it, especially when you're a woman in public). I used to wear noise-canceling headphones until I realized that they worked so well, I'd disassociate while walking around and almost get run over (usually by cyclists because they never seem to obey traffic laws).

* **Pills.** I have an old travel-sized Tylenol canister I rubbed the label off of to just keep filled with generic ibuprofens or other OTC painkillers. Nothing's worse than being out in the wild with a headache. But then someone gave me weed mints, so I put them in the pills canister. And then somebody else gave me mushroom capsules, so I put them in the pills canister. And now I don't know which one is which, except for the ibuprofens, which are all gone by now. So . . .

* **A portable iPhone charger.** A beauty brand gave this to me in a swag bag on a press trip, and these things are great! It's

the size of a slice of cheese and it juices up a dying phone so quickly, so I never have to use my own brain for GPS again.

* **Sunglasses.** (When I remember them.)
* **A tiny Jiji plushie.**
* **Hand cream.**
* **A brass plasma lighter.** It looks like a Zippo but it emits an electronic X of plasma for lighting things on fire. I don't smoke but maybe one day someone will ask me if I have a light. I hope they're hot.
* **Dust.** So much dust. How does it get in there? It's an enclosed space! Bags are gross.
* And last but not least: **The Audacity.**™

No Fun in the Fun House

S ometime in the winter of 2015 I and seven other women were flown first class to Rio de Janeiro for a weeklong shoot about our hair. We were all meticulously selected for our unique hair colors, textures, lengths, and nuanced multiethnic appearances. There was a woman with long, wavy lengths of silvery-gray hair; lots of girls with curls of different textures; girls with chemically straightened hair; a girl with long blue hair; and there was me—the blonde. Specifically, the blond *Asian* woman. We were all Real Women* selected by Dove to tell our stories about how we wear our hair however we damn well please without the conventional attitudes of how society thinks we *should* wear our hair. We shot in different film sets made to look like the streets of New York City, open fields of the Midwest, or other locations American women might ostensibly walk in slow motion while casually flipping their gorgeous hair.

The advertising agency in charge of the campaign took care to attempt to represent each of us as authentically as possible while still aligning with the Dove color palette. For me that entailed a lot of light-wash denim, creamy beige knits, and gauzy white linens. For one sunny afternoon, I was filmed lounging around a beautiful villa that was so closely shot it just ended up looking like a light brick wall in the final cut. But that's fine with me because the other shots entailed me

---

* Real Women is how Dove referred to talent in their campaigns that featured real women and not models, actors, or otherwise commercially pretty people—they even did background checks to make sure none of us were secretly models or actors.

pretend-playing an acoustic bass guitar* on a hammock (something I would probably never do because I refuse to be that guy at the party who whips out an acoustic guitar and subjects everyone to elementary licks of Dave Matthews Band or whatever).

I was playing "Asian woman with dyed blond hair." There are many Asian women with dyed blond hair, but my platinum-blond head was all over the first page of a Google image search under terms like "blond Asian hair," "Asian with blond hair," and "can you bleach Asian hair?" My cache of beauty stories about becoming the blonde, the maintaining of the blonde, and generally any beauty story with my byline and my blond-headed mug in it made me the dominating SEO image result for "blond Asian woman" (at least in 2015), ultimately convincing the overworked casting agency that I am clearly *the* blond Asian woman to fit the bill.

On set there was a hairstylist, makeup artist, wardrobe—the glam squad responsible for making every Real Woman's hair look really, really good. The whole thing was a fun hang. It felt like summer camp, spending a week with a bunch of other women who also found themselves in the same spontaneously privileged position of exploring the beautiful beaches of Rio while getting pampered and paid, all of which resulted in a YouTube ad running less than two minutes long where each of us uttered one voice-over tagline having to do with our hair (scripted and edited based on our initial hair stories during the casting process). Mine was something about how I didn't think Asian women could have blond hair "because Asians just didn't do that," which probably had more to do with my own cosmetically conservative upbringing than speaking for everyone of Asian descent (I mean,

---

* I made the mistake of revealing that I played bass in a band in my initial meeting with casting, and it was clear the anecdote was a tantalizing bit of "fun fact" flair to pitch to the brand.

all the most colorful hair colors come out of Japanese and Korean hair salons, according to my Instagram Explore algorithm). When I saw the final cut, I was like, *Oh, that's the one they went with? Hmm, okay, I guess.* It wasn't an untrue sentiment, but I thought I had *way* better sound clips regarding exercising your right to chemically melt your natural hair pigment away.

Dove is known for these kinds of emotionally uplifting campaigns that don't directly sell products. They promote an *Everyone deserves to be beautiful!* sentiment meant to win over a modern consumer base with values that were undoubtedly market researched to reveal women's affinity for authentic self-expression and self-acceptance. It's easy to suggest beauty is for everyone when you are selling beauty products because ideally everyone is your target demo. But for a brand like Dove, owned by one of the biggest global beauty conglomerates, there is profit to be made and there are products to sell, whether those products align with the sentiment of *You're beautiful as you are* or not.[*]

It's framed as if beauty is as inalienable a right written in the Constitution. Everyone is beautiful. All bodies are beautiful. You don't know you're beautiful; that's what makes you beautiful (okay, that last one was One Direction). But if we're all beautiful already, then why is there still so much beauty we're expected to be doing all the time? If natural beauty is best, then why does it require so many makeup products? If all bodies are beautiful then why am I always being goaded into training like a Victoria's Secret model (or detoxing and dieting also like a Victoria's Secret model)?

Beauty culture's official response thus far has been expanding its

---

[*] Dove has received public backlash for a racially insensitive body wash ad in which a Black woman appears to turn into a white woman; for releasing a series of differently shaped bottles of their body wash to mirror (or condescend to) women's different body shapes; for selling skin-whitening products in South Asian regions, and . . .

industry to as many niche demographics to address as many niche concerns as a brand or product can ostensibly solve. The culture of beauty has, in so very many ways, come to encompass how we choose an identity and then how to decorate it. Our lifestyles revolve around our chosen aesthetic practices and how they reflect our values. One might assume that our age of celebrating authenticity and individualism has championed the age-old, oppressive beauty standards of yore, but the tricky part is that claiming your "right" to be beautiful is just as much an inclusive invitation as it is a cultural mandate—one that seems to fall largely upon women to uphold.

Beauty culture today is a fun house in which you're the main attraction. It's a mirror maze of warped reflections showing you all the versions of yourself you could be or feel that you *should* be, all generally under the guise of a good time. Given the sheer magnitude of ways you can self-optimize in varying degrees of invasiveness and expense, beauty is now for everyone, whether they want it to be or not. It can sometimes feel like terms and conditions you're forced to agree to just to participate in society now. And opting out of beauty can feel like more of a deliberate and fraught choice than opting in. Even so, beauty culture's progress has not eliminated its stigmas; instead, a new capitalistic paradigm has absorbed them. Every perceived flaw becomes a platform for marketing new beauty values. Our modern beauty discourse champions a woman's right to aesthetically (medically) upgrade without social stigma while simultaneously promoting sentiments of self-love and how we are all beautiful just as we are. The "because I'm worth it" edict obscures our complicity with the same patriarchal and oppressive ideologies we may refuse but are willing to negotiate with insofar as what doing so will gain us. Irish author Emma Dabiri writes on this contradiction, "All of these new innovations and their complicated pleasures have distorted already indistinct boundaries between beauty operating within a system of oppression, and beauty as an expression of agency and autonomy."[*] We live in a world that has no shortage of tips, tricks, hacks, and tutorials you could do to look better.

Having more options is not without its perks, most of which are material. The industry has granted all the things we demanded of beauty for so long—inclusivity, accessibility, affordability, variety, novelty—only with slightly ironic results. The representation we've earned was because enough of us had to buy into it, to convince an entire industry that historically neglected demographics (non-white, queer, gender nonbinary) were willing to put our dollars toward it. Dollars are the most effective way to communicate with industries whose economic interests inform their politics and products. Inclusivity is table stakes for the beauty industry now that we've allegedly championed diversity—well, enough to intimidate brands into launching with no less than thirty-plus complexion shades. "POC-" and "WOC-owned" have become marketing terms to give brand stories an inclusive *edge*. But introducing inclusivity into an unchanged system just serves to distribute the labor and the expectations of that system to a more diverse set of people. It rolls out a dubious path toward attaining beauty ideals with tools and resources for all genders and skin colors, with no mention of the historic reasons they were excluded in the first place.

The boom of so many beauty brands launching so many new products is fueled by our multi-mirrored beauty fun house, every mirror a new channel for a different look, a new trend, and the next way you can optimize your appearance. It makes beauty a performance of class when every new option we have dangles the carrot of social and economic mobility.

---

[*]   Emma Dabiri, *Disobedient Bodies: Reclaim Your Unruly Beauty* (Wellcome Collection, 2023).

One of the contradictions of beauty culture is that as much as we aspire to (and invest in) beauty, we're not meant to acknowledge the labor and financial toll it takes. Why do you think we've referred to our grooming practices as "beauty secrets" for so long? Yet beauty's validity and merit are still undercut by the effort involved in achieving it. Celebrities are always criticized for gaining weight or not wearing makeup, as well as for being too thin or for getting any cosmetic work done that looks too obvious or "overdone." The pressure of being famous for one's beauty is that the expectation to uphold that reputation is paramount; failing to do so often makes them an outlet for our (the public's) own internalized frustrations with beauty standards. Anybody who relies on their looks as their meal ticket understands how much labor and maintenance it requires to keep up appearances. And a person's beauty doesn't make them immune to insecurity and appearance anxiety—in fact, it can easily amplify those feelings. The more important beauty seems to be, the more unfair it seems as well.

This contradiction is the age-old rivalry between beauty and vanity. Beauty is many things: a concept, a goal, an ideal. And vanity is the driving force behind it: the preening, primping, and varying degrees of body manipulation or punishment. Vanity is evidence, in many ways, of beauty's importance, the machinations of self-optimization people find so off-putting despite enjoying the end results. It's like seeing the strings of a puppet show; it can obscure the glamour of the fantasy. Investigating and interrogating beauty's relationship to vanity is where many of us get tripped up. It's only natural that an obsession with our looks is the first response to the anxiety of our appearance, especially if our looks are considered our most important asset. But vanity that was once reserved for the privacy of the home is now glamorously on display. There's no part of anyone's grooming, hygiene, or beauty habits that can't appeal to some voyeuristic audience—often becoming the mechanism of success for many beauty entrepreneurs and content creators.

Vanity has been manipulating humanity since the beginning of time. She's reinvented herself more times than Madonna, but don't ask how old she is because you will not get a straight answer. What you *will* get is the looming instinct that you should do everything in your power to pursue beauty. Vanity's breakout hit was a Greek guy, Narcissus, who was so obsessed with his own handsomeness that he couldn't stop looking at himself in some dirty pond until he *died.*[*] Narcissus's desire for his own beauty was so overwhelming, it surpassed all other life-sustaining imperatives (like taking the occasional snack break).

In Chinese mythology mirrors can be portals to a parallel dimension where your reflection is really a demonic twin who learns how to mimic your gestures perfectly the more you look into the mirror so they can one day pass over to our world and replace you (which you'd know when you look into a mirror and don't see a reflection—creepy!). Wildly different tales, but the message is similar: there is danger in vanity because there is danger in desiring beauty. Folklore spares no gory, twisted, and downright wacky detail to convince people that spending any idle time looking at themselves is bad news—while also telling us that being beautiful makes you better than other people. That contradiction is what binds modern beauty culture together, creating no shortage of morality traps surrounding beauty and what must be done to achieve it. And now, even as standards of beauty are expanding to include more than just one type of ideal, they're still expanding, nonetheless.

✹

I THINK ABOUT LIVING IN BEAUTY'S FUN HOUSE AS HAVING TWO ERAS: BEFORE DIGITAL and social media,[†] and the now. Before I was constantly confronted by my self-image via technology's gaze, my sense of self was mostly

---

[*] I heard he got turned into a flower, which honestly doesn't sound like the worst, but still.
[†] BDSM lol.

formed by the community directly around me (you know, family, friends, school bullies, et cetera). Before YouTube and Instagram, you were an Autumn, Winter, Spring, or Summer. You were either hot or not. Everyone looked cool in Polaroids, rendered softly with the chemical mercy of film. Even the early model digital cameras gave everyone a cool, arty, high-contrast treatment that blotted out any skin texture, blemishes, or detail with the flash. Beauty was static—a barrier of celluloid between oneself, magazine cutouts, and movie scenes on repeat. Beauty in analog, for better or worse, stayed in its lane.

In a post-internet world, beauty has become a many-headed hydra—a global revolution of newness opened in infinite tabs. It eclipsed the relevance of beauty authorities like magazines; there was a wider perspective to be found online. If you wanted to find beauty idols who looked like you, it was possible. Our new idols weren't just industry-selected models, but also pretty people with a blog, a YouTube channel, or an Instagram account. By the time beauty vloggers had become a dominating presence on social media and in public interest, legacy media had reluctantly started "pivoting to digital." Our attitudes toward beauty also shifted—celebrating authenticity and individuality gave beauty a personality, it made it fun, and the inclusion felt more sincere. Framing beauty as fun made it less intimidating, even if the intentions weren't entirely changed. *Look how fun it is to do beauty, you're the star of the show, the world is your oyster!* But sometimes oysters betray you.[*] The beauty fun house has a way of making a content forum out of the body dysmorphia it's inspired.

The earliest memories I have of being perceived online is on MySpace or LiveJournal, some of the first editions of the blogosphere and social media. It's amazing how you can be a local five, post some

---

[*] Like the ones at my brother's wedding that gave me and several other guests food poisoning. I call it Mollusk Mayhem.

arty-looking pics on your blog and suddenly you're a Tumblr eight. The internet really plays fast and loose with egos. It wasn't until I got into the beauty writing game, contributing to a site called xoVain, that I began to really feel comfortable owning that eight-ness. It was a sister website to xoJane; ostensibly the beauty vertical for xoJane with a handful of contributors who all had their own "beats." The posts were diaristic and contained tons of self-taken imagery. Personal anecdotes and oversharing was encouraged. You had to take your own photos (phone selfies not allowed—camera only!) and you weren't allowed to alter them in any way beyond minor lighting or color correction, as was the site's authenticity policy. My face was all over that site (and Google image search results since digital-first sites like this one got a head start on dominating keywords). It had a robust comments section of loyal (and highly critical) readers. It was a great lesson in self-photography, beauty editorial strategy, and voice-y writing (and not reading the comments).

Thanks to (and exacerbated by) the internet, we've never been looked at more than we are now, *and* we've never had more unfettered access to watching the lives of others. Or the lives other people want to project, anyhow. Living in a surveilled society is not to be confused with a sudden obsession with vanity. Left to our own literal devices, beauty culture has exploded to include so many more of us than it ever has before while also upping the stakes of what it takes to be considered Beautiful on the grand global scale. It's become almost impossible to separate individual ideas and desires about beauty from that kind of broadscale programming. But beauty is long overdue for a reboot in our hyper-digital era.

If we all remember, the first emerging social media sites were beauty focused. Facebook (now Meta) started out as an Ivy League exclusive "hot or not" ranking website, if you can believe it (and now it's mostly where your aunt goes to vent about a poor experience at the local Starbucks, and where you can buy decently priced furniture from local civilians). The community that internet and social platforms granted us was great for forming a broader global perspective in general, but once we started realizing that the internet gave us more direct access to worldly hotties, our priorities were set to ogle.

Beauty found a new arena—one of connection, service, education, and a whole lot of #inspo. Connection and content have benefited us in tons of ways, but what we didn't exactly anticipate then was that abundance begets abundance, and the more that beauty imagery dominated social platforms, the more our already very appearance-based culture extended lookism into the network of our digital economy. Global connection created a worldwide beauty network that broadened the scope of what beauty could be. This also had the effect of blending that scope into a racially ambiguous ideal that wasn't universal so much as it was à la carte. It formed a baseline average of global beauty decontextualized from what it means to be in a human body by isolating appendages and features as if each whole was only as worthy as its ideal combination of parts (like Frankenstein's monster if he was remade as hot). Internet culture's hive-mind behaviors have a unique ability to make anyone famous, as well as dehumanize those who are swept up into its current, based on what goes viral. Andy Warhol was right: in the future everyone will be famous for fifteen minutes.

Beauty's fun house is fueled by content, and lots of it, most of which we put out there ourselves. People born after 2010 likely have Instagram accounts made for them by their parents when they were infants. Technology indulged our wholesale voyeuristic tendencies, connecting us to a global worldview, but it has also introduced many more unignorable and uncomfortable truths, one being if you want to participate in the modern world, there is no escape from being perceived anymore. Privacy and FOMO have become one and the same.

There isn't really a passive way to create a presence online; it requires a performance of self that, even when it does feel authentic, is incrementally and increasingly swayed by who's viewing you and what for (and if there's a comments section, even more so). Being a person is fundamentally odd enough when you don't have potentially hundreds or thousands of strangers perceiving you doing it, so it's only natural that the personas (and neuroses) we develop are in self-preservation as much as self-expression.

Engaging with beauty online means you have most likely gotten ready with many a person through personal videos of them doing their beauty routines. Watching a person transform is always compelling, but usually way more than makeup and skincare tips are being shared. There's something inherently intimate about getting ready with an audience, as is maybe chattering on about your personal life as a way to fill dead air, but this beauty video format has taken off to now share any anecdotal experience, rant, or stream of consciousness diary update. It can feel like hanging out with a friend in their bedroom. When it comes to personal sharing, vanity has become the most universal mechanism. (That's why those "What I eat in a day" and "How I got fit" YouTube videos are so popular.)

The behind-the-scenes B-roll of the way you present yourself to the world is usually always more interesting than the final product. In my editor days, any time a beauty article involved unexpected results, a transformation, or tutorial, the accompanying imagery that included an in-process shot (even if it was lo-fi) would up the click rates way more significantly than a happy, polished "after" result. It feels like all anyone wants to ever know about a person is how their persona measures up to their appearance; if we consume enough of someone's content, we believe we can really get to know a person. And that isn't entirely untrue. Posting online means our habits are on display just as much as our faces and bodies are. In many ways, you are what you post. But how others perceive you is only in your hands so much.

Vanity's centuries-long reputation as a deadly sin did not stand a chance against visual platforms like Instagram and YouTube. Vanity won. It became a main character, fleshed out with complex backstories and holistic narratives that included the in-between processes and the ugly fails that appealed to our morbid curiosities about beauty, its risks, and its rewards. Anyone could be the star of their own show.* Contouring with wacky objects like a shoe or wine bottle; applying a hundred layers of foundation; demonstrating things that are not makeup (hot cocoa powder, glycerin soap bars, or activated charcoal tablets) as makeup; and close-up pimple-popping videos all became new ways to entertain with beauty (except maybe that last one). And these stunts done by regular civilians with increasingly large online platforms led to a whole new job: being an influencer.

In terms of beauty, influencer culture's boom began with YouTube in the 2000s and then its success was spurred on with Instagram in the 2010s. Influencers (originally referred to as bloggers or vloggers) cannibalized digital media in a way that no one anticipated, and everyone is currently doing their best to capitalize on. As someone who was a beauty blogger† during a time when bloggers were *not* considered aspirational at all (bloggers were initially thought of as cringey, self-obsessed, model wannabe try-hards by the general public, not unlike the initial cynical perception of influencers before they began to out-earn our most recognizable Hollywood figures), redemption came in the form of economic dividends that validated their ambitions and a

---

* And when you grow up in America there's an intrinsic belief that you already are.
† Well, it wasn't *my* blog, but back then web writing was broadly referred to as "blogging."

whole new category of media career.[*] These are the people launching beauty brands now, some to great success. Some of the most popular makeup lines were launched by influencers—Kylie Cosmetics, Kat Von D Beauty, Huda Beauty. The beauty industry quickly became eager to partner with influencers as brand ambassadors and satellite marketing figures. And the tiers of influencers[†] took the shape of whatever seemed like the most genuine way to engage with potential consumers.

Anyone can be a content creator, and anyone can go viral. Not everyone who posts beauty content takes off, but most people who have experienced virality on TikTok eventually try their hand at dabbling in beauty content (this is usually where the "getting ready with me"s and the routine videos come most frequently into play). All consumers who engage in beauty content become influencers in their own way. Influencer culture is the result of inclusivity capitalism. There are no more gates to be kept. When done well enough, it can lead to a very lucrative career. Monetized YouTube channels, sponsored posts, affiliate commerce links, and for the especially successful, career opportunities beyond social media, have all made the lifestyle of an influencer economically aspirational for those willing to devote the majority of their time and personhood to it. But the stakes of such a glamorous life have risen to the point of perfection overall, often obscuring the transparency and authenticity promised in favor of successful contents' best practices.

The ubiquity of Instagram flat-lay posts of one's "holy grail" products, or *shelfies* (basically the same thing, but sometimes not so flat),

---

[*]   Which technically did not benefit me in the same way that it did for career influencers, since being a beauty editor pays considerably less.
[†]   Shopify logs them into five categories:
    Nano: 1,000–10,000 followers
    Micro: 10,000–100,000 followers
    Mid-tier: 100,000–500,000 followers
    Macro: 500,000–1 million followers
    Mega: 1 million+ followers

became a visual beauty language of its own. Naturally lit shots featuring Aesop Resurrection Aromatique Hand Wash, half-crunched tubes of Laboratoires Embryolisse Lait Crème Concentré, Byredo candles, and so many Glossier products on a bathroom sink, a vintage vanity desk, or artfully strewn across fluffy linen bedding (sometimes with a cappuccino delicately balanced on a saucer as well) broadcasted being in the beauty "in" crowd. You didn't even have to necessarily show yourself wearing any of them—just the products themselves. UGC (user-generated content) became some of the most effective marketing for beauty brands because it looks like personal promotion rather than an ad when in reality it's both. There was something aspirational and inviting about such aesthetically casual luxury, like getting a (literal) snapshot into someone's beauty routine.

Once beauty became my occupational playground with dermatologists, makeup artists, hairstylists, and aestheticians happily offering their services to me, naturally, the first thing I did was explore all the ways I could be classically hotter. I went platinum blond, for Christ's sake. It's way too tempting not to indulge what you could look like when it's available to you. My limit was always at the brink of permanence—if I couldn't grow it out, wash it off, or let it fade on its own, I was hesitant to engage with it. I think that's why the most successful beauty brands are ones that promise to make you a hotter version of yourself, usually in some "five minutes or less" format; most people want to feel transformed without much sacrifice (of time, effort, or ethics). And while the choice to transform is on you, the Beauty™ in question still feels compulsory—like you have to do *something*—when our visually obsessed world demands to see you in every context: your everyday glam, your going-out glam, your before-and-afters, and above all, your real and authentic self. And if you're not sure what that looks like, there are plenty of blueprints to try. The whole world is waiting to GRWM at all times.

Beauty's digital media age got a burst of energy with the rise of reality television stars—perhaps most notably with the Kardashians. Since their cable TV debut in 2007, the family of sisters now has become a global beauty, fashion, and lifestyle conglomerate simply by televising every glam and unflattering detail of their lives. The Kardashian-Jenner aesthetic of filled lips, dramatically contoured complexions, and lifted, almond-shaped eyes inspires equal imitation as it does criticism from the global public. Their ubiquitous look, most replicated on Instagram, introduced a modern beauty aesthetic that is only as attainable as it is financially feasible—but no less unrealistic. Not that everyone in the world wants to look like a Kardashian-Jenner, but even those who are vocally against the beauty standards they promote (many of which were already well established by Black women but made popular by the Kardashian-Jenners) also continue to pay them the attention that grants them that influence. It's a contradiction that makes me suspect it's not authenticity we're after; it's access. Anything is made authentic with constant surveillance anyway—or at least that is the illusion when you think you're getting the whole narrative.

The Kardashian-Jenners helped to promote selfies as a currency for social metrics. Now Instagram is the number one source for looking at hot people as well as hurting your own feelings. I suspect that the app caught on to this snag, offering something to curb the sting of being perceived barefaced or just not with the current trends: filters. The filters that were created to paint all kinds of aesthetics onto your face made people more likely to post. Even the silly ones, like the dog-face filter, contort your facial proportions to be cartoonishly cuter and your skin smoother. They serve as a preview for what you might look like with no under-eye bags, CGI-smooth skin, bigger, poutier lips, and more angular eyes. Filters are ubiquitous to the point everyone doubts that anyone actually looks like what they look like online; in fact, the filters are an assumed part of being online. And while most of us who are very online are cognizant of the fact that so much of what we see is postured, filtered, and edited,[*] that awareness does little to minimize the sentiment of seeing so much of it: you'd better keep up. We're constantly subjecting our egos to the blunt strokes of a pixelated portrait reflected flatly back at us from our phones and computer screens. When we see each other that way more than in real life now, it's not surprising that many of us seek out ways to match the filtered version of their faces.

Beauty brands jumped on the filter wagon, offering complexion makeup and skincare products that blur pores and blemishes so you can post a perfect selfie on Instagram, "no filter needed." With that, filters took over the stigma traditionally placed on makeup—that women only wear it to hide what they really look like. And then wearing filter-mimicking makeup to make filters redundant became the work-around. When selfies are a primary mode of self-expression in a digital landscape, perfecting them feels important. I've reaped the benefits of many a well-lit, well-angled selfie—mostly in little dollops of dopamine with every heart or fire emoji comment. Our appearance insecurities, some of which we may have never even realized we had, come to the forefront simply because we think about our appearance in so many more meticulous ways now. It intensifies the already felt anxiety that social media is only for pretty people.

With our modern techno-vanity we have the ability to edit our reflection to appear exactly as we want to be perceived. Mirrors have evolved into screens, creating a fourth dysmorphic dimension of another self—your meta mirror. Whether you're an influencer or just an app user consuming their content, it's difficult not to compare yourself

---

[*] I don't know why everyone assumes Instagram was created with the intent to broadcast reality, considering how obviously *artistic* those original filters were.

with other people's lives or feel bad about your own based on what appears to be real and so often isn't (at least not entirely).

Filters have gotten very good now, so good you don't realize how apps have sneaky default filter settings that subtly soften the fine lines in your skin and the slight bags under your eyes. Even Zoom has a "beauty filter" to better serve your own reflection back to you as you're staring at your own little square in back-to-back work meetings. Zoom fatigue from the early days of the COVID-19 pandemic inspired an uptick in beauty treatments like injectables and a newly invigorated obsession in skincare products to combat the digital insult of pixelated self-reflection. It's hard to track those exact numbers since in-person doctor treatments weren't permitted in the most stringent lockdown days, but any plastic surgeon or dermatologist I've spoken with since has told me that their inboxes and DMs were brimming to the point of capacity, all with people asking to discreetly be seen for Botox and filler (none of them obliged, at the risk of losing their medical license).

The digital reflection has become the dominant force setting modern beauty standards, ironically giving us free will (or the illusion of free will) to decide what looks gain traction as well as applying the same pressures to conform to them. We have access to so many more varieties of embodied beauty now, and yet I'm sure you've noticed that the figures and faces social media celebrates the most often look like ones who always have been. Meanwhile, our self-esteem is held hostage by a mysterious algorithm that decides whether your selfies deserve to be delivered to your full follower count or not. The entire production requires so much of your emotional energy for the anticipation of a reward that, even when it does come, is often robbed of the satisfaction by the fast-paced attention economy of the platform itself.

Every technological innovation is a mirror; anything that reflects human image can reflect human behavior as well. There are cameras now that can "see" the sun damage or lack of hydration in your skin (some of this imaging technology, like UV photography, is used as a health monitoring resource since the dangers of sun damage are well-known). Artificial intelligence may become the next research and development department and creative director of the beauty industry. Beauty brands are hopping on the tech trends to create devices that examine not just the health of your skin, but also the quality of it, and monitor how people engage with beauty online. I used to think being ugly was worrying enough, but now that anxiety has extended simply to being perceived.

✳

AND YET! AS OVERWHELMING AS BEAUTY CULTURE CAN BE, IT'S NEVER BEEN AS DI-verse and representative as it is now. Consumers demanded representation, so now we have foundation collections launching with no fewer than forty shades. Beauty campaigns include faces of all races, genders, and sometimes ages. Cosmetic formulas have innovated to serve and address any skin or hair concern. We demand that our beauty products represent us as well as our values, while simultaneously providing us with a means to optimize whoever that is. As satisfying as it is to finally be recognized and celebrated by mainstream media, being seen also means being assessed with the same eye that reinforces beauty standards to begin with. There's money to be made from exploiting insecurities as well as celebrating individuality, and often the only difference between the two is marketing. Beauty sponsored by capitalism makes its pursuit a never-ending list because the ways that one can participate in beauty culture are now endless.

Economics aside, beauty is incredibly complicated to deconstruct, let alone discuss, now. It is difficult to remove our own desires for beauty from their history of patriarchal sexualized ideals and the moral contempt toward women's bodies throughout Western philosophies and religions. How does a person reset or unlearn aesthetic preferences? Our fixation on bodies—women's bodies especially—makes it so difficult to separate beauty from our self-worth because historically, our appearance has always heavily impacted how we are judged in ways that have nothing to do with our character. This is also how beauty is coded into our bodies. It is a familiar language we understand intimately, one capable of inspiring feelings of affection, insecurity, envy, love, and desire. Yet more and more, I feel that reframing how we engage with beauty can be the antidote to the pain it's caused.

Perhaps it's my own morbid curiosity, but getting nearer to it has always been my chosen method of investigation—I often push myself to explore all the ways hair and makeup can be an expressive and transformative creative outlet (one devoid of its original intent). Having a career in beauty has been illuminating to me; it really is all made up, largely by marketing and advertising agencies, sometimes by editors like me, and increasingly by everybody with a social media handle. With great power comes great responsibility, as the saying goes.*

Beauty's secret skill is the connective tissue it forms between us— especially women. There has never been a time when I could not get to know a person better through a conversation about their grooming and hygiene habits, their cosmetic choices, or even the scents they like. I've met some of the most brilliant people through beauty's town hall (the internet). The community women find with one another through

---

* Something to remember if I ever get bitten by a radioactive spider and gain the opportunity to avenge the death of my beloved uncle Ben.

beauty is a strong one; it may appear to be superficial product recommendations or swapping makeup tips, but each one exchanges the kind of vulnerability that engenders a path to intimacy and support—both foundational to forming meaningful connections with others. We hold beauty's messaging in our bodies in ways we aren't even aware of until its tautness is released, at least for a little while. To be in company where I am not constantly aware of being watched—to release the tension of an arched back and a sucked-in abdomen—is a haven that must be protected.

The economy of being a woman is one that conflates appearance with the value of one's entire being—it is possible (and encouraged) to improve upon your appearance, but often at the cost of being taken seriously as a person once you do. Put more concisely by lexicographer Erin McKean: "Prettiness is not a rent you pay for occupying a space marked 'female.'"[*] But it can be confusing to accept that you don't owe anyone beauty when everyone seems to expect that you do. Beauty's standards are coded into so much of what's involved with being a person in society: class, for starters, dress codes, getting a job, finding a partner, smiling, not smiling . . . Beauty can sometimes feel like the Hotel California—you can check out, but you can never leave.

This chapter could easily be a bummer, and to be honest, it's been a doozy. I'd love to just pretend that beauty is just for fun and isn't it so great to be a woman because we get to paint our nails, dye our hair bright colors, and put on lipstick to Shania Twain? There is no shortage of self-proclaimed experts and authorities on beauty, and even as someone who held a pretty privileged position in one of the most authority-type roles one can have in beauty, I'm still like, *Welp, it's up to you to do whatever you want in the one body you get in this one life.* Hopefully you don't treat it poorly. It'd be a shame to spend any

---

[*] Erin McKean, "You Don't Have to Be Pretty," A Dress A Day, October 20, 2006, https://dressaday.com/2006/10/20/you-dont-have-to-be-pretty/.

time feeling bad about your body when it's doing what it's supposed to most of the time. But that doesn't stop me or anyone else from feeling shitty about the way we look, when the way we're allegedly supposed to look is so specific and not really all that easy to maintain. Doggedly charging at the pursuit of beauty is so often an impulsive response to life's frustrations, as if it is the solution to feelings of inadequacy. But to ignore its shadow sides paints yourself into a corner that eventually eclipses the light beauty promised in the first place.

I never want to tell people how they should feel about themselves, especially not how they should feel about beauty. Offering "But you're beautiful!" as a form of reassurance for the lack we feel that lots of times is based on all the entities telling us we are not beautiful enough . . . is not actually that comforting it turns out. It's optimism through a fragile lens of impersonal positivity—one that insists upon hope without examining the doubt. "Everyone is beautiful" only compounds beauty's importance in defining a person. Why should beauty be the central defining characteristic of our identity? And why should a global soap company—or any brand—be the one to give us that permission? Even in our modern, inclusive, diverse beauty culture, objectification remains the outcome. Upholding its ideals serves mostly as an investment in future grief because eventually we all age out of the ideal. And now these ideals are changing in even more niche and fundamental ways—soon no pore will be safe. We have to rein it in before it gets subdermal.

Beauty is many things, but I must remind myself that it is, above all, a choice. It's how I play with identity, how I visually communicate who I am, and in some ways how I care for myself and others. It's how I appreciate the body I live in now, more than ever, to make up for all that time misspent criticizing it in my youth. I could easily change the things I don't like about my appearance (again, occupational perk), but that doesn't feel like the win to me. Adorning myself in ways that feel reverential of my own desires and pleasures is much more satisfying. As is visiting spaces where bodies can exist just as they are.[*] It is highly advisable to interrogate how beauty serves you, especially in times when you're triggered by it. In the interest of authenticity, if that's what we're still doing, isn't it worth getting straight with that first? This way, even if you don't feel like you measure up, at least you know where you choose to stand, rather than being swept away in the riptide of inadequacy. It's important to take inventory of the things that occupy space in your mind.

Beauty's fun house is just that: fun—but mostly in small and deliberate doses. It may promise so many shiny, alluring, options for how you can self-optimize and experiment with your look, but it doesn't give you much nuance and it cannot deliver satisfaction (that's on you). At a certain point you just have to hit pause. Your attention is a finite resource. In the absence of resolution, I'm holding space for changes inching toward a beauty culture that cares not just for self-optimization but for everyone's comfort, acceptance, and pleasure. And in that space, there are way less mirrors. With virality determining trend cycles even more rapidly with "problem areas" that definitely sound made up—strawberry legs, over-boob chicken cutlets, TrapTox, neck grins—there are more insecurities being spawned than solutions.

A house of mirrors is meant to be unreal. Nothing about it intends to tell you the truth; in fact, its main draw is your own self-curiosity. Luckily beauty thrives on inquisitiveness, play, and ephemera. Nothing is permanent. Hell, even most waterproof makeup is not as impervious to wetness as it advertises. Try shit out—anything that amuses you and feels good to you—and it can only bring you nearer to the satisfaction of self-becoming. And then a little while later, you might change your

---

[*]   Korean bathhouses are such a relaxing way to be among other naked bodies with no posturing, just resting and relaxing, and absolutely cooking like an egg in those hot tubs and saunas.

mind, and that's fine too. Vanity is a portal toward self-discovery; it's a process that often requires coddling your deepest insecurities while simultaneously indulging your fantasies. Its momentum makes it more difficult to hang on to stagnant ideas of what beauty is for. It's best practiced with patience, a good sense of humor, at the hands of professionals in some chemical cases, and above all, with compassion.

The Job a Million Girls Would Dye For

eing a beauty editor will take you lots of places that absolutely ruin you for civilian life. My second month as a beauty editor at *Allure*, I was sent to report on the launch of a makeup brand's clay-based foundation stick. This involved sending a handful of editors, including me, to Costa Rica, where I was put up in a private bungalow at the Four Seasons, taken zip-lining, went river rafting, toured turtle and butterfly sanctuaries, and *pura vida*'ed my best life for the duration of a long weekend. The penthouse bungalow we stayed in had an infinity pool and a cupcake tower with colorful makeup compacts for decor. As I treaded water in said pool, overlooking a cliff lush with tropical greenery, I distinctly remember thinking, *This is probably the best day of my life* (it's easy to forget all those other best days of your life in the presence of nature's glory and five-star accomodations). Drunk with passionfruit-derived dopamine and Central American sun, it was easy to forget that I was there for work.

The next year, I was sent to the Coachella music festival with VIP passes to collect some social content for a big beauty store's sponsored hair-braiding tent that featured its brands' products—glitter and colored hair sprays and unicorn-hued hair accessories. The big beauty store also budgeted a buddy, so I was able to take my best friend Alle (hi, Alle!), who doubled as my de facto cameraperson. Among the LSD-soaked tech bros and influencer entourages in the VIP tents, we were decidedly over- as well as underdressed (turns out, nobody wears pants at Coachella. It's cheeks out everywhere) as we roamed the fields aghast at the sheer level of hedonism at this Instagram playground.

My last year as a beauty editor, I was flown to Singapore in business class to write about the "wellness menu" on the flight that was curated by an elite hospitality group where the likes of Bill Gates and Martha Stewart went to abscond (a lot of well-being involves absconding, it turns out). For the duration of the nineteen-hour flight, I sampled a menu of twelve different low-calorie, gluten-free, and vegan courses, all of which were five-star. And then I spent three days in Singapore between flights demolishing my guts with street food and hawker market meals (totally worth it) in between exotic beauty treatments like a crystal reiki facial and a vulva rejuvenating treatment. My labia have never been so pampered in their lives.

Working in beauty has been responsible for most of the stamps in my passport. When not flying business class around the globe, I was regularly smearing my face with creams that the general public would liken to the blood of virgins or sacrificial lambs, given the price tags and ingredients. I had the personal phone numbers of the beauty pros who did Meghan Markle's wedding makeup and Ariana Grande's ponytail in my phone. The contents of my medicine cabinet would likely fund one of those Mars rovers. But if you asked me what my job actually entailed, the answer would differ based on what financial quarter or season it was, which brand was doing a launch, who was on the cover that month, or what film franchise was trending.

I didn't know that at the beginning; all I knew was it was seemingly *that job* a million girls wanted and the one I got. But it did not start off very glamorously.

It was the spring of 2017 and my first day working at *Allure*. I had to continuously excuse myself several times throughout the day to hack phlegm loogies in the bathroom toilet because a few days earlier, I let someone spit in my mouth who I probably shouldn't have, and had the makings of a cold coming on fast. I managed to keep the bacterial tempest at bay as I went about my first day on the job. I wore silvery pleated Issey Miyake–inspired H&M trousers, a black lettuce-hem mock-neck crop tee, and my green, patent leather Maryam Nassir Zadeh Sophie slides. I had my cerulean-blue hair roughly waved and tossed over to one side. (I have never known how to properly dress for an office and still don't, but the fact that I remember exactly what I wore that day surprises even me, now.)

They never tell you this, but every office job in New York City post-9/11 requires a photo ID key card to access the building, and they always take the photo on your first day, so you'd better treat it like picture day at school. My Condé ID photo looked *good*. Even the lady taking the ID photos was like "Ooh girl, you really nailed it!" when it came out of the little printer, magnetized for access to One World Trade. For once in my life, I was very pleased with how my grainy laminated likeness turned out—a promising sign I belonged here! My hair at the time even matched the blue of the One World Trade Center logo.

Another first-day good luck charm was discovering the secret, fancy executive bathrooms on that floor. When you work at a place like Condé Nast, work-life balance is an urban myth. You're going to be spending way more than your salaried forty hours a week in this building, so you're going to need to accommodate whatever bodily functions may insist upon happening there. Also, it's a rite of passage that everyone gets food poisoning at least once from the Condé cafeteria, so it's in your best interest to find a private bathroom.

One unique feature of using the restroom in a skyscraper tall enough to charge admission for is that all those stories require plumbing powerful enough to reach upward of ninety stories. To efficiently collect waste from the height of the heavens down to the bowels of New York City's sanitation system, the toilets flush with the intense efficiency of those unsettling salmon cannons meant to redistribute fish over dams. The sound of the flushing alone requires protective gear over your ears, like those construction site headphone mufflers—but *not* in my secret oasis.

Nestled in the center of the thirty-fourth floor between the elevator banks and the corridor of conference rooms, the bathrooms were quiet, elegant, marble-clad atriums with recessed lighting and Malin+Goetz hand soap. Each stall was its own private chamber with a sleek Toto toilet that managed to flush politely and efficiently. There was rarely a time when someone else would even pass by those restrooms, so you could take all the time your nervous bowels needed to evacuate, or to rehearse your budget presentation. Honestly, a pooping bathroom totally transforms your quality of office life, whether you work at one of the world's most preeminent legacy media conglomerates or not.

The question I've been asked the most in my career is surprisingly not how to find the ideal pooping bathroom at work, but: How did you get your job at *Allure*? (Often asked with the same fervent curiosity that chronically single people in New York City ask couples how they met.) But my beauty career did not start off all that glamorously.

The year was 2012. I was desperate for a new roommate tout suite, after receiving a rude two weeks' notice from my current one. I wrote a long-winded, detailed apartment listing, waxing hyperbolic on all the attractive features of the convertible two- to three-bedroom apartment and surrounding neighborhood. At the time, I was working very part-time as an assistant at a friend's design studio, and it wasn't the kind of wage that could cover the entire $2,500 monthly rent; plus, my savings at the time were nonexistent. So, I was posting the listing on every apartment share site I could at the time: Craigslist, several local Facebook apartment forums, word of mouth, whatever. The ad was a hit. It could've won the Pulitzer of Craigslist ads, if that was a thing. Most of the comments it received were about how funny the ad was and how I sounded like a really fun roommate (I'm not). A beauty editor responded,[*] saying she worked at a newly launched beauty site called xoVain and was looking for writers; she enjoyed reading my ad and wondered if I'd be open to pitching her.

I'd never heard of xoVain at the time, but I was aware of Jane Pratt because of *Sassy* and *Jane* magazines, so if xoVain was the beauty outlet under her, I was interested. The articles on xoVain.com were *very* loosely beauty-related—it was essentially a blog with multiple contributors who re-created all of Lindsay Lohan's mug shots (wigs, fake tan, and all); tested how Nars Orgasm blush compares to the blush from an actual orgasm; and what your portrait would look like if you described yourself to a sketch artist using only the most gorgeous descriptions of yourself. Beauty was the anchor to the posts, but the topics ranged broadly. They paid fifty dollars per post, which required original photography and in-depth, personal takes on the topic at hand. Photoshopping was forbidden. This was an acceptable rate to me, someone with zero journalistic cred and mostly expired makeup I had shoplifted years ago. I pitched something about doing a morning-after-inspired makeup look, thinking I was being *edgy*. Either way, it flew, and I became a freelance beauty writer. Some memorable pieces include: "I Created a Makeup Look Using Only Shades with My Name" (Sable); "Going Platinum Blond Required a Visitor's Pass Through the 9th Circle of Hell but Was Totally Worth It" (questionable but fair); "How to Cover Bruises and Swelling from Getting Completely Clobbered in the Mosh Pit" (probably should've consulted a medical professional for that one); and "Let's Make Weird Girl Hair a Thing" (an ill-conceived response to the "cool girl hair" trend of the time). XoVain was truly the underdog of beauty sites. I don't think most of us felt qualified to call

---

[*] She had no idea if I was ugly or not, which I naively thought might be some deciding factor in writing for a *beauty* publication, but it turns out it's not, because women are never ugly.

ourselves beauty writers, so much as we were professional bloggers on a 1099 basis. The timing couldn't have been riper, though, because I found myself right at the beginning of the YouTube and vlogger era, and brands started to realize just how influential bloggers could be.

I found that the scrappy underdog role suited me. I was used to hopping from miserable part-time job to slightly less miserable part-time job that would gain me an extra two to three dollars on the hour with each leap. I'd never had an annual salary until I was twenty-eight, let alone my own health insurance since being yeeted from my parents' plan two years prior (thanks, Obama, you tried), let alone an employee ID card with a hot photo of me on it.

By the time I was hired at *Allure*, the brand was going through a near-total revamp of its digital presence. Michelle Lee, the editor in chief at the time, championed a digital-first, global perspective—the ambitions of which would involve Phillip Picardi, *Teen Vogue* and Condé Nast wunderkind, to lead the digital editorial team and select his writers.[*] In a very media world fashion, Picardi sent me a Twitter DM asking if we could talk about a position for me, and even though I was just getting into the groove of freelancing, you don't *not* take the call when the King of *Teen Vogue* beckons.

Working at *Allure* was in some ways just as glam as I imagined it'd be, and in many ways not how I expected at all. It wouldn't be out of the ordinary to bump into celebrities in the elevators, on the photo studio floor, and swanning about the corridors of our floor. One time I accosted Aubrey Plaza and fangirled over her in a restroom on the photo studio floor as she was attempting to zip up a gown for a shoot. And one time an extremely attractive and charming young male celeb from some popular teen show tried flirting with me at the sinks in our newly gender-neutralized restrooms, which might've worked if I hadn't just

---

[*] Fun fact: I interviewed for Phillip's job at *Teen Vogue* maybe a year prior. Didn't get it.

gotten an earful of his powerful stream. One time I tried interviewing James Franco at a Coach fragrance event, and his handler wouldn't allow him to answer a single question about his skincare routine ("I use, um, Kiehl's, I think?"), and then a venture capitalist tried to abduct me to his Hamptons estate via Blade helicopter. A handful of times I've even taken the elevator with Anna Wintour, and she would curtly nod at me in acknowledgment that I am a person sharing an elevator with her. Glamour!

Despite that, it's also a job that requires jobbing in ways that don't wholly make sense to the outside world. Like when Emily Ratajkowski's* cover shoot required an editor on set with no instruction other than "just to make sure," so I was sent to the shoot. While I *made sure* to eat as much on-set catering as possible, I'm not sure what else, exactly, I was supposed to make sure of. Or when it came to awards season—the Oscars, the Golden Globes, the Emmys, the Met Gala—editors worked a double shift with no overtime, posting up in a conference room "war room," feverishly pumping out articles until well past midnight, writing up the most minuscule of beauty-related crumbs with the urgency of a crisis call center. This annual workday marathon is necessary because as the beauty industry continues to grow, the ever-growing demands for commerce and online traffic goals (click-through rates, affiliate link purchases, et cetera) have only increased.

That's the thing about working in digital media—any journalistic integrity is constantly being held hostage by the traffic goals that validate or invalidate the kind of work we're able to do. That's why you're sick of reading about the Kardashians, and J.Lo's makeup-free selfies, and the hidden meaning behind Cardi B's manicure; everyone loves to click on the things that annoy them. The landscape of digital media is a true reflection of the culture's interests and impulses. We are giving

---

* She was very nice and professional!

the people what they want! The more you click on things, the more data you're giving all our creepy analytics programs that this is what is of interest to the masses and therefore what we must consistently cover. So, really, all of you are deciding what media covers. If only the annoyed commenters beneath shared articles about Kylie Jenner's wig-or-not-a-wig hair color transformations knew that they are always contributing to the proliferation of content they despise with every "garbage" and "who cares" comment. There is such a thing as bad press, but all engagement is good for the gander.

My one grudge against the Jenners is that they *always* post sneak peaks on Friday afternoons during work hours in Calabasas, but ends up being Eastern Standard go-the-fuck-home hours. And inevitably it would come down to a game of editor roulette to see who will take one for the team in either writing a rapid report about Kylie Jenner teasing a new eye shadow palette including blurry screenshots from her Instagram story (requiring a headline workshop for article title, SEO headline, and social media headline) or assigning it out to any available freelancer at the ready, and then editing it to post as quickly as possible. This was trickier if the Kardashian-Jenner squad posted anything juicy on the weekends, pre–weekend editor days, because before we had a budget for a weekend editor the team would occasionally get work emails on a Saturday evening like: *Can someone please write up this tiny tidbit about Khloe Kardashian's new highlights? It would be suuuuuper helpful for the team.* Unfortunately, the lower you are on the masthead, the less boundaries will benefit you. The higher up on the masthead you are, the more boundaries work in your favor. You can leave every day at three p.m. to pick up your kids from school or just never come in Thursdays and Fridays because you're at your summerhouse in the Hamptons for the weekend and responding to emails with no more than five words, signed with "sent from my iPhone." And that's just corporate culture.

Being a beauty editor is a job with its own very specific lifestyle. There are the press trips (definitely the best part) where I was zip-lining, dining at Michelin-star restaurants, and staying in five-star resorts on the clock. But of course it isn't always like that. The not-so-glamorous part of the job involves a whole lot of experimentation with products, and the courage (or dissociation) to sacrifice your body in the name of beauty, trying out the newest products and procedures for a first-hand account that will later be narrated through an editorial lens. No one really complains about this, considering how *prestigious* a lot of that stuff is—that is, until you become the victim of an injectable gone wrong, several bouts of contact dermatitis, chemical burns on your scalp, and eyebrows permanently microbladed in a shape that won't be on trend a few months later. You really have to be a good sport about your ego. No one exits Beauty™ unscathed.

It's not necessarily a beauty editor's job to dictate what's beautiful and what's not, even though in my early magazine-reading days I assumed someone just decided something like *French manicures are out! And messy eye makeup is in!* and that's how magazines got made (not entirely inaccurate, but it's never without substantial reference). Beauty editors are meant to oversee the whole beauty landscape—what innovations the industry is making, how culture is shifting, and what people are actually wearing and paying attention to. Beauty editors communicate the significance of beauty, whether that be economical, cultural, or personal, rather than determine what is or isn't beautiful. The hundreds of daily press releases and product launches we receive citing trends and breakthroughs aren't proof of concept—they're more like an omen, a swarm of squawking ravens (Lip flip! Curtain bangs! Shade range extension! Hailey Bieber nails! Retinol!) to be deciphered and their meaning extracted and validated through a wider scope of experience and observation of culture.

Beauty editors are not aestheticians, dermatologists, makeup artists, or hairstylists. We're more like a conduit to all of them, armed with encyclopedic knowledge of marketing stats and what's *working*. We are mouthpieces who shape the narrative of why all those things are worth caring about for our readership (or whoever we think that readership is, and what they care about). As the title of "editor" implies, the job involves having a point of view that informs the curation of content and tone; we are responsible for dissecting and validating (or debunking) beauty trends and the resources required to achieve them. We're also responsible for serving our readership the kind of content that engages and titillates.[*] Many times, these two things are in conflict. Lots of beauty writing involves the same product-peddling and trend-reporting as a brand might do, geared toward steering the readership toward the product we want them to notice. Often, this comes in the form of hyperbolic headlines that will make whatever the product is seem most relevant to the cultural conversation at the moment. The digital landscape, in short, is the wild west.[†] We are all positively *howling* into the void of social media. There are SEO editors and social media managers who filter everything through the most click-y headline formats and posting conventions, which is why clickbait is a thing (because it works).

Beauty writing is often geared toward selling solutions to issues that aren't problems, so much as they are new benchmarks of what's *in*. These solutions to invented problems then become implicitly—or sometimes explicitly—endorsed via media acknowledgment and coverage. Beauty editors are just one reflection of the beauty industry just as much as they are cocreators of it, and the industry would like to have as much control of that image as possible. But the thing about wealth-

---

[*] Optimized for commerce affiliate links, so our corporate overloads can reap as much commission from purchases made through our little articles as possible.
[†] That's what the "www" stands for: wild wild west.

driven industries is that sometimes being inside and being included is conflated with expertise, when it's mostly just access. Living up to or performing the reputation of its uber-glam lifestyle is what perpetuates those perceptions as well as establishes us as "experts," because to an outside eye, access is everything. And ever since social media and influencer culture became another conduit into the beauty sphere, that access has opened to a much wider audience, making beauty its own entertainment, as well as a service-oriented channel. The beauty editor title alone grants you an authority backed by the publication behind you, which influencers don't necessarily possess as self-employed personal brands. In practice, though, successful influencers get the same perks as editors without the salary caps and nine-to-five hours. Considering how much editorial content is bolstered by influencer posts and trends, the divide between them is shrinking.

I came into the beauty editorial world after media's glory days but before the new digital era *really* took off. Getting my start at a site like xoVain was exciting because beauty was being parsed through a much more personal lens than most beauty publications at the time (even today). Our coverage involved experimental and skeptical narratives and individual voices. It's no wonder that beauty bloggers took off—they gave us the kind of voyeuristic (and sometimes messy) entertainment we craved from beauty coverage. Even as I onboarded at *Allure*, editors were taking on more voice-y assignments as well. The big difference between being at a smaller blog versus a media giant was that *Allure* had the legalities of corporate employment as a leash. If you work for a corporation, you can only keep up so much with folks who are willing to go to legally unadvisable lengths in the name of beauty content before your employer discourages things that could possibly get them sued.

Don't get me wrong—magazine jobs still retained plenty of the glossy and luxurious reputation from their pre–great recession days of town car service to-and-from work (for the high-up editors), designer bags as holiday gifts, dinners at Cipriani, and galas all the time. Back then, upward mobility was all but guaranteed for those who stuck with it and mass layoffs were rare. Some editors' entire careers included a decade at one publication, having interned their way to the top (I've known a few who have done that).

Nowadays, many people working in media in editorial and creative roles are underpaid, doing more jobs than they signed up for, and they see colleagues being easily laid off every financial quarter. (If you work in media, it's never wise to tie your job title to your sense of identity because it's entirely too easy to have it stripped away one unexpected morning in a conference room with stony-faced HR personnel and your fellow fallen comrades.) Those super-glamorous perks are fewer and far between; while you may be sent to jet off on an assignment, the salary is low and the daily perks are significantly more limited. And depending on which brand* you work for, sometimes your employer will demand a cut of any sponsored content opportunities you're given through your personal social media accounts as a result of being an editor there, while also denying you a cost-of-living raise or any other yearly bonus, merit-based or otherwise. No wonder everyone's unionizing.

It's not all economic distress, though. One of my favorite parts of the job (aside from the swag, swag, swag) is the camaraderie. The bond of beauty editors is a strong one, as it requires sharing your vainest aspirations and most vulnerable insecurities, as well as allowing your colleagues to enable your most frivolous pursuits and validate your impulsive changes in appearance (for the plot!). At *Allure*, the intimate knowledge we shared of one another's personal lives was borderline unprofessional, having witnessed so many bodily functions: crying, being physically sick, panic attacks, UTIs. If anyone was visibly upset,

---

* Magazines refer to themselves as brands now because the illusion that what we're doing isn't just an exercise in glossy capitalism has been fully dispatched.

your colleagues would descend upon you with affectionate concern, a hug, sometimes whatever cake or sugary treat in the shape of a brand logo was sent to the office that day, or just a hand to take you on a walk to air out.

When you're a beauty editor, the idea of work is quite different from lots of conventional notions of toiling away for the corporate overload. Believe me, we did plenty of toiling, but with regular breaks to swatch Pat McGrath lipsticks on our hands and spray clouds of Caudalie Beauty Elixir in between editing and meetings. The biweekly dissonance comes in the form of your paycheck and its pitiful after-tax net, which is barely enough to cover your living expenses for the month—a reminder that this job can only go on for so long before you're ostensibly priced out of it. It's not unusual to get flown first class to Paris to sniff Lancôme's latest perfume while living off Trader Joe's frozen meals back home and mopping up your employment anxiety sweat with Christian Dior blotting papers.

The organization of our little open-plan cubicle setup meant that the four or five other people who sat in your pod became fast friends and fiends. I sat next to the wellness editor, which meant that I often got first dibs on all the sex toys and fitness accessories and equipment sent from brands she didn't want. Sometimes we would use the several gratuitous yoga wheels and yoga balls to race down the corridors or drape ourselves around dramatically in a midday brain fog. If anyone expressed want for a *zhuzh*, a refresher, or a hand, someone would pipe up with just the thing from their desk—a spritz of Urban Decay All Nighter setting spray, a LED-lit makeup mirror, various sticks of natural deodorants, the latest Tom Ford fragrance, cooling eye masks, a Theragun, someone who knew how to do fishtail braids—anything. Camaraderie through beauty has always been the easier way for me to connect with people who I otherwise don't have much in common with. Friday afternoons sometimes devolved into all of us getting ready at our desks to go out after work, lingering after hours to primp before the evening's plans would commence.

Allure was where I discovered that beauty is the cornerstone to connection; there is a true intimacy to uncovering people's deepest, most private vanities.[*] Most beauty editors become quite chummy after attending the same events and trips together over the years. You really get to know and understand people's inner lives with beauty, because for so many of us beauty is our first line of defense and self-preservation. Editors just get to try way more stuff. We all have unique approaches to beauty, vicariously experiencing certain aesthetics or styles through one another. I don't really care about teeth whitening and self-tanner in the way our one sorority-bred social media manager did, but I would trust her with my life, and vice versa, even though she'd never dye her hair green or wear eye decals on a daily basis. Aesthetics can often obscure a lot of underlying similarities.

After a few months on staff, every beauty editor was like the post-makeover version of themselves. To work in beauty now is a fast way to indulge your vainest aspirations.[†] A unique privilege is that once in a blue moon, a licensed plastic surgeon or a neurotoxin-sponsored dermatologist would do an office visit, offering Botox or filler for any staff desiring a top-up. Even so, gratis injectables were just an email away to the right publicist. When there are no limits on access to products, it's easy to beauty too close to the sun, even for those of us innocently reporting on how not dangerous and totally easy all these products are. It's something that newbies learn quite quickly.

Media brain corrupts your thinking patterns to exploit any idea, nuance, or reaction for the sake of content. Sometimes it prompts you to dress up lukewarm opinions with clever portmanteaus or made-up

---

[*]   Plus sharing the same corporate working woes.
[†]   Until a celebrity hair colorist burns off all your hair and a million-dollar aesthetician leaves you with a tragic case of blepharoptosis.

labels to court clicks with hot takes, regardless of it even aligning with what the publication allegedly stands for. It treats long-form opinions that nobody asked for like academic thesis papers. And for some sad little psychological reason, a published story's emotional accomplishment value degrades rapidly once it's published, posted, and shared. I always get a little dollop of dopamine when sharing a story I've worked on and enjoyed on social media, only to feel a vast emptiness not even six hours later. I suspect most digital journalists feel similarly, robbed of the feeling of accomplishment by the riptide of the digital pace. As soon as something is published for all the world to consume, it begins its steady descent into the void of an endless scroll.

As much as beauty editors are expected to be at the cutting edge of all things beauty, gazing into our glittery orbs to forecast the future of beauty, so much of digital beauty reportage involves cleverly exploiting evergreen SEO. Basically, you're creating a robust database of content and articles catered to the most searched beauty terms (which required outsourcing to a sneaky SEO analytics team to discover!). Every month we'd be given a list of terms to write articles about, and I was initially shocked to learn that the most searched beauty things are also the most basic. Reigning at the top were things like:

How to wear red lipstick
What is the difference between concealer and foundation?
Best eye cream

As I penned something clever to cover a "where to put highlighter" search term, I realized that the entry to beauty was fraught with sheer overwhelm. The data was a reflection on where people approached beauty, and it's not that people were seeking the next big thing in beauty, so much as they wanted to know how to simply do beauty at all. At work, we spent so much time trying to be the first to report on big trends, when the bulk of what people were seeking were answers to basic how-tos.

Once you've been in the industry for long enough, you realize that the dissonance between what the beauty industry is covering and what people actually want is like the Grand Canyon of missed opportunities. If you want to make the most money in the beauty industry, cater to the most basic demand: providing advice and product recommendations to help people look like themselves, *but better* (at least in my experience, that's what the resounding universal call to beauty seems to be). "Better," of course, is totally subjective—but it explains why the "no-makeup makeup" trend stays in the zeitgeist. The trick for me and the other beauty editorial elite is how to disseminate that information in a way that incorporates the knowledge and expertise of the pros (makeup artists, hairstylists, dermatologists, cosmetic chemists, nail artists, et cetera) and collect it into easy-to-digest directives to tell you exactly what to buy, and what it's for. That's why listicles and awards are so popular.

At the beginning of every year, the *Allure* team would start collecting submissions for the annual Best of Beauty awards, which are basically like the Oscars of beauty products. And yes, we really do test everything on ourselves. For the first four months of each year, a team of specialists (aka freelancers) is brought in to collect products from any brand that wants to submit to the dozens of categories for superior product performance, chemistry, or innovation. There are a *lot* of products, so it's an all-hands-on-deck operation. The editors select the categories they want to test and then we are inundated with the hundreds of samples to vet in the remaining time frame. And the time frame is usually pretty tight.

Have you ever tried testing forty-eight self-tanners in the span of eight weeks? Neither have I, because that's insane. But some poor chump had to do it. After the mistakes of my first year, I learned to go for the makeup categories, which are way easier to test than skin- or hair care.[*] To this day, I still have crates full of blushes, highlighters, eyeliners, and powders in my closet somewhere from my last Best of Beauty test batch. Cosmetic chemists, makeup artists, hairstylists, and dermatologists get involved for some of the categories. It's one of the few awards that I feel confident in its vetting, since there are actual studies on the product ingredients.[†]

Beauty marketing loves to lean on impressive stats, studies, and trials to leverage the efficacy of their products. But learning how to read a study is wild—turns out there's so much context to how these trials are conducted, all of which affects how certain products or ingredients are perceived. Clinical trials are the gold standard, and they're very expensive to do. But even so, clinical trials don't guarantee accurate results; the trial groups could be too small—not enough people, not enough information, you know? And if a trial is funded by the brand or someone with a stake in the brand, there's an element of bias in the results; they're not going to publish studies that steer consumers away from buying their products, you know? A lot of data is shared in a way that manipulates perception to be favorable when trials are conducted in a way that minimizes the risk of negative outcomes.[‡] That's why there are asterisks and fine print.

On the one hand, I think it's great how beauty has become something defined by the people who invest in it the most. On the other hand, the individualistic attitudes of any given moment quickly fuel niche markets, so the industry continues to produce *new* things, instead

---

[*] People would have to tap out after suffering bouts of contact dermatitis from trying on sixteen different chemical exfoliators or retinol serums nightly. Grisly.

[†] Even if there is some bias shown to advertisers' products, which, perhaps by the time this book ages, will require disclosure.

[‡] Percentages seem to hold a lot of authority on product pages but, honestly, what does it even mean that "88% of people using this hydrating serum for a week reported feeling more hydrated skin"? You don't know how many people were surveyed, and you don't even know if the people involved had used any other kind of product besides this one. If it's the difference between using this serum vs nothing at all . . . well, of course you'll feel more hydrated.

of working on solving the underlying issues driving the market. The way we talk about beauty often overlaps with what we value about our health, and as such, consumer criticism doesn't so much *change* existing products as it inspires the creation of new alternatives. It's important to be careful what we consume when our consumption sustains what we may not support. There isn't much criticism that the beauty industry can't absolve by making a new product about it, even when in most cases, it shouldn't.

Our $500+ billion beauty industry contributes to a majority of plastic waste on the planet, environmental damage, as well as resource depletion.[*] It's beyond the point of individual embargo; it requires industry regulation. Of course, a kill-switch solution like quitting beauty seems the obvious strategy, but our wholesale reliance on personal care products is fully ingrained into our hygienic practices—it's not realistic to expect everyone will readily ditch it without an equally promising alternative. It requires critical thought to navigate the beauty industry without losing your mind. Despite the anxiety-inducing overwhelm of new launches, new treatments, trends, and procedures being reported on for your knowledge, beauty culture itself hasn't evolved much past its original tenets. There's just way more stuff now for you to try out.

The best beauty editors are inquisitive weirdos with a talent for personal metaphor, an astute awareness of cultural and global context, and a robust vocabulary. This job requires respect for the process and a curiosity-first approach—you can't be too jaded or snobby about new, wacky things, because there are new and wacky things happening in beauty every day; and not for nothing, but curiosity always makes a better story than judgment. That said, possessing a healthy skepticism to separate ill-conceived marketing and advertisement from the meaning

---

[*] "Beauty & Personal Care – Worldwide," Statista, updated September 2023, https://www .statista.com/outlook/cmo/beauty-personal-care/worldwide#:~:text=Beauty%20%26%20 Personal%20Care%20%2D%20Worldwide&text=Revenue%20in%20the%20Beauty%20 %26%20Personal.

behind it is an invaluable trait, otherwise you fall for everything. Also, a streak of rebellion is required, especially in a corporate environment. It will not make your job easier, but it will make the work better.

Much like that saying about learning the rules in order to break them, working in beauty requires (well, it should) a deep understanding of beauty standards, their performance, and their cultural origins. It gives meaning and context to the habits we've blindly followed for so long. To study beauty is to take a magnifying glass to what you learned of it from your childhood, explore your personal connections to it, and to watch how the world shapes beauty as much as beauty endures whatever the world is going through. Glamour can be a tricky goal; it's enticing on the outside but getting close enough will often undo its charms when you witness what's behind it. Sometimes it's a bummer, and sometimes it's just way more underwhelming than you thought. You have to keep an eye out for the little quirks, the nuances, and the humanity to appreciate beauty's meaning and context to you—an instinct that's easily anesthetized when you're caught up in the swag of it all. That's why fresh eyes and new vendettas are necessary to shake it up. The beauty industry can only benefit from more people coming to it from a totally unrelated field—sometimes even disgruntled former shopgirls and minor kleptomaniacs like me.

Fuck Around & Find Out: Beauty™ Edition

THERE IS NO SUCH THING AS "UNIVERSALLY FLATTERING."

Whenever I see this description for any beauty product, my eyeballs morph the words into a muddled sentiment in the shape of *I don't know, it's makeup, just put it on your face!* At this point in time, it's a lazy assumption about what people find flattering. Maybe the copywriters are checked out, defaulting to the familiar language of what entices a customer, or maybe there were so many cooks in the kitchen that this is the most inoffensive term everyone could agree with. When you see this phrase, remember it's a cosmetic anomaly. *Nothing* can be universally flattering if it's not taking the universe into account. (Speaking of the universe, I wonder if aliens wear makeup . . .) "Universally flattering" is *usually* used to describe makeup products that cater to paler skin tones, sometimes medium skin tones, but almost never to the deepest skin tones.

YOU'RE NEVER GOING TO NEED AN EYE SHADOW PALETTE WITH MORE THAN A DOZEN SHADES IN IT.

Even if you *think* you want the whole palette, let's be real—you're probably only going to use three, maybe four, shades in it, tops. Maybe there were one or two *really pretty* shades that drew you to that ninety-dollar eighteen-shade palette, and maybe those shades are packaged "exclusively" to that one product. Big Makeup knows *exactly* what it's doing. And if that's the case, you've got to pay to slay. Most of the time, you *can* find a similar shade from another brand, if you're willing to do some digging. I mean, sometimes an entire console of eye shadow is fun to have—I'm not going to tell you how to live your life. But I'd love to know the editing process for palettes with upward of twenty-four shades.

BEAUTY HAS A VERY EFFECTIVE (AND EXPENSIVE) PLACEBO EFFECT.

When it comes to product hype, most of it is marketing. Why are moisturizers $300? Because if it's so expensive, *it's got to be good*. Inflated cost is a very effective marketing tool. At some point strategizing product differentiation, some marketing genius went "What if it was *too* expensive??" and they've never looked back (spawning a new luxury to the luxury beauty category, dubbed "ultra-luxury"). Also, there are literally no laws limiting how much you can charge for a beauty product. When it comes to hype and virality, so much relies on the idea of desirability, status, and sometimes more than performance itself. All it takes is the right marketing—or a celebrity endorsement—for something to become *viral*. Remember: samples are offered freely and widely at most beauty retailers. If you ask me, there isn't much reason to pay for a moisturizer over forty dollars, unless you want to (but I reserve the right to change that number once scientists start making cosmetics from pure alchemy or alien DNA).

EVERYTHING COMES BACK AROUND.

Trends, karma, exes . . . Rest assured that just by living long enough, that thing you like will totally be cool one day. Or that thing that was cool when you were in high school will come around again (butterfly clips, chunky highlights, white eyeliner—so far, I'm three for three). You may as well just do whichever ones you want to regardless of their relevancy. Who knows, you might even bring back a trend.

THERE IS NO SUCH THING AS "EFFORTLESS" BEAUTY.

Beauty requires effort, a lot of which comes down to basic hygiene. Effort includes brushing your teeth twice a day, showering regularly, brushing your hair, washing your face. It's all just a matter of the way you do those things. And how fancy your toothpaste is. Remember, if a style guide is pitching "effortless beauty" and requires a billion steps to get there . . . use your brain. We've got to think of a better term for "effortless" that actually makes sense.

ALL "ANTIAGING" SKINCARE PRODUCTS ARE LYING.

You're still going to age if you use it. I know, it's crazy how Big Skincare is able to get away with printing a *clearly* false claim on their products. I'm honestly surprised there isn't a huge class-action lawsuit about this. You know how litigious we like to get. Aging is a result of living. It is also the way we learn to appreciate the ephemeral and transient stages of life. Forever isn't a familiar concept to beauty the same way youth isn't a familiar concept to life.

BEAUTY STANDARDS ARE MADE UP.

And mostly by Western hegemony. If your definitions of beauty are only informed by Western standards, you limit yourself to beauty defined by a myopic, imperialist, and patriarchal viewpoint. It's like having only one channel on TV and it's broadcasting nonstop miserable programming such as: Eurocentric features are the ideal; thinness is ideal; aging is unsightly; and performing femininity is the goal. Consider alternate cultures' values of beauty like the wabi-sabi philosophy of Japan, the ceremonial beauty in rituals of indigenous tribes, and the West African philosophy of combining physical attributes and behavioral characteristics in defining one's own unique kind of beauty. Free yourself from the limitations of visual optics being beauty's only incarnation. Beauty flourishes on the emotional spectrum. Let it.

SO ARE FLAWS.

If you think about it, flaws only exist in opposition to an idea of a beauty ideal. These so-called flaws are, in fact, evidence of your ancestral inheritance, your lived experience, and ultimately markers of your life-long story.

SO ARE "BEAUTY RULES."

See above.

YEAH, YOU SHOULD WEAR SUNSCREEN EVERY DAY.

I know I'm anti-should, but this is just good medical advice because the sun is out every day (even the cloudy ones). It's the same good medical advice as don't smoke and get enough sleep. It's your life, so you're going to live it how you want to, but this is a beauty book, so I must assume you, the reader, have at least a passing interest in aesthetic preservation techniques. They say the best sunscreen is the one you'll wear every day, so find one you like. There are so many nice ones out there now that don't leave you with a pale, ghostly veil of zinc on your face. If it helps, think of yourself as an undercover vampire and the only way you can go out in daylight is if you wear enough SPF. That's what I do.

YOU DON'T HAVE TO DIY.

Co-opting things that are not meant to be beauty products and using them as beauty products does not necessarily mean that they're better. Sometimes finding a good DIY feels like pulling a fast one on Beauty ™, but there are some things best left to the chemists—like anything that goes on your eyes, anything that requires a chemical combination to work, or anything where bacteria could set up shop. You're better off just using water or something cheap and gentle like Cetaphil rather than expensive honey from New Zealand to wash your face (the difference is . . . negligible). Putting lemon juice in your hair and then sunning yourself for highlights is a good way to also fry your hair, as well as your scalp. Using food as makeup probably feels very romantic and cottage-core but food is best ingested than left to rot on your skin.

THERE'S NO SUCH THING AS A LOOK THAT ISN'T FOR YOU.

If you like it, wear it. And if after you wear it, whatever it may be—neon eye shadow, a mullet, black lipstick—you come to consider that maybe you don't like that, well, now you know! And you can move on to try something new, no lingering thoughts of *What if . . .*

SOMETIMES YOU JUST HAVE TO LOG OFF.

You ever hear that phrase "one woman's beauty is not the absence of your own"? It's kind of an obvious statement, but sometimes one that bears reminding when you're microdosing dysmorphia on your daily scroll. Since when did everyone become twenty-two and also impossibly bombshell hot?? The reality is that some twenty-two-year-olds are bombshell hot, and it's the ones on Instagram who are algorithmically punted onto my Explore page to trigger my insecurity on some days when I'm not feeling so hot. When you start getting agitated by someone else's beauty, or start feeling insecure, it's a healthy choice to log off until you chill out.

DON'T BE BULLIED BY MAKEUP.

One of the most common questions I see regarding products, trends, and routines is: What's the right way to . . . ? When it comes to anything chemistry-adjacent, like skincare, (or anything involving high heat with hairstyling), there are indeed some more correct methods than others. But when it comes to makeup, it is a wild west out there. Sure, you might find some helpful tips from YouTube or Reddit, but whatever works best for you is the right way. There's no right way to wear lipstick. There's no right way to do your eyeliner or blush. It's a lot of trial and error, and then success. There is rarely a "right" way to do beauty.

NOT EVERYONE WHO FAKES IT MAKES IT.

The most powerful transformations come from within. They don't always adhere to your desired time line and they definitely don't happen all at once. But little changes eventually form bigger ones, and before you know it you're a totally different you. I mean, you're technically always in flux, always on your way to something, and always able to change course as you see fit.

PERFECTION AND BEAUTY ARE NOT THE SAME THING.

Perfection has always struck me as dismissive. It's a grand finale. It suggests that at a certain point you're done. And beauty isn't the kind of thing that is ever "done" because beauty is a reflection of living, of spirit, and in large part, the memory of both.

The Pretty Privilege Is All Mine

Forgive me for assuming that everyone's seen *Mean Girls*, but even if you haven't, you've probably seen the best parts of the movie memed to death, so here we go. *Mean Girls* is a great film about the contradictory nature of being a pretty young woman, and how the line between being pretty and owning your prettiness is some allegory for the dangers and treachery of indulging the power that beauty affords women. One of its most memorable one-liners comes after Regina George (reigning queen of the high school hotties) tells new girl Cady that she's really pretty. When Cady says thank you, Regina challenges her with a riddle: "So you agree? You think you're really pretty?" It's an iconic moment in the movie, and one that brings to light one of the fundamental trappings of pretty privilege: The first rule of pretty privilege is you don't talk about pretty privilege. You can be pretty, but you aren't supposed to own it.

When you're young, you come to know quite quickly who's pretty and who isn't. If you're pretty, people will tell you often and upfront. And if prettiness isn't your overwhelmingly defining feature, people will use other complimentary adjectives to encourage you: smart, clever, fastidious, well-behaved, creative, talented, funny, loves to read, et cetera ("creative" was a big one for me). It's not like *nobody* told me I was pretty when I was a young kid; my parents did, but they made me, so obviously they're biased (plus my parents' friends, but bias is also at play here because you can't tell your friends that their kids are uggos and expect your friendship to remain intact). One would think that doing child modeling would make it clear that I was pretty privilege incarnate, but this was the nineties and mainstream media could always find another peg to knock me down throughout my awkward adolescence. An adult told me once when I was about twelve that I would understand I was pretty when I was older. I remember at the time feeling a kind of dread in the futility of an unformed future and its uncertain promises.

"Pretty" is wholly subjective, of course. Back then it was mostly defined as being thin, white, cisgender, and feminine. And while that lens has broadened quite a bit now, those markers are still generally the easiest to benefit from if you hit them. Prettiness makes its importance known to many twelve-year-old girls, though, especially once it begins reaping social benefits beyond the privilege of being the first person among your friend group to choose which Spice Girl you wanted to portray in your Spice Girls dance group—meaning, who would be the first one to be kissed or have a boyfriend.

Some people are born hot. They often share a few telltale markers that will let you know that this is a person who has enjoyed the glow of pretty privilege for most of their lives. For one, they always know it, even if they don't mention it, because everyone else around them has told them all the time. The born-hots will often have a solid sense of confidence and self-assuredness. Many of them may self-identify as lucky. There's a natural ease in everything they accomplish, and things usually work out for them. People who see themselves as attractive may hold certain self-evident beliefs that their looks entitle them to the power and status they possess. And in belonging to a higher social class, they're more likely to support ideologies that contribute to the inequality that they benefit from.[*] Basically, hot people who know they're hot are very likely to think they're better because of it.

The social advantages of pretty privilege are well known: for one, your dating app matches will never run empty. People will buy you

---

[*]   Peter Belmi, "Mirror, mirror on the wall, who's the fairest of them all?" Science Direct, April 12, 2014, https://www.sciencedirect.com/science/article/abs/pii/S0749597814000223.

drinks at bars, randomly do nice things for you, give you gifts, and generally go out of their way for you. There are many economic advantages as well. Attractive people are more likely to receive raises, promotions, and be heard in the workplace. The perception of their productivity and value to a company is outsized. There are several studies that examine the power of pretty privilege and the unbalanced life experiences of those who have it. Conventionally attractive people are perceived to be more competent, likable, and trustworthy than the general population.[*] Before we even get to the numbers, all that excess hype instills a kind of self-worth in attractive people that they are indeed deserving of everything they desire, which makes their endeavors that much more persuasive. After all, believing in yourself is necessary for others to believe in you too. That confidence compounds upon its existing privileges, which explains how pretty people get ahead professionally so much more easily than their comparatively "plainer" peers. That's also why the best scammers are always hot. If you're a successful con artist, you probably have pretty privilege to thank for that.

Unlike many material privileges, pretty privilege is somewhat inextricable from personhood. You can get kicked out of boarding school and excommunicated from your wealthy family, but you can't actually quit your face or your body (not without significant self-sabotage). You can, however, gain pretty privilege by acquiring attractive features through any means of cosmetic manipulation. I've never been more assured that pretty privilege is real and powerful than when I've intentionally and laboriously leaned into perceived femininity—long, flowing weaves, false lashes, makeup, and heels. The reception is *loud* (and sometimes dangerous when you remember that some men feel entitled to touching women's bodies as they see fit). But there are certain

---

[*]   Gregory Ciotti, "The Surprising Power of a Beautiful Face," *Psychology Today*, December 7, 2014, https://www.psychologytoday.com/us/blog/habits-not-hacks/201412/the-surprising-power-beautiful-face.

provisions to the ways that pretty privilege works—generally it calls for a kind of beauty that appears convincingly "natural" in order to imbue positive associations of goodness and moral virtue with beauty. And we all know that "natural" is as subjective a word as "pretty."

We don't really have a collective name for whatever the opposite of natural beauty is, but the word "fake" (implying all kinds of undesirable traits like untrustworthiness and dishonesty) is liberally applied to those who choose to wear visible makeup or cosmetic enhancement. The most neutral terms we manage are "low maintenance" and "high maintenance." And "high maintenance" is always used in a pejorative sense when describing a person. "Low maintenance" implies the kind of virtue inherent in a lack of vanity (or beauty routine). If you only ever buy beauty and personal care products marketed toward "normal" skin and hair—and no one ever tells you *You'd look so much better if*—congratulations, you can enjoy a peaceful, low-maintenance life. "Normal" is a made-up term when it comes to beauty products. There is no normal police; it is not a benchmark regulated by any governing scientific, industrial, or medical body. Rather, it instead refers to the larger culture at hand's idea of what is baseline acceptable—much like *natural*. Opting out of beauty's machinations is something that mostly people with pretty privilege can manage without social stigma. You're considered low maintenance if you don't fuss over your appearance beyond basic hygiene while still appearing appealing, but you've let yourself go if you don't fuss over your appearance beyond basic hygiene and *don't* fulfill a certain level of conventional attractiveness.

If you do possess pretty privilege, you're expected to keep that knowledge to yourself. I mean, how many times has the ideal woman (written by men) been described as "beautiful but doesn't know it"? Beauty is praise given with the assumption that one's looks are not an earned asset and therefore undeserving of acceptance. It's why most times whenever a stranger has given me an appearance-related compliment, I feel compelled to deflect with a cheeky "Oh, this old thing?" or "Compliments to the chefs." It makes the whole issue of appearance bias a taboo that undermines ownership of one's own appearance and maintains the systems that put appearance on a pedestal to begin with.

Pretty privilege is an uncomfortable topic, both for those who are overlooked or dismissed in favor of more preferable looks and for those whose successes and individual agency are undermined as a by-product of their appearance. It is not a pleasant or necessarily fair allegation to make that one's looks are primarily responsible for any professional and social advancements they may benefit from. But looks certainly play a part. And for women, pretty privilege plays a much more outsized role because women still remain broadly objectified by society; our looks are often the most prioritized asset we have to bargain with, and looking the part is always requisite to getting the part. I like to think that my ample skill, experience, and charm make me a qualifying candidate for most jobs, but I am willing to bet from experience that optics have always prevailed where doubt may linger.

Those optics are informed by a collection of assets that haven't changed much in the last century or so. British philosopher Heather Widdows named four major tentpoles that women are expected to achieve in the name of Western beauty ideals today: thinness, smoothness (aka hairlessness), firmness, and youth.[*] The more of these that you possess, the more you benefit from pretty privilege. There's no one perfect image to aspire to, rather a combination of these tenets is negotiated, given a certain culture's affinity toward body types, skin tone, emphasis on youth, and tolerance for body hair. A lack of one is forgivable in the possession of the others, depending on the level of compliance to that majority. They're an invisible scaffolding that guides how far beauty standards can stray from their original blueprint.

---

[*] Heather Widdows, *Perfect Me: Beauty as an Ethical Ideal* (Princeton, NJ: Princeton University Press, 2020).

Pretty privilege provides certain advantages on how much you can stray from those principles. I mean, there's a reason you mostly see alternative beauty looks praised as aspirational on young, thin people (who are also more than likely white or ethnically ambiguous). I imagine sporting my unshaven armpits would be seen as more slovenly than edgy were I thirty pounds heavier or thirty years older. The older one is, the less there is to leverage within the remaining constraints, and the same goes for the other perceived aberrations. Beauty's ethical imperatives can only be bargained in so many ways. We all gamble our assets at whatever level we're willing to risk invisibility—the consequence for opting out of performing beauty.

Pretty privilege also plays a significant role in informing the kinds of beauty trends that obscure our perception of beauty. The year after I began my beauty writing career, Marc Jacobs plopped black, shaggy, Joan Jett–esque wigs on his models and sent them down the runway totally barefaced for his 2015 spring presentation. François Nars, founder of NARS Cosmetics, pulled an "emperor's new clothes" beauty concept for the show, swiping some NARS Skin Luminous Moisture Cream on the young models' faces for a radiantly dewy finish (and admittedly a little dab of concealer for a few who looked a bit less than fresh-faced). Minimal makeup had slowly been making its way back into the beauty zeitgeist, a trend that championed showing your true, authentic self, freed from the rigorous aesthetic of heavy contouring and face-baking made popular on Instagram just a couple years earlier. And while I'm of the opinion that no one, save for people in the industry, really cares about Fashion Week's beauty trends (since the hair and makeup seen on runways is often not the main event, just a supporting accessory to the clothes), this validated that movement. Media coverage doubled down on the sentiment with headlines like:

The Models at Marc Jacobs Wore No Makeup Whatsoever—
*   None!*
Models Walked the Runway at Marc Jacobs with Zero Makeup
#NYFW Spring 2015: No Makeup at Marc Jacobs, You Won't
*   Even Recognize Kendall Jenner!*
There Was Absolutely No Makeup at the Marc Jacobs Show

I guess it could be considered a beauty stunt, more artistic concept than imaginative confection, implying that beauty isn't created so much as it simply *exists* as is. It's a very chic suggestion that's easy to sell when the control group involves runway models—humans employed selectively for their excess height, lack of body mass, and youthful features. So, while the beauty mags declared a modern movement toward barefaced beauty, barefaced was the idea, not the execution. Glossier, champion of the "you but better" beauty movement, happened to launch the same month, giving the world exactly what it just learned that it wanted: makeup to give the appearance of not wearing makeup.*

The "no-makeup makeup" look isn't new; it's the way most people use makeup, as far as I've known. But giving it a name and an attitude shift allowed for it to be marketed and branded to even greater success. The rhetoric changed from discreet makeup to hide your blemishes to makeup that *reveals* your true beauty—unfettered by spots, uneven tone, or sallowness—so you can look like yourself, not like your makeup or your flaws, which is basically saying the same thing but with a "glass half full" attitude. Make it seem easy enough that technical skill is no barrier, and just transformative enough that we *feel*

---

* In fact, initial criticism of Glossier's launch was that it was for people with perfect skin already, makeup for pretty people, which did nothing to curb the overwhelming amount of user-generated content despite the sentiment.

changed even if we aren't visibly all that different looking—it's more of a shift in perspective than in appearance. The transformation should be able to conceal itself, as well as your blemishes. It suggests that makeup disappears when applied correctly, even though no, it doesn't, because otherwise we wouldn't wear it. Makeup is tasked with covering our flaws, highlighting our assets, uplifting our self-esteem, celebrating our authenticity, and doing it all undetected (a big ask from a skin tint that launched with three shades). Ironically, the heavily contoured and cut-creased, glam aesthetic of "Instagram makeup" and the *effortless*, no-makeup makeup looks are two aesthetics both alike in dignity. They often both involved just as many products, with the latter doing double duty to cover its tracks.

Part of what makes acknowledging pretty privilege so prickly (other than our social conditioning that acknowledging one's own attractiveness is vain and vanity is in and of itself unattractive) is that accepting its existence also means conceding that you benefit in ways that you may not deserve and that others do. It tends to keep women at odds with one another, constantly negotiating their looks in comparison to one another. *(Don't hate me because I'm beautiful. She's probably just jealous of you. She only got ahead because X wants to sleep with her. Is his ex prettier than me?)* It's very *Highlander* "there can only be one." This kind of toxic femininity stems from the age-old scarcity mentality that one woman's beauty negates another's. It's a misogyny-coded mindset that perpetuates the way we value women by their appearance first and their humanity second, and it maintains silence around pretty privilege that keeps us arranging ourselves in a social hierarchy based on looks.

Holding appearance in overly high regard has a way of also diminishing a person's lived experiences and talents. I'm sure many good-looking people are familiar with their achievements being minimized and dismissed as a result of their looks. Once, a guy I went on a couple dates with told me that before he got to know me, he assumed I was a vapid bimbo because of how I looked and dressed; he meant this as a compliment, by the way. I keep a mental tally every time anybody uses the word "actually" when complimenting my talents or skills. And yet, I remain highly employable and widely desirable because of the way I look—that I'm also talented and experienced just means I get to keep those jobs for longer than if I wasn't.

The "halo effect" is a psychological term for the cognitive bias we have when making judgments about a person, brand, or place—our initial positive impressions tend to influence how we judge them overall. Simply put: good-looking people come off as smart, capable, trustworthy, and generally morally virtuous. It's why even when hot people commit crimes, they are less likely to serve time (or serve less time). Their plights are seen as more sympathetic, and they are much more likely to be granted clemency or second chances. Such is the case of "the hot convict," Jeremy Meeks. His mug shot went viral on Facebook in 2014 after he was arrested during a gang sweep in Stockton, California. Meeks is now a professional model and actor after having served half of his twenty-seven-month sentence. Not many people know what happened to the other purported gang members who were also arrested and incarcerated from that sweep, presumably because their mug shots were not as noteworthy. Ted Bundy, an American serial killer who kidnapped, raped, and murdered at least twenty women in the 1970s (he confessed to more than thirty, but the total count is unknown) is a media mainstay, mostly owing to the fact that his looks and charm were what granted him access to so many victims. There are several documentaries and films about Ted Bundy, casting him with attractive actors, none of which bear much resemblance to Bundy but share a similar mechanism of fascination (Zac Efron, Chad Michael Murray, Mark Harmon, and James Marsters are a few).

When you consider that attractiveness, according to conventional standards, is overwhelmingly favorable to whiteness, you can understand how certain criminal cases pick up steam in ways that similar ones do not, based on who's at the center of them. (There are not nearly as many true crime documentaries or dramatizations about Black or Indigenous women who are murdered or go missing at rates much higher than white women.) Eurocentric beauty standards work to maintain whiteness as the epitome of not just beauty but of moral virtue, heightening the perceived wickedness of crimes against them, and contributing to the ways that punishment is doled out in our judicial systems. It's also how a fake German heiresses can spin a Netflix series, reality TV show, and book deal out of defrauding hundreds of thousands of dollars from the New York City elite, after ample splashy media coverage.

Race has a way of complicating our lived experiences. And the racism inherent in how we define beauty contributes to massive inequality when it remains unacknowledged within our governing systems. Which is likely why it makes validating pretty privilege even more fraught; once we start to dissect what and who is considered pretty, it unearths much uglier truths about the power of the beauty we value. Beauty has always been the easiest way for people to humanize women, especially. It's always made clear to me what kind of women are most protected whenever a pretty, young, white woman goes missing. The news travels far and wide; everyone is up in arms. Accordingly, hoarding beauty can be an act of self-preservation, especially for those of us who don't fit the image of the perfect victim.

It took me well into adulthood to detangle my ethnicity from my beauty, to understand that they're not at odds with one another, and that existing in the body of an Asian woman doesn't mean I'm beholden to negotiating the stereotypes about Asian women. Growing up in America, I'm reminded much more frequently how my appearance fuels assumptions inherent to the local perspective—assumptions about where I'm "really from," my demeanor, my interior world, my sexual accessibility, even the validity of any beauty I might possess in contrast to my ethnicity ("You're pretty for an Asian girl" or "You're pretty in that Asian way" are common remarks uttered as compliments). You don't have to be called ugly to feel ugly—a constant interrogation of why you look the way you do will fuel your suspicions plenty. Had I grown up in Asia and not America, the pressures to be beautiful would still be there, just differently targeted. Ironically, it's overwhelmingly Asian American people who compliment me based on specific features like my double eyelids, my high nose bridge, and the idealized ways my genetics obscure my own race. "I thought you were mixed" or "You don't look fully Asian" are intended compliments I've heard more than a few times; they reinforce that beauty cannot be defined by Asian features, and that my perceived mixedness inches me closer to a more palatable attractiveness on the racial spectrum. Occupying a third culture space usually involves an innate estrangement with the idea of "normal," as we are constantly negotiating disparate identities. Beauty is no exception; it becomes a governing principle that always reminds me of where I stand—usually acting as a buffer or some form of compensation for the detrimental circumstance of my race.

Ironically (or confusingly), when it comes to the appearance bias (pretty privilege in a lab coat) in romantic and sexual partners, being an Asian woman puts me at a disproportionate advantage, at least online. A 2009 OkCupid survey that collected info on the implied racial preferences of men and women (based on which race got the most messages or responses from which race, broken into four broad racial groups of white, Black, Latino, and Asian) found that Asian women and white men were the most messaged/responded to, and Black women and Asian men were the least messaged/responded to.[*] A similar data survey from Facebook's dating app Are You Interested? (which utilizes the Tinder-standard swipe method of *yes* or *pass* to match) found that Asian women and white men had the highest right (meaning yes) swipes.[†] While I've never had a shortage of matches when I've had an active dating app profile, an app match is pretty low stakes when it comes to pursuing a romantic interest. Anyone who's been on the apps knows the collective frustrations with non-intentionality and flakiness. And my preferential status online doesn't seem to translate into offline dating for me. Unsurprisingly, seeing a person in the flesh is very different from viewing their dating profile. (I've gone on dates with people I met in real life, who, after seeing their dating profiles, I don't think I would've swiped right on—and vice versa.) In person, there are three whole dimensions, you can witness their body language, how they move in their own skin, hear the sound of their voice (so important for me!), and observe the way they navigate social situations. Also, you can see if they chew with their mouths open before becoming enamored with their textual prowess. Something I've been made to be aware of, just by being online and having a career that relies on being online, is that the way I present digitally is very different from how I present IRL. I've been told this many times, that I'm "hotter" online. And by hotter, I mean without my personality getting in the way, my image is one of a woman who may or may not possess any number of traits you can project onto me based on your contextual impressions of my digital presence. I would be insulted by this if I didn't get a kick out

* https://web.archive.org/web/20150207064642/http://blog.okcupid.com/index.php/race-attraction-2009-2014
† Ritchie King, "The Uncomfortable Racial Preferences Revealed by Online Dating," Quartz, November 20, 2013, https://qz.com/149342/the-uncomfortable-racial-preferences-revealed-by-online-dating. Interestingly, all men preferred Asian women, except for Asian men, who responded most to Latino women; and all women preferred white men, except Black women, who responded most to Black men. Black men and women received the lowest response rates.

of reminding people that one good photo of a woman does not a dream girl make.

I get it—personality can complicate chemistry. Who among us hasn't been stoked to go on a date with an online hottie only to be met with disappointment when they're rude to the waitstaff or regale you with stories that reveal a certain lack of critical thinking? But based on this information, I often find myself wondering if my relative popularity on the apps is perhaps due to a sexualized perception of my ethnicity; if stereotypes about Asian women's docile nature and sexual submissiveness (or hyper-sexuality) precede any of my individual charm; and if the entire Western hegemony doesn't have some wholesale Asian fetish. The quickness with which some friends have warned me, "He has a lot of Asian ex-girlfriends" or "Be careful, he might have an Asian fetish," leads to a general assumption that any non-Asian man romantically pursuing me has—or likely has—an Asian fetish. This all makes it clearer that my presumed desirability lies in my race far more than any other attractive traits I might possess.

Bafflingly, a person can be pretty and not necessarily derive privilege from it. Beauty and attraction are incredibly subjective, but privilege is often based in institutional and established cultural beliefs, much of which blend racism and colorism, sexism, fatphobia, ableism, ageism, and other appearance-based discriminations into their perceptions of beauty. The further out a person is on the spectrum of prettiness, the harder they must work at proving their reasoning. Those who experience these prejudices often spend so much of their time performing their value, reassuring others of their capabilities as they navigate their own self-doubt. They're burdened with the onus of proof that they belong. It's exhausting. The virtues projected onto beauty work just as much against those who don't fulfill beauty's ideals. It's not ugliness that is the assumed opposite of beauty, it's abnormality. A lack of beauty (and evidence that effort is being made toward beauty) is pathologized as a defect of character. Anytime someone says you look tired or asks if you're well when you haven't done your makeup for the day; when fat people are assumed to be lazy; when frizzy or just naturally textured hair is seen as unprofessional—it's all pretty privilege in reverse, an interrogation of one's place in society.

An absence of pretty privilege doesn't necessarily condemn you to a life less extraordinary, though. People are dynamic, attraction is fickle, and charm, intelligence, and wit will get you a lot further than looks can (even if you have to put more effort in it). Our appetite for beauty demands some variety, and if everyone looks the same then the pretty becomes redundant and boring. Humans aren't *completely* shallow, despite unflattering evidence that suggests otherwise. It's our experiences and privileges that grant us access to resources for individual resistance; how we're born into the world and how we're taught to perceive ourselves determines how much we can cash in on those privileges.

And it turns out that the halo effect works both ways. If movie makeover montages have taught me anything, it's that attractiveness is malleable. And it turns out that your personality and behaviors play a big part in how attractive you're perceived. Being cool, kind, and doing "good things"[*] can change how a person's attractiveness is perceived, namely by increasing it. Talent bias, wealth bias, good-deed bias, BDE (big dick energy)—they all contribute to people thinking you're hotter than the sum of your physical attributes, according to a 2023 PLOS study.[†] In the study, subjects were shown images of the same person with different personality descriptors. Images accompanied by verbal descriptions of their generosity and kindness resulted in higher scores of facial attractiveness than when the same images were accompanied by negative traits like selfishness and unfriendliness. Personality per-

---

* Goodness is also a malleable concept, so this is just as subjective.
† Ryosuke Niimi and Mami Goto, "Good Conduct Makes Your Face Attractive," PLOS One, February 13, 2023, https://journals.plos.org/plosone/article?id=10.1371/journal.pone .0281758.

ception affects facial attractiveness, as do other contextual elements like prior knowledge of a person and their role in your social community, but generally speaking, good behavior and positive attributes make you appear hotter to other people.

But the thing about beauty is that it often usurps other positive qualities a person might possess. Prettiness is a passive trait. It's a common assumption that classic hotties must not have had to develop any other redeeming characteristics because beauty is the ultimate redemption.* Looks do matter—sometimes, a bit too much, it feels like—because they're a conduit to power. There's a reason pretty privilege is, in fact, a privilege; it makes life easier. But it's important to remember that hotness and desirability are made up of so much more than the sum of your most desirable physical features. They're encompassed by a host of nonphysical attributes that contribute to how you're perceived, including the idiosyncrasies and quirks of your personality.

I have a theory that everyone is hot, it's just that some people know it and some people are not yet aware of it. Often the difference between the two is confidence—it doesn't even have to be real; fake it till you make it, as they say. Plus, with so much applied aesthetics in our faces all the time now, the beauty fatigue is *real*. We crave personality, unique quirks, and the kind of charm that comes from a life less polished. I mean, there's nothing less *cool* than conforming to society's standards, and that includes beauty. Sometimes all it takes is enough time to pass for that thing you were insecure about (freckles, gap teeth, too-thick eyebrows, no eyebrows, scars, et cetera) to have its moment in the limelight, and for you realize that your insecurity doesn't define who you are. If anything, it proves to you that it's all made up, and you can release yourself from appearance anxiety, bit by bit as time goes on. Owning your individual quirks and what makes you *you* is always

---

* As a casting agent once told me, "God doesn't give with both hands."

hot behavior. When I think about what attracts me to people, it's always something about their outlook on life, their warmth and generosity of spirit, how comfortable they are in their own skin and the solidness of their presence, which is often some enigmatic thing that tells me they know what's up. Energy always pulls where beauty falls short. There are no ugly people, only bad PR.

Die Hot with a Vengeance

The first time I got dumped superbad was in college, when I was twenty-one. We'd been together for only seven months—not all that long of a relationship, right? That's not even enough time to gestate a baby. But alas, you never forget your first heartbreak (or baby, probably).

He and I had been friends for a couple of years before we got together, and it was one of those friendships where you have so much chemistry that romance seemed like an inevitable conclusion. I wish I'd known at that age that the way to go from friendzone to bonezone is not to petition someone with a list of reasons why *it makes total sense* you should date, as if you're selling a time-share. If someone is not already enthusiastically wooing the crap out of you of their own volition, do not pass Go, babe. But I was young and convinced this person was my person because we were both into the same cartoons or something twee like that. All it required was the Facebook official status.

The relationship didn't work out for lots of reasons that relationships between twenty-one- and twenty-three-year-olds don't work, including that he had just graduated from the college we both attended and was figuring out postgrad life, and I perhaps had conflated what I considered good chemistry for good communication skills. He broke up with me one wintry evening while I was visiting him at his Brooklyn apartment. I cried through three subway transfers and on the Metro-North to drag my sorry ass back to Westchester where I was still living on campus at college.[*]

---

[*] If you have never wept so viscerally on public transport that passengers avoid sitting or standing near you the same way they avoid unhoused people on the train, you have not yet truly dipped into the depths of your own humanity (or the New York City subway system).

As someone who grew up with the belief hammered into them that anything was achievable if you just work hard enough at it, this was shocking to me. Another devastating realization: not only was my ass dumped for what I firmly believed was wrongful termination, but I also had to reckon with this new, horrible knowledge that the people you love can hurt you, sometimes without meaning to, and there is little you can do to prevent that from happening. There are, and will be, situations where it doesn't matter what you do or think—some things just will not work out, despite your best efforts. This remains the spookiest thing I've ever learned.

I spent the spring semester of my senior year crying myself thin. I had ZERO appetite, which is an anomaly for me because I love food— truly, madly, deeply. It sustains me not just physically, but also spiritually, mentally, and emotionally. I understand that's a redundant statement in this post–food blogger era, but experiencing flavors and smells are some of my favorite activities. Every morning when I wake up, I have a new opportunity to make one decision that never fatigues me and only excites me: *What am I going to eat today?* There are few tasks that cannot be completed by a delicious treat as incentive and also reward. Eating is a celebratory, social activity for me. There truly is no experience that can't be enhanced with good company and good food.

But in these dark and sulky times, I was feeling maximum anti-social and extremely life-avoidant. When I did spend time with friends, I wasn't fully present, and my eyes were glassy and puffy nearly all the time. I'd report to my on-campus work-study job at the admissions office, glumly opening the mail and filing applications. My grief was so palpable that the clerk who usually scolded me for being slow or bad at my job was even like, "Honey, what *happened* to you??"

To live for several weeks and months thinking *meh* at the thought of things that I'd normally salivate over is a pitiful half-life I wish upon no one. A month later, I was the thinnest I'd been in my adult life, hovering slightly under ninety pounds. I developed under-eye circles despite depression-sleeping thirteen hours a night because the natural padding that normally filled in the hollows of my eye sockets was AWOL. People were legit *concerned* for me. My mom asked my brother if I had a secret coke addiction.[*]

This was, however, the mid-aughts, when *thinspiration* was a Tumblr personality, hot on the heels of the nineties' heroin chic, and I had unintentionally found myself within the bounds of both. I wasn't trying to, but my deeply dysfunctional sadness had manifested in disordered eating, which manifested into a very on-trend body type (especially when you go to an arts school).

Having gone from a size six to a size *gaunt* was apparently more noticeably transformative than I even noticed, considering the amount of amorous and complimentary attention it garnered from my peers and other dudes around campus. Guy-friends as well as guy-crushes who had previously never looked at me twice suddenly expressed intense interest in me. Compliments regarding significant weight loss from men always seem to carry this entitled subtext like, *I'm so glad you've finally decided to conform to the aspect ratio my eyeballs consider attractive.*[†] The frail and depressing nature of my concave midsection fed into every cultural message that romanticized thinness, something I was only dimly aware of as I cried myself to sleep most nights.

I was discovering my body now held clothes differently, in ways that everyone thought looked great and volunteered to tell me often. I experimented with more body-conscious fits, feeling sharper and more potent in my tautness. I mean, sure, maybe I felt hot in some Hervé-Leger-by-way-of-Forever-21 bandage dress, but that was merely

---

[*]   To date, I have still never done coke. Mostly because I am not cool enough for anyone to have offered me coke and even if they did, I have enough sinus issues as it is to snort solids.
[†]   I can't remember any time a man has ever said to me, "Wow, you look so happy or confident or like you've really come into your own," you know?

some ill-conceived consolation prize that fell apart after the first wash, much like my emotional constitution.

Even though I had a lovely and patient therapist from the school's student counseling center talking me through processing those feelings, it was strange that I could feel so absolutely miserable and have people praising what that feeling had done to my body. They were all like, "Cheer up, you look SO HOT!"—a refrain greatly at odds with what was happening beneath that veneer. Though my friends were generally great sports with redirecting my sullen disposition into partying the weekends away, they weren't bringing me any closer to emerging from the emo sunken place I was fully plunged in.

Being fashionably skinny didn't make me any less sad or heartbroken, it just made it more illogical to me that I should be heartbroken in the first place (if more hot, why not more happy?). I remember many aimless nights out in those hunger-less times, recklessly running on fumes of external validation while applying another glossy topcoat to any part of me that hurt, convinced that this was some kind of workaround to confronting my own painful vulnerabilities. Sometimes beauty is self-love the same way french fries are vegetables—satisfying and enjoyable but not necessarily the most nourishing in, you know, important ways.

On the one hand, it was helpful to have friends and potential suitors hyping me up at a time when I needed the attention—and distraction. Romantic attention at random can be a very effective distraction for the specific ego bruise of romantic rejection. It's a momentary high, but it feels like a suggestion of hope that there is, in the words of Cher, love after love (*after love after love*).[*] Maybe I *won't* die alone after all. But it also reinforced the idea that my self-worth hinged upon

---

[*]   *After love.*

how many dudes found me desirable at a time. When you are young and have yet to fully embody yourself, sometimes the presence of another person wanting you, feeling you, can give you enough footing to inspire a likeness of confidence. Wanting to disappear and actually, incrementally disappearing can be an intoxicating feeling to a young girl who still relies on a conventional witness to grasp a stake in the world. The smaller I became, the easier it felt to pull myself out from that pit.

Little did I know that this was my first introduction to "revenge bod." Revenge bod is a tabloid-y turn of phrase that takes self-improvement and weaponizes it against a person who romantically fumbled you. It makes glowing up a misguided and petty enterprise. It's getting sexy in the face of romantic wreckage. You know, girl stuff.

The subtext: *Look what he's missing out on.* The subtext's subtext: *Because women's primary value lies in their desirable appearance, and damn, her stock just rocketed.*

Revenge bod is a beauty pageant for feminine rage that insists satisfaction—and vengeance—be found through your reflection. It not only frames beauty as the antidote to pain, but also a weapon to do unto others as they have done unto you. None of us may be able to escape love unscathed, but getting hotter does not solve the particular grief of heartbreak or help us to regain love that was lost. And yet the pathology of revenge bod continues to be bizarrely celebrated and encouraged. And even if you do enact your very specific revenge . . . Okay, well, now what? Glamorizing pain doesn't do much to soothe it so much as circumvent the stigma of emotional distress and crystallize it into its own kind of neurotic vanity.

For women especially, beauty—or a lack of it—is always the first thing to come under scrutiny in the case of romantic rejection, so of course that's going to be the first objective for imagining defensive strategy. It's a reactionary instinct, and if nothing else, it's a way to recover one's own dignity when your ego's been knocked down a peg.

I mean, sure, looking amazing in the presence of your ex is not a *bad* idea, especially in a city like New York where despite there being eight million inhabitants, you're guaranteed to run into that one ex at the most unexpected time and place—like the waiting room of an urgent care clinic or the back seat in an Uber pool. Feeling put together can soften that sort of spontaneous emotional pang (or at least not add to the grief). But it's one thing to make sure you've run a brush through your hair or mascara through your lashes before leaving the house, and quite another to *Pimp My Ride* about it, figuratively speaking.

Unfortunately, revenge bod and Revenge™ are not the same thing; the vast differences between the two can only be learned through personal experience. After my initial collegiate heartbreak experience, it *did* feel good to have people telling me how great I looked, even if my "hotter" self at the time was emotional devastation manifest. But, of course, it stuck in the back of my mind at the time that going out was dual purpose: see and be seen, and I knew that my ex would be checking on whatever Facebook party photos I was tagged in.

Of course, working on your fitness and getting your health and well-being together is a positive direction to reach toward postheartbreak—what's going to make you feel better other than doing stuff to make yourself feel better, you know? But revenge bod is not really that. It's empowerment in reverse, anchoring your self-worth to a sunken ship, thinking you can save it by going full throttle at feminine performance for the sake of (a particular) male gaze.

Once the emotional dust settled after that big breakup, I realized that my life generally wasn't so bad. More than that, I realized how grief gets heavier the longer you hold on to it; you've got to set it down every now and again. A shift in perspective (and, okay, therapy) gave me better insight and self-compassion to gradually return me to a more regulated and less embittered self.

The satisfaction I gained from any amorous attention post-breakup was really just a form of triage. It wasn't real, sustainable healing. But I think that's the effect of revenge bod, that it redirects vengeance and vanity toward a kind of pain that would better be tended to by compassion. It forges beauty into a specific kind of aid and armor meant to charm and seduce others in service of placating and patching up your own ego. It dangles empowerment and the getting of one's groove back like the carrot on a stick in front of an already very depressed horse. But does that solve any underlying sadness or fear? Maybe for a little while, but not really in any lasting way.

Vengeance, like any initiative born from the complicated emotions of pain, has a way of alienating you from your own needs by prioritizing crisis management over thoughtful reflection. But the core essence underscoring revenge bod's machinations aims to seek a deeper meaning from your suffering than simply getting hotter and fitter (even if those are the mechanisms). The workism[*] embedded in our meritocratic society valorizes labor as a foundational means to constructing—or reconstructing—identity. We may be more secular than ever, but within our practices of capitalism, everyone worships something (even ourselves). There must be some meaning to suffering because without it, what is the point of *all this* (I ask, gesticulating wildly around myself)?

Contrary to what Revenge Bod™ might have you believe, my streamlined new figure did not inspire such remorse in my ex, making him realize what he'd lost. Of course not! Attempting to rebuild your

---

* Workism "is the belief that work is not only necessary to economic production, but also the centerpiece of one's identity and life's purpose; and the belief that any policy to promote human welfare must *always* encourage more work." (It is a term coined by Derek Thompson in a February 24, 2019, *Atlantic* article, "Workism Is Making Americans Miserable," https://www.theatlantic.com/ideas/archive/2019/02/religion-workism-making-americans-miserable/583441/.)

confidence by any measure of approval from an ex-lover is truly the Hail Mary of playing yourself. In events of romantic distress, it's natural for instinct to lunge toward hardware upgrades.

Sometimes insecure pangs of *What if I had abs, or boobier-looking boobs, and a perkier butt?* will crash my brain as uninvited intrusive thoughts. Wouldn't that just make this whole "having a body" thing so great? Maybe. But it's not a failure in body confidence I'm experiencing, so much as the cognitive futility of trying to repair a relationship with self-worth via beauty. People don't fall in love with individual appendages; that would be weird. And I wouldn't want to date anyone who just wanted to be around me for my rock-hard abs and inches-upon-inches of perfectly highlighted extensions.

The deep, underlying fear I have is that perhaps I am someone who, even in all my multifaceted charm, wit, and heart, will eventually inspire apathy and indifference in everyone I love. It keeps me subconsciously taking inventory of all the ways I can stake a more permanent claim in the hearts of everyone around me. And because that fear is partially substantiated by past experiences and made bigger than it is by the bone memory of grief, it looms large enough to wind me up like a kinetic watch, powered endlessly by the drive itself.

A body can be a weapon when it intends revenge, but we often end up punishing ourselves instead. By its namesake, the only legitimate revenge bod would be a body capable of exacting the deserved brutality and devastation that was enacted onto you in the first place.[*] I want a revenge bod with all the bells and whistles. Give me fingernails so sharp they can cut through metal. I want vocal cords that can shatter glass and biomechanical limbs that transform into extendable and articulated hooks so I can fuck up your shit to the degree that will make Beyoncé's "Hold Up" music video look like an episode of *Supermarket*

---

[*] The most ironic depiction of revenge bod I've seen is the 1996 film *Thinner*, based on the novel of the same name by Stephen King.

DIE HOT WITH A VENGEANCE

Sweep. Give me tits that launch mini heat-seeking missiles and eyes with infrared sensors that can pick up a specific body heat fingerprint, like the Predator. Vipers for hair? Climb aboard. My revenge bod would be like an evil Inspector Gadget or a lawful evil femmebot. Medusa for the modern world. Without the hardware to back up the claims, a "revenge bod" is of little use to me.

What Glows Up Must Come Down

ecoming "your best self" feels like the modern mantra of being a person today. It's one part self-competition and one part redemption arc. It's also a widely encouraged goal for nearly everyone, at any point in their life, because what are you even doing if not striving to be your best self? Anytime I don't feel like I'm in control of my own narrative, fucking with my appearance is usually a reliable first response to reclaim my physical self. When I look like a different person, I feel like a different person—someone more capable, formidable, perhaps even intimidating—and that's always the feeling I'm after. The beast must be fed, by which I mean my ego and its sometimes inconvenient cravings for external validation—the mortar in between the bricks of my pride and resolve.

I know I'm not alone in this. I mean, that mentality of glowing up is baked into our culture. Just look at Hollywood and how makeovers are depicted as fun, glamorous, and an extremely successful fuel for a character arc. They were a very common cinematic device to show women stepping into the power afforded them by the culture that determines what power women are allowed to wield. Plus, makeover scenes always have the best soundtracks in movies, consecrating them into our impressionable little hearts and minds. *She's All That, Clueless, Grease, Miss Congeniality, The Princess Diaries, Cinderella, The Fly*—all makeover canon from my youth. They taught me that all it takes to find true love (or become super popular and asked to prom) is removing your glasses, chopping your overgrown coif into a cute bob, dyeing it a cherry-cola red, cropping your tops, ditching the farmer clothes, and eliciting the help of a benevolent witch (or Larry Miller with a Mason Pearson hairbrush). The fluffy makeover plot device is great for convincing teens that all you have to do to stop being invisible and *finally* catch the attention of the guy—or many guys—is straighten your hair and trade your glasses for contacts. And then you can finally learn to love yourself . . . once you realize you were indeed hot the whole time.

The year I graduated from high school, the reality show *The Swan* aired to great fuss. It was a makeover reality show where contestants (all of whom were women) underwent several invasive plastic surgeries to transform these "ugly ducklings" into beautiful swans (metaphorically, not literally). Significant plot point: These were all healthy, able-bodied women. They hadn't suffered any disfigurement or been born with any diseases that *required* surgery (which wouldn't be appropriate either but would perhaps be some kind of hooky-hook to justify the show's brutal agenda). Each contestant had a tragically depicted backstory containing carefully edited footage with pointed questions about their lack of confidence around not fitting into conventional beauty standards and sometimes being jealous of other women who did. Then with the help of a team consisting of a coach, therapist, trainer, cosmetic dentist, and some plastic surgeons, they were whittled away into their final form. At the end of each contestant's months-long transformation and recovery process, there was a big reveal party with all their family and friends in attendance. They'd almost all cry when they saw their new-and-improved, carved-up selves, as their husbands and mothers would look on, glowing with approval and pride (and sometimes well-intentioned shock). Each episode featured two contestants, one of whom was selected to go on to the final competition of becoming *The Swan*. (I don't remember if or what anyone actually won at the end, aside from thousands upon thousands of dollars in cosmetic surgery.) The show was canceled after two seasons due to public outcry for all the reasons that your brain is probably outcrying right now, reading that. In a 2023 *GQ* profile of Terry Dubrow, *The Swan*'s head plastic sur-geon, Dubrow explained an instance during the show's tenure where after three months of not seeing her kids, one contestant reunited with them just as she was seeing herself for the first time after her surger-ies. "They wanted her kids to see her as she saw herself," Dubrow told *GQ*. "And they open up the mirror and they're supposed to go, 'I'm so happy.' She turns to her kids and her kids look at her like, 'Who are you?' and they started crying." After that, he said, "there were no kids at the reveals anymore."[*]

My childhood was *full* of such glamorously transformative narratives—they were a tried-and-true reliable form of entertainment in that time especially (but still is now). When *America's Next Top Model* debuted in 2003, it easily became appointment television for me. Led by supermodel Tyra Banks and a team of experts, the competition real-ity show attempted to transform a dozen pretty girls into supermodels over the course of a dozen episodes (and twenty-four seasons). *Ambush Makeover* debuted the same year, doing exactly what the name implies, taking strangers off the streets and commandeering their day to the salon and the mall for a total costume change. And in 2017, there was *Revenge Body with Khloe Kardashian*, which was similar to *The Swan* but with less scalpels and more *I'll show you!* The entertainment factor made it fair game for virtual software. I remember being a tweenager and using virtual makeover software (well, the trial disc because my parents refused to buy the program for me) to upload photos of myself to the family PC so I could try on a bright red French bob or long, dra-matic layers. I suppose these were the earliest renditions of filters and Facetune, except no one would see them unless you brought them over to your computer and were like, "Look at me with bangs!"

Makeovers are simply a rite of passage for nearly anyone engaging

[*] Eve Peyser, "How *Botched* Star Terry Dubrow Found His Higher Calling," *GQ*, April 12, 2023, https://www.gq.com/story/botched-terry-dubrow-profile.

in our appearance-based society. The gratification of a good makeover montage relies on the happily-ever-after images being a dramatic distance from the befores. The drama is required to reinforce empirical proof that anyone can be hot if they just try hard enough (or thin in the case of the reality competition show *The Biggest Loser*—which ran for seventeen seasons, it was such a hit). We are always rooting for everyone's secret hottie within, shrouded under a layer of bad clothes and excess body mass. It's almost as though all you need is a charitable new high school friend (or Tyra) to show you how hot you are on the inside, and subsequently how to manifest it on the outside. With all the abundantly consistent messaging of love, validation, and self-esteem earned in a post-makeover life, the glowup has become mythologized as a virtuous pursuit—the one thing that stands between you and Your Best Self™.

Glowing up is a softer and more vaguely optimistic rebrand for makeover madness. Glow-up culture may have similar intentions as revenge bod, except it's not necessarily wielded as any specific form of damage control. Glowing up has no deadline. There is simply no end to how you can self-optimize in all parts of your life—professionally, romantically, personally, creatively. It is *The Achievement Show*, renewing itself season after season, with some implicit reward at the end in the form of empowerment—the value of which is generally determined by how much overall external validation can vouch. Extreme makeovers require a kind of capital that adds up and can also be costly to maintain. And their most recognizable blueprints are usually always the flashiest: expensive workout regimens, expensive salon visits, expensive new teeth, new wardrobe, aesthetic treatments—it's so much lead-up to a "new me" that may appear shiny and renewed but doesn't necessarily guarantee any sort of profound revelations. (Because and then what? AND THEN WHAT??) In the words of Kacey Musgraves, *healing doesn't happen in a straight line*. But some paths are better tread with thoughtful compassion for oneself rather than frantically glamorous flailing. The resources you'll sink into chasing a transformation that finally feels *complete* can be a sunk-cost fallacy. Art may imitate life, and media can often be propaganda—usually when it's in favor of antiquated cultural values that are increasingly unsustainable the more you invest in them. The empowerment you're meant to gain from all this can easily become a scam when it conflates external validation as the proof of success. I am not immune to external validation, of course. But it does hit differently when it's about something I've defined on my own terms. The empowerment rewards supposedly granted in your post-makeover and post-glow-up self is not without value. But again, it's power gained by conforming to systems that also disenfranchise you by determining your self-worth by appearance.

Measuring how being yourself and how you prefer to look, against the existing messages about why something looks good (or doesn't look good), introduces a lot of cognitive dissonance. The relevant truth that the patriarchy's all-day menu of attractiveness hasn't changed in centuries (thinness, femininity, youth) narrows your options between conventional standards and however much your personal authentic expression strays from them. If you haven't defined the latter, it's almost always easier to slide right back toward the first, impersonal though it may be. Beauty isn't in the eye of the beholder so much as it is in the *power* of the beholder, which classically, historically, and boringly has been a male gaze. It sets the stakes by stoking tension between those who strive to extricate themselves from the ideals of beauty's standards and those whose entire agenda involves embodying the shit out of them. It's a very effective patriarchal device that validates beauty by devaluing other women's appearances, establishing an automating system in which comparison and competition keep us all scrambling to outdo one another. A woman choosing bodily autonomy on her own terms is chaotic, beyond control, and unpredictable. And since controlling women is pretty much the entire job of the patriarchy, it's a bit useless if it can't do that. It's useless even when it can. That the entire basis of makeovers, glowups, and revenge-bodding rests upon a well-established foundation of patriarchal lust, the idea that you can glow up out of it feels naive at best and self-defeating at worst.

But! It's important to know that makeovers are not practices of self-hatred by nature. And changing yourself isn't inherently self-betrayal. Sometimes we've outgrown certain styles or looks and want to be intentional to reflect who we truly are or who we want to be. I am fully a new person, year after year (every seven of which I fall into the trap of thinking bangs will work for me, when I have ample proof that they always annoy me). We're constantly striving to evolve as people, and for better or worse, makeovers are about chasing transformation. More drastic transformations may promise greater rewards, but it's not all that realistic to transform our bodies, minds, or habits overnight or within some ideal optimized schedule. You must be your own true north because you can't underestimate how deep the hooks of many toxic beauty standards are sunk within your brain as you innocently believe something so simple as glowing up is without influence. Nobody glows up in a vacuum—the scripts are written far before you even make a go at it.

Having the body of a woman (and presenting in the body of one as well) is constantly politicized, as you have probably noticed from the ample laws and rights around healthcare we are subjected to or denied simply by presenting as female. There is never a shortage of ways to discuss a woman's body. In all these centuries you'd think they'd get bored, but nope! Our bodies may be temples, vessels, and threats to be consumed, revered, or reviled as weapons of mass seduction. What we do with our bodies seems to always be in service of some perception of femininity. That women visibly reap the most superficial benefits of pretty privilege is so often brandished as both reward and reason for playing the part. It's a red herring to the gendered power dynamics at play that always seems to bear the most criticism from those who put those dynamics in motion in the first place.

I sometimes notice this most jarringly in women-dominated spaces—in the ways women discipline themselves with the choices they make in their diets, their lifestyles, the way they wear their hair, the makeup they choose to wear, and how they judge women who make different choices than they would. The language of maintaining thinness and of being pretty is so normalized that women reinforce those ideals, lovingly, kindly, sometimes rudely, but most of all efficiently and without second thought, as if we are looking out for one another. The YouTube fitness vloggers, the beauty salon staff, photographers—anyone invested in image and appearance knows the tips and tricks for enhancing flattery. We speak of beauty ideals as if they're a normal default that all healthy and capable bodies should align with.

What does "pretty" even mean when it's on your own terms? How can we even imagine a world devoid of a male gaze—it's impossible to retroactively unknow. It's something I always think about when doing my hair or makeup, deciding what looks "pretty" and why. Who am I dressing up for and what am I trying to communicate about myself? Not to say that loving yourself and your own appearance, even when they're on someone else's terms, is void of value, but it bears reminding that our choices aren't without influence. It's also important to remember that validation isn't the same as peace or contentment, just like revenge is not satisfaction, and just like pain is not progress.

And yet of course, in the face of mortality's anxieties—the external being the primary way we communicate with the world—it's the external that gets the polish. I'm aware that I say this in my relative youth wherein I'm still in the age bracket appearing broadly desirable by some measure of conventional expectation. Glowing up can feel like a way of delaying the aging process. And since I am not yet reckoning with the cumulative angst of time and gravity in my late thirties,

I default to relying on my excellent exterior to try and stake some guarantee of security against loneliness and abandonment. While we may all be loosely aware that there is no warranty or promise for those efforts to pan out, the cognitive dissonance often spurs many of us to plow further down the rabbit hole that beauty will save us, and as long as we possess it, we will have at least some immunity from grief. What beauty grants in personage, however, it lacks in mercy. And in its pursuit, we often make martyrs of our own bodies. No matter how we strive to overcome them all, the result is the same: We're all going to die one day. Even hot people die eventually. If we are lucky, we have the privilege to live throughout the entire span that our telomeres can sustain, to earn the experience of age and spend our lifetime learning to love ourselves on our own terms, and to love others on theirs as well.

And not to get even more morbid (I'm about to get more morbid), when you die, as your body decays it will return to the earth as recycled energy that goes on for infinity throughout the cosmos. Consider it the ultimate glow down. Sometimes I think about how everyone who was ever alive on this earth is still around in the dust you breathe, the dirt that brings you flowers, and the trees that make the atmosphere livable (for now). We all become food for fungus, joining the ultimate mycelium hotline (which from what I've learned about mushrooms sounds really cool, by the way). It's a comfort to know that no matter how I spend my one precious life in this one bod, I'm only borrowing it for a little while anyway. I'll be sticking around here, one way and then in many others.

So, for the blip of time that you get to steer your body around the universe, it seems like a better idea to enjoy it. Why spend your life resenting your body for someone else's gain? Or body-ing at anyone spitefully? There is no satisfaction to be had resenting how the length of your life is in opposition to impossible standards that (so far) nobody immortal gets to hold over you because nobody is. Bodies are always changing, sometimes of your own accord, and always of its own. Seems more pleasurable to make it a team effort, innit? Celebrate smile lines, shave your head, grow a wig collection, get freckles, show some skin—stretch marks, scars, wrinkles, cellulite, and all. Be gentle with your soft spots (the ones held with affection by others). Flip your hair in the face of danger or color it some hue not found in nature if you want to. Grow some abs if you want to, and don't worry if they go away because technically, they're always kind of there underneath. Get a cool tattoo. Get a stupid one too. Smile with lipstick on your teeth. Die hot with a vengeance.

The Flawless Industrial Complex

It took years of being a beauty writer and editor before I had anything injected into my face. Four months into my position at *Allure*, lured by the exciting novelty of complimentary lip filler (occupational perk), I hauled myself from Brooklyn to the Upper East Side, where the fanciest plastic surgeons set up shop. I don't think anyone who stumbled into this lobby would assume this was a medical facility at all—it looked more like a luxury boutique hotel or a town house. The place was upholstered, wallpapered, and appointed to reflect the comfort of a well-designed home. Any distaste for the body mods being performed there is easily cushioned with bouclé upholstery and Gucci wallpaper—that's the luxury of cognitive dissonance. You know you're in a fancy-pants establishment when it doesn't look like what it is at all. So charmed was I by the original crown molding and Georgia O'Keefe hanging on the wall that I almost forgot why I was there, until I was presented with a medical intake form by a cheerful receptionist (lest we not forget that acquiring DSLs also requires medical intervention).

My injector, a lovely American Board of Plastic Surgery–certified (very accomplished) doctor, perhaps sensing my nerves, insisted that there is no way to overfill a lip unintentionally because the injector can see exactly how much they're injecting and where—the stuff doesn't swell up like spray foam insulation.[*] This was a house of conservative tweaks. At least that's how she referred to what most of her clients

---

[*] Which was a little bit how my mind imagined it, since my earliest memory of being aware of lip filler was Goldie Hawn saying "fill 'em up!" in *The First Wives Club*.

requested, just wanting subtle changes to their face. (Subtlety, funnily enough, is also a spectrum.)

There are, in my experience, two ways to get your kisser filled: You have a targeted injection technique, like little bee stings with a fine-tipped syringe to inject filler into certain spots only. And then there's the ol' plumbing snake technique (my description, not theirs). A nurse pricks a hole into the corner of your lip with a needle, and then your seasoned injector will feed a long cannula into that opening, inward toward the center of your lips, and then pull it out slowly while depressing the syringe's plunger to dispense filler in its wake. Given a choice between the two, I say go with the latter. The bee stings cause more bruising and swelling, which I know because that's what happened after I got them.

Pink gloves on, the doc slathered my mouth with a lidocaine gel that soon made my lips numb to the touch; they felt like two dead slugs, mobile but unfeeling. I poked and pinched at my lips making sure I couldn't feel anything before we got down to business. I sat still like a stone in the chair, doing my best impression of a human pin-cushion, head leaned back against the chair as a bright overhead spotlight shone onto my face, blinding me to anything beyond its halo.

It took less than ten minutes to have my mouth sensually buttressed with hyaluronic acid fantasies. I didn't notice it in the moment, but I must've been nervous because my underarms were *soaked* when I got up. Soon I was on my way back to the office with a branded tiny pink pillowy ice pack to ward off swelling. Later that afternoon at my desk, once the lidocaine wore off, I was very *aware* of my mouth. Pressing my lips together, I could feel soft little lumps squidging around. *It's just the swelling, they said there would be swelling!* I reminded myself. And when the swelling subsided, those lumps remained because they were indeed filler. *Just massage them gently and they should melt into your lips so you don't feel them anymore,* the dermatologist suggested.

She'd used Restylane Silk (the "Rolls-Royce of filler," as I was told at the time). It's a kind of filler with a firmer texture—great for shifting the shape of lips, making cupid's bows a bit more peaked and the overall outline a bit more tented. But liquid scaffolding that it is, you can *feel it* in your lips. Also, to my mild horror, they were slightly uneven. Other dermatologists would turn their noses up at the mention of Restylane, shaking their heads that they'd never use that kind (meanwhile their practice is affiliated with a competing filler brand). The tragically redundant part of this whole event is that in the end, I didn't even look *that* different. You fill, you learn.

Plastic surgery may seem like a novel invention to cater to the vain whims of modern culture, but it has actually been around for centuries. It predates things like modern plumbing and vaccines. Wild, right? It became a serious medical study in the twentieth century, when wartime medics and doctors were like *We gotta do something for these brave soldiers*, who had suffered facial disfigurement in the line of fire. The first facial reconstruction techniques were developed with noble intentions aimed at restoring dignity to those who had served their countries, giving it an honorable ambition, devoid of vanity.

In the 1960s, a Brazilian plastic surgeon named Ivo Pitanguy became the patron saint of plastic surgery and the first celebrity plastic surgeon, for using his advanced skin reconstruction techniques to treat burn victims of a big circus tent fire in Rio de Janeiro. Many of the victims were children. Pitanguy offered his services gratis to relieve them of the stigma of their disfigurement. Witnessing how his patients' emotional and mental health vastly improved, he was moved by the restorative effects that cosmetic surgery could have on a person's quality of life. His medically reconstructive techniques were soon adopted for standard cosmetic procedures as well, as he developed many of the plastic surgery techniques used today. He is perhaps most notable for being the doctor who invented the Brazilian butt lift (or BBL, as it's known). Pitanguy went on to become Brazil's most prolific plastic surgeon, and an advocate for beauty by the blade.

Having a prestigious figure in the medical community rally against the stigma of ugliness not only normalized plastic surgery but gave it a compassionate agenda. In a well-meaning plot twist, Pitanguy petitioned the Brazilian government to subsidize the cost of plastic surgery to make it accessible to less economically flush folks, opining that beauty is a human right. It shifted the narrative from vanity to . . . well-being (which isn't dissimilar to how medical aesthetic treatments are marketed today). It sounds like the plot of some futuristic sci-fi tale when body mods are as accessible as buying a new dress, but reality has a way of preceding fiction, doesn't it? The Pitanguy "right to beauty" philosophy conceded that access to beauty improved a person's confidence, self-esteem, and quality of life in all the superficial ways that matter to us social creatures. Pathologizing ugliness as the source of bad psychological vibes, including depression and poor self-esteem, clinically normalized cosmetic surgery (despite not taking into account all sorts of things that could be the source of those bummer vibes that aren't so easily eighty-sixed via injection or face-lift). His philosophy was that no one should have to suffer a life less beautiful if they had the medical means to do something about it.

Now, Brazil is the second most popular cosmetic surgery destination in the world; the government subsidizes about half a million cosmetic procedures annually,[*] thanks in part to Dr. Pitanguy. Of course, it's not just one dude with a medical license who lionized *plástica*—cultural uptake involved the Brazilian president getting behind it, as well as the media and influential celebrities.

Like Brazil, South Korea's government supports cosmetic surgery,

---

[*] Poh-Chuin Teo et al., "Cosmetic Surgery Industry in Brazil," *International Journal of Academic Research in Accounting, Finance and Management Sciences* 10, no. 1 (April 2020), https://hrmars.com/index.php/IJARAFMS/article/view/7050/Cosmetic-Surgery-Industry -in-Brazil-An-Assessment-Using-Cause-and-Effect-Model-and-Risk-Assessment-Matrix.

insofar as it helps elevate its national perception to the rest of the world. When it comes to beauty by the blade, South Korea's hyper appearance–based culture has made it a global force for cosmetic enhancement. The nearly homogenous look of K-pop idols is evidence of a very specific beauty algorithm at work—that of cuteness, youthfulness, and a pale, blemish-free, and pore-less face. Basically, if everyone in your country is superhot, that raises its social capital and economic standing in the global purview. Rather than conforming to other norms, Korean culture has dominated music and cinema by perpetuating its very own unique aesthetic and style. I mean, it's a worldwide flex, for sure, but one shouldered by its inhabitants subject to the most stringent expectations for perfection. Things that are considered flaws to Koreans (freckles, frizz, suntans, for example) can be considered attractive or interesting to Western eyes. The beachy saltwater hair sprays, freckle pens, and self-tanner of a certain California girl aesthetic would *not* fly over there.

Aesthetics may be culturally and regionally unique, but pressure to conform to them can be universally felt. Tolerance for flaws ranges subjectively between *I can live with this, it's not a big deal* to *I'm a monster and I hate myself* (sometimes vacillating between the two on a daily basis). There is no universal benchmark for what is considered a flaw, but the pressure to do something about it is where we are globally aligning.

In practice, you can't really tell most of the time when people have had injectables, unless they want you to be able to tell (and that may be a regional spectrum of what is aesthetically considered able to pass for "natural"). In a city that demands you grind yourself half to dust just to get by, the tackiest thing you can do in the eyes of the New York elite is appear to be trying too hard. There, plastic surgery's greatest stigma is often its obviousness; the "best" work is largely invisible. In New York City, the tolerance for artificial beauty is mostly limited to its discretion. Wealth affords the most sophisticated kinds of cosmetic treatments that mask any trace of artifice, as well as all the products and maintenance to keep up with it. That's why "effortless" beauty aesthetics are always a traditional aspiration; effortlessness conveys the kind of life of leisure and ease that privilege and wealth grant, and conversely, visible effort reveals that not only is beauty a construction, but it also emphasizes the amount of labor required to achieve it. *Effortlessness* is less about actual effort and more about proximity to class. Money may always be the easiest way to escape the stigma of aesthetics, but those same stigmas eventually funnel us toward choosing between the greater offender: the artifice of cosmetic treatments and unbridled aging.

But we're not all on the same page, globally. In fact, one of my first beauty events as an editor was attending a breakfast with an esteemed Eastern European plastic surgeon, who mentioned to me that his clients in Russia and Poland prefer a super-taut, very lifted, and plumped look. Showing off the work (*his* work) was actually a status symbol, akin to carrying the right designer handbag (which they also probably owned as well). The look symbolized the lifestyle. He was positively bored to tears working in America, with its comparatively plain requests.

When appearances are everything, that also includes the appearance of your appearance. Even the signs of recovery like a bandaged nose can be a status symbol.[*] Aesthetic enhancements take on a performance of their own, especially the faces in the entertainment and reality TV industries; they wear a kind of hyper-glamour geared specifically for the screen, fashioned to really "pop" under bright lights and flashy sets. Beauty becomes a uniform for the narrative. The uniform often includes blindingly white, Chiclet-looking veneers, a perpetual tan, full-faced makeup, and perfectly styled hair (and hairlines). Now that way more people live their lives on-screen, more of them

---

[*] Made even more glam by a number of international *Vogue* editorial shoots putting models with bandaged heads and prosthetic facelifts in haute couture, shot by Steven Meisel, Tom Ford, and Jamie Nelson.

adopt a similar aesthetic, one that mirrors the look of success of others in the same field. It's like ordering the Deluxe Success Special at the plastic surgery HQ.[*] Circumstance informs context when one's job is to be glamorous on-screen—it's why so many celebrities succumb to the pressure to get work done in a hypercompetitive visual industry and why so many Instagram influencers have the same *yassified* look of plump lips, dramatically high, angled cheekbones, slim noses, and tautly-tugged up eyes and brows. These kinds of beauty ideals are structured less like a pedestal or pyramid and more like a vortex funneling everything into its center.

The Flawless Industrial Complex is what I call our current era of late-stage capitalist beauty culture, where achieving beauty standards is championed as aspirational, and self-optimization is framed as self-empowerment (both of which have become access points to social cachet and economic success). Meanwhile, the divide between the filled and the filled-nots grows wider by the cost and class barriers between them. It's a structure built from our massive interconnectedness through visual-based digital platforms, hyper-individualistic culture, and the socioeconomic rewards that give us all incentive to continue the feedback loop where we all perform beauty at each other to the effect of intensifying beauty's urgency, potency, and relevance. The pressures people feel to be pretty now often eclipse things that might give one pause, like critical consideration, personal safety, and budgeting. Lacking the funding doesn't necessarily prohibit people from seeking cosmetic procedures; it just narrows their resources. People who can't afford reputable plastic surgeons will generally find a way to get what they want from a discounted avenue, succumbing to medical frauds and dangerous malpractice.

---

[*] Like "success perms," which were popular with Asian Americans in the nineties as a status symbol of what material wealth—and a combination of glycerol monothioglycolate and ammonium thioglycolate—can afford.

This is where beauty is seized by Beauty™—where looks are sponsored by capitalism, multiplied through algorithms, and achieved through a rigorous dedication to a specific kind of aspirational conformity that grants status or at least proximity to it. It's reflective of the kind of industrial expansion of high-rise condos cropping up at record pace in major cities; they share the same sleek, ultra-modern architecture and design that communicates luxury over taste. With status as the aesthetic goal, the result is a tell-tale homogenous signature of its own that undermines the meaning of status itself; it's a very earnest class cosplay. With that in mind, aspirational beauty is not necessarily meant to look natural as much as it is to look *expensive*. Both beauty and flaws are subjective perceptions, but flaws are much more easily recognizable than beauty seems to be. They eclipse beauty even as they serve to define it. We have plenty of specific names for flaws, but mostly a handful of polite terms for beauty. It takes an abundance of beauty to conceal a flaw and just a minor flaw to spoil an abundance of beauty. Beauty's inability to sustain a neutral or middle ground raises stakes where stakes never even were.

The Flawless Industrial Complex is based on a rewards system that relies on the commodification of bodies. Its intensified manifestation in our culture is in many ways the result of an uncertain economy and the fact that everything has become increasingly expensive to the point that "cost of living" has become a polite phrase to describe the economics of survival. Since beauty has always been an aesthetic currency for women, we are rewarded the more we go to extreme lengths to attain the kind of capital that can keep up with such living costs (or quality of life standards). As long as appearance alone can be a conduit to romantic prospects, economic mobility, and social clout, the FIC will dominate our beauty culture, and beauty culture will come to cannibalize our own sense of self-perception. Having your beauty constantly praised in real time is addictive. The attention feels a lot like love, the same way that filters look a lot like beauty.

✳

NOT TOO LONG AGO, I WAS ASSIGNED A STORY FROM A MAGAZINE THAT REQUIRED I VISIT a plastic surgery practice. I was there to write about a new noninvasive treatment that was meant to lift my face and neck heavenward without using any needles. On the ground floor of a classic New York landmark building, the practice was all beige and muted pink walls. Frosted glass doors separated practice rooms as classical music pumped softly through the reception, mirrored wall-to-wall creating that infinity effect. The waiting room walls were peppered with framed images of patients' before and after photos, listing what procedures they'd had done and a fun fact about themselves: *Linda had rhinoplasty and— fun fact—she's really good at tennis!* All the before photos were taken in bland, mug shot–style lighting from a front-facing, frowny angle. And the after photos appeared to be selfies nabbed from their Instagram profiles, well-lit, posed at dynamic angles, in full glam, blown up past any dimensions their pixel resolutions would recommend. All the women in the "after" photos could have been related, if you clocked their similar features; they all had the same high, pronounced cheekbones, slim noses, full pouty lips, and taut almond-shaped eyes. It's the same face that Instagram has introduced and proliferated, one enhanced with *tweakments* indicative of the kind of beauty crafted by medical intervention. They're the same features seen on the face of the doctor whose name was plastered on the practice's door plaque.

When I asked her what most of her clients requested, she told me that most people want to look like themselves but better. "The camera favors drama," she said, matter-of-factly, describing the facial dysmorphia of real life and on-screen. "Better" holds no loyalty to self-perception now that the screens in our lives have become the dominant reflections of how much better we can be. Knowing your angles may help you not totally loathe the photos taken of you, but in lieu of that I've learned that with ample funding (or access) you can create them exactly as you like.

✷

DOLLY PARTON HAS THIS QUOTE I LOVE: "THERE'S NO SUCH THING AS NATURAL beauty."[*] *Natural* is simply a concept with subjective meaning to everyone—including the lash tech who once gave me eyelash extensions so long they grazed my eyebrows and audibly clickity-clacked against each other like wind chimes when a strong gust blew, after I'd requested a "natural" look. (I'm curious what the glam set would've looked like, but I honestly doubt my poor follicles would have the strength to hold them up.)

Stick around the beauty sphere long enough and you'll discover just how impotent the word "natural" is. Natural beauty's objective is less about beauty in its unadorned state so much as it is a campaign for understated beauty and a stratagem for invisibility of effort. Nature takes time; ask any late bloomer this and we'll tell you. But nobody has the patience for nature in our age of Amazon Prime. Natural beauty—or our idealized version of it—is the main reason we go to such unnatural lengths in the name of beauty. And when you see how the sausage is made, the romance of it all goes out the window.

No aesthetic practitioner or dermatologist has ever looked me in the eyes when speaking to me. We'll have entire conversations, including complex explanations on how Botox can be used to the same effect as lip filler, how radio frequency ultrasound works under the skin, or

---

[*]   Said by the character she played in *Steel Magnolias*.

the benefits of platelet-rich plasma injections, as their eyes flit about my face in microseconds, taking inventory of all the ways it has succumbed to time and stress, like some sort of Terminator for blemishes. Once, a cheerful medical aesthetician put a large mirror in my hands as she used one of those dramatically long Q-tips as a conductor wand to do a PowerPoint tour around my lagging facial features, tugging up the places to demonstrate where Botox and filler could *freshen* it up: some fine lines in my nasolabial folds; a slight loss of elasticity under my brow bone, asymmetrical eyelids; an upper lip that disappears upward when I smile; and the beginnings of jowls around my chin—all things I never really took note of on my face, which can be tweaked back to how I presumably looked maybe ten years ago. There is no roasting quite like a dermatological assessment. The language is savagely clinical, damning without being judgmental, and a total sucker punch for anyone with a wobbly sense of self-esteem. And yet, the optimism lies in how flippantly they address signs of aging or asymmetry as if they're an easily vanquished nuisance on the same level of a zit. From what I'm told, clients are often most satisfied with their own faces from their youth reflected back at them, more or less. Rarely are people slapping cutouts of Bella Hadid on the counter, going, "Hadid me, doc!" but certain public figures (like Hadid and the Jenner-Kardashians) have an influence on what aspects of beauty become a larger cultural fixation. My nasolabial folds already occupy far too much of my mental energy.

All beauty editors in their careers produce a prolific portfolio of anecdotal records inventorying their vulnerabilities, insecurities, issues, and beauty "journeys." That we get to interrogate and investigate them without the ethical and financial dilemmas of budgeting personal resources or the challenges of access to the appropriate vendors isolates the experience to a procedure, a product, or a treatment—devoid of contextual personal stakes. The journalistic angle fulfills a public voyeuristic desire while absolving the individual from most personal hang-ups or social stigma. It's our job, after all, to explore beauty's in-accessible offerings, and what more authentic way to do so than volun-teering our own bodies for the sake of beauty journalism?

Sharing my lip filler experience was just another performance of the job title—a timely one, considering that public interest in inject-ables had been peaking ever since Miss Kylie Jenner publicly opened up about hers. Lip filler was by no means a new thing at that time, but it was experiencing a surge in popularity and curiosity as a symptom of our new investment in celebrity beauty. That one Calabasas teenager could inspire such injectable frenzy is indicative of a much larger force at hand in our beauty culture.

At first, when plastic surgery was being revealed to be something more people were opting into for themselves (removed from the kind of pressure that a public career where appearance is paramount applies), it felt radical to admit without shame the measures you take to maintain your appearance. It's a vulnerable confession to admit one's own short-comings. But now we're in an era of beauty culture that is so beyond reproach from vanity's age-old stigmas that we've overcorrected toward sharing for the sake of content. The valorization of transparency when it comes to what you've had done to your face and body in the name of optimization does more to reveal one's economic and social privilege than it does to destigmatize cosmetic surgery or treatments.

Confessing that one gets filler, Botox, or other expensive medically administered facial treatments is further proof that there's no stigma that capitalism can't champion, and there's no taboo that cannot be manipulated and declawed by turning it into the right kind of content. And with less and less stigma, transparency becomes endorsement un-der the guise of empowerment. I'm not entirely sure what it's meant to prove anymore, other than that vanity has become an accepted form of entertainment. Taboos usually do, in time.

✳

ONE DAY CIRCA 2014, BEYONCÉ PROCLAIMED "I WOKE UP LIKE THIS," POSTING A makeup-free selfie on Instagram that implied exactly that. Because she is Beyoncé, of course she looked radiant, not puffy, no eye boogers in sight, hair just the right amount of bedhead. Maybe it was meant to be relatable, chill, possibly even vulnerable, but the truth is no one wakes up as Beyoncé. When I wake up in the morning and see my reflection, the first thought I tend to have is: *I have got to start sleeping on my back.* I don't want to have to think about how I look when I'm unconscious. That's my little restorative eight-hour break (if I'm lucky) from the constant tyranny of incessant self-perception.

To appear flawless in a post-Beyoncé world is to afford a Beyoncé lifestyle where one's health, physical form, and appearance are not just taken care of but prioritized. Wealth is a hell of a skincare routine. Industry titan that she is, when Beyoncé makes "Flawless" an anthem, we salute it. And even though I am sure she meant it in a self-empowering way, there is no sentiment that cannot be commercialized and sold to an idol's audience. For the next seven years, the term "flawless" and the phrase "woke up like this" would become the top terms you'd find in beauty marketing (other than "all-natural" and "Like your [appendage] but better"). The hyperbole of Flawless™ made it a rebellious anthem for anyone subject to the stigmatized lens of beauty ideals. "I'm flawless!" "She's flawless!" "We're all flawless!" But as it wormed its way into our digital vernacular it became a mantra, and then soon enough, a goal.

To be *flawless*—rather, to perform an interpretation of Flawless™ that claims ownership of your own beauty—is, ideally, a state of mind and a lifestyle choice where self-acceptance and confidence can overtake any beauty standards. Banishing beauty standards, smashing the patriarchy, and self-love are optimistic anthems that apply gusto and bravado where quiet introspection might also be meaningful. It's a nice way to take a holiday from the narrative that beauty is a constant oppressor of your self-esteem, holding your self-worth hostage on someone else's terms. But we can't exactly dismantle beauty standards by just deciding they don't affect us, because we still live in a world where they absolutely do. To say otherwise would be too easy, and totally inaccurate. And trying to fake it till we make it backfires often. Even body positivity's valiant efforts to eradicate shame around your corporeal form demands a blind commitment to disregarding your own very complex relationship with your body, which can double down on your inability to love yourself when you experience a negative thought about your body because *your entire life* you've been taught all the specific ways that your body is not good enough. Feeling bad about feeling bad about your body is not helping anyone.

Resorting to "cheats" like Ozempic (a prescribed semaglutide medication intended to help treat type 2 diabetes) to lose weight raised ethical issues around those who use it for what is considered vanity purposes versus medical purposes (or those who are sick and those who just need to lose weight and can't they do it the old-fashioned way with diet and exercise?). The shaming debate of weight-loss medication isn't new—there have always been diet pills, laxative teas, and other "lose weight fast" products with as much stigma as avid users. But shame aside, Ozempic and other semaglutides present a kind of ominous wish fulfillment in that anybody can be thin by sacrificing pleasure. That is how the drug works—it deafens our dopamine receptors to our cravings.[*] We've ostensibly found a way to inject ourselves with discipline. It reveals how body positivity never stood a chance against our wholesale fatphobia, not when this magical cure for obesity means we no longer need to unpack our cultural attitudes about bodies now

---

[*] https://www.ncbi.nlm.nih.gov/pmc/articles/PMC6520198/

that we don't have to tolerate any increment above "ideal" weight if we so choose. And why wouldn't anyone choose it? It's a common theme throughout many dystopian speculations.

Beauty offers mobility beyond one's original upbringing and class. That's how you can know for sure that beauty is power—no one bothers to gatekeep things that aren't. But beauty's empowerment is mired in a constant negotiation between individual benefit and communal care. One can only girlboss their way so far past the centuries of white supremacist and patriarchal rule that define our culture's values, before some real-world scenario knocks your ass back into our current time line where natural hair is politicized, and the amount of melanin in your skin and your body fat percentage can influence how much of a salary you're offered.

Conventional beauty standards have always existed to preserve the ruling class, which is why they probably seem much more easily surmountable when you already conform to them because often the biggest chunk of the assignment is possessing Eurocentric, feminine features. Modern plastic surgery trends cherry-pick which features and to what extent, removed of their original context, they can be used to enhance your appearance. If you aren't born with them, sometimes they can be bought, which is where we find ourselves reassessing beauty in a modern globalized world. While slimmer noses with a tip like an accent, pert round breasts, and flat torsos have always been house specials, global views are expanding the menu to include more globally ethnic features. Post Instagram boom, full, plush lips and dramatically curvaceous hips and butts are in—features usually found on Black and brown women. While maintaining an hourglass shape and a small waist, the new slim-thick aesthetic is a mash-up of Eurocentric and ethnic that few people are ever really born with, requiring surgery to achieve that middle ground. Ultimately, it's extreme measures for what may very well be a flash in the pan of chart-topping ways to be hot. The same famous bodies that made an exaggerated hourglass shape desirable have been quietly getting their BBLs reduced and implants removed, signaling a retreat back to thinner silhouettes. It seems unrealistic for an entire population to determine what bodies are "in" based on a few popular people, but if you think back on it, historically it's always been like that.

We appraise beauty so granularly now—uneven skin texture, visible pores, loss of elasticity—that corrective measures have all advanced accordingly to apply to all ages, doled out in demographically friendly forms that live in your medicine cabinet to caress your mortal anxieties away twice a day. What flaws a retinol serum can't solve, a microcurrent device can, and what a microcurrent device can't solve, an injection will. Flaws include anything that indicates you're a live human in a flesh vessel subject to the erosion of time and biology. It all becomes a bit of a dark comedy once you realize that the origin of error is simply remaining alive. Even for the very wealthy and privileged, the passage of time on a body is something to be obscured from view. And with more easily accessible solutions to the visual evidence of one's years, there is less reason to tolerate these alleged defects. Some of it works, some of it doesn't, but what it's most effective at is offering a sense of control. Rituals can be powerful that way, regardless of what they're meant to evoke.

Cosmetic surgery's generally cost-prohibitive nature has spawned a whole new trend of semipermanent beauty treatments like laser facials, chemical peels, lash lifts, lash extensions, microblading (getting eyebrows realistically tattooed on), and even lip blushing (a lip color tattoo)—basically, expensive but not bankrupting beauty treatments to make one's lifestyle that much more "I woke up like this" for a time. It's high-maintenance beauty for a low-maintenance lifestyle, the only difference between the two being who you ask and how much money they have.

Flawlessness easily becomes a sunk-cost fallacy because it's a forever moving target—these days more than ever. At some point, you have to check yourself. Throwing all your money at aesthetic treatments and beauty products may boost your confidence temporarily but in the long run relying on mercurial external metrics for validation doesn't bring you lasting comfort. But the tricky thing is how difficult it is to have confidence in a constantly changing landscape of beauty that exerts marketing where meaningful cultural changes would serve a greater good, rather than just some corporate bottom line. Also, nobody can anticipate how they're going to feel in the future. It's entirely possible that you just won't care after a while. Most of the insecurities I had in my teens and twenties (flat chest, no thigh gap, crooked teeth, et cetera) I barely ever think about now.

Sometimes, when I do actually get adequate sleep, some cocktail of eating enough fiber and drinking enough water is keeping me on a regular streak, *and* I'm in whatever hormonal cycle isn't out to sabotage my skin or my mood, I experience a momentary potency of persona that fills in all the gaps that beauty easily mends. It's then when I realize how beauty is a great companion tool to feeling my best; conversely, when things aren't going well, my appearance is usually the first to bear the burden of picking up the slack. Has that ever solved any issues besides the superficial ones? No, but too often we resort to beauty to inure ourselves to the mysterious chaos of living in our hyper-digital world. Beauty gets way more credit for future-proofing when in reality, it's most potent in the present. Beauty wielded for control is an illusion with diminishing returns; what it grants us tends to be more in consolation than control. No matter how many antiaging products and treatments you use, you're still going to age until you die.

There is no such thing as a static or complete beauty, but that's easy to forget when the Flawless Industrial Complex's feedback loop is an endless one. And yes, while beauty has always been a resource for self-advancement, it's also a source of personal enjoyment. Defining beauty by an absence of flaws does more to validate its standardization than it ever does in expressing beauty. And ironically, it's our perceived flaws that give meaning and personality to beauty. If everyone was a picture of conventional beauty ideals, that would be very boring and meaningless. And, sure, there are some cultures that demand that kind of homogeny (South Korea, looking at you), and if there is one thing you will learn from aesthetic adherence, it is that it's a very effective control method. But conformity can also be a bummer. It keeps you from exploring your own personal preferences and commits you to ideals that you had no part in forming.

Living in a culture that claims to champion individuality and uniqueness while encouraging conformity to a specific aesthetic should inspire a healthy amount of skepticism. I mean, doesn't it seem weird to you that so many of us have an encyclopedic mental catalog of very specific flaws, but when it comes to an absolute ideal of beauty, there's no one singular image (and if there is, it may only last a moment)? I mean, why are these "flaws" so defective anyway? Beauty and flaws are subjective, placed in opposition of one another, when in truth they serve to define one another. It's bad beauty math. If I think about what a flaw is long enough, it starts to lose all meaning in my head, like semantic satiation. We all have things we like about ourselves and things we don't, but when I think about where I learned of my alleged defects, it was always through someone else's opinion, never an original idea and definitely not within the same value system of beauty at all.

When I find myself deafened by the cacophonous echo chamber of gua sha tutorials, before- and-afters, injectable content, GRWM videos, and any #hotgirl content, to the point that my brain starts to disassociate from my body, I have to just log off for a bit. Sometimes even keeping up with my own beauty ambitions relegates participation into the "maybe one day" and the "too rich for my blood" categories.

It's good to air out your own desires for a bit and see where they fall, and if they burn as hotly after too long (especially when it comes to anything permanent or even semipermanent). It bears reminding that trends change, and that whatever is popular now won't be popular forever. Who knows—maybe in the next couple of years, things will shift once more and some Brutalist-inspired beauty aesthetic will take hold of the zeitgeist, giving my LEGO-shaped face a turn on the aspirational charts. Sometimes patience is the best way to deal with flaws. Lots of times you'll come to realize that what's flawed was your perception.

No Gore, No Gorgeous

eauty is pain. It's a timeless mantra, as if acknowledging your own discomfort makes it more bearable or you any more valiant. The truth is that being in a human body subjects you to pain. There will be stubbed toes, fractured bones, paper cuts, and migraines, and to be a woman means that pain is a built-in feature. The additional female-oriented organs we bear in service of biological imperative never seem to make their presence known in pleasant ways (um, cramps). But that's not what anyone's talking about when they say *beauty is pain.* Beauty is on the outside, silly.

I learned this most viscerally one unfortunate summer afternoon many years ago, as I found myself in a trap of my own making. Sitting on the bedroom floor of my old Williamsburg apartment in front of my full-length mirror, naked from the waist down and sweating profusely, I gripped a particularly thick slab of GiGi Brazilian Body Hard Wax crystallizing onto my mons pubis. I had about less than fifteen seconds to let 'er rip before it would solidify too hard to effectively do its job of grasping and forcibly evicting my pubes from my body. I inhaled deeply and exhaled shakily, pressing the lower end of the strip taut as I gripped the other end, and on the end of that breath, tugged hard. It came off in my hand right where I held it. Shit. Most of the strip was still there, its ripe flexibility quickly succumbing to rigor mortis. I flicked and scraped up another edge to tug again and when I did, I heard that horrific human Velcro sound of hair popping out of follicles en masse before that strip also broke in half, mid-pull. Fuck. Once again: flick, scrape, tug, sweat, *fuck*. Learning to efficiently wax yourself requires your tuition be paid in agony.

The trick to the perfect pull involves a generous smear of hot-but-not-burning-hot wax, smoothly applied in a strip in the same direction as hair, like you're buttering toast. Flick the little wooden stick upward at the end to create a little surf wave, which will become the tab that you pull. Allow it to cool until it's firm but still a bit flexible. You can tap your nails on it, and it should make a dull, semisolid thud. But only a little. Flick that tab upward a bit to get a good handle on in, hold the skin below it taut and pull parallel to the skin, not upward. Pull hard, all the way. No wishy-washy test tugs. You need to yank that bitch off like it's a leech you just discovered after falling into a swamp. Weak pulls = more pain. Do whatever breathing exercises will help you finish the job. You'd be surprised at how efficiently this ancient method has held up to the test of time. I mean, if it was good enough for Cleopatra, it's good enough for me.

I wax my own bikini line about twice a year, usually in the spring and then around the middle of the summer, the times of year when my bikini line will be occasionally in view of the public. I have the whole waxing kit—the warmer, the hard wax, a set of popsicle stick applicators, and some gummy pre- and post-epilation oils and cooling gels. Every time I break it out, swirling the warming wax in its little Instant Pot, I brace myself for about twenty minutes of uncomfortable slouching in front of a mirror with my legs spread open, and I think to myself, *I guess I have to do this for some reason*. Having done it multiple times now, I can confirm that there is no shortage of weird ways to position your legs to gain access to your crotch with a fast-cooling glob of wax on a popsicle stick. Like a cat licking itself, your limbs look sculptural, artistically akimbo.

Before I learned to wax my own crotch, I didn't know shit about my own pain tolerance. The first attempt probably took an hour or more and I didn't even finish because it was such a mess. But once you realize that when the wax is on, there really is only one way it's coming off, I don't know, something happens in your brain and you're like *Okay, we just have to get through this.* I imagine it's the same psychosis one undergoes in a Jigsaw trap in a *Saw* film. I mean, yeah, you're going to lose some flesh but if you want to get out alive, you've got to rally—and fast.

When I think about all the minor surgery I've done in the name of beauty, the scalp-eviscerating peroxide root touch-ups, routine pore extractions, microneedling facials, microblading, tweezing—the meaning of "mild discomfort" gets scrambled in cognitive dissonance. Now, nobody can hurt me. I am invincible.

When you see an immaculate, beautiful, gorgeous, traffic-stopping, eye-popping, *AWOOGA* hot, Hot Girl™ you might first notice her hair, her eyes, her lips, her figure, the accumulation of attractive features that check all the pretty privilege boxes, launches ships, and all that. To be in a body so agreeably hot requires a lifetime commitment to hot maintenance, which very often requires many unpleasant, off-putting, and downright painful processes and procedures. Little do you know that the hottest hot girls are also most likely to have the spiciest pain tolerances. They're basically bulletproof. They are the femmebot blueprint. And maybe you're thinking, *No way, high-maintenance girls are always complaining about minor inconveniences and things that don't look like they hurt that much. And they always have tummy aches!* And I can assure you, it's all a ploy. It's why they seem to move through life so easily—they've really nailed the whole "mind over matter" thing. It's an unfortunate trope of horror movies that the hot (promiscuous) girls always get killed first, but assemble a bad guy-killing vigilante operative team from beauty pageant contestants and I can assure you, no Vorhees, Krueger, or Meyers stands a chance.

Don't get me wrong—being a woman is often great. I mean, we get first dibs on lifeboats on sinking ships and endless variety in footwear options. Being in a woman-looking bod, however, means we are subjected to so much more scrutiny about its appearance (and sometimes its function). And managing your appearance can be a chore, especially when it involves hot wax glued to your crotch. Pain is a currency for the kind of beauty that's considered valuable and worthwhile, the kind most people in Western civilization agree on. Pain is also considered just an annoying side effect to tolerate in pursuit of an ideal.

My earliest memories of pain in the name of beauty started in the bathtub. When I was a just a wee baby, I'd be plunked into a half-filled tub before bedtime, and my mom would get to scrubbing the ever-living skin off me with a red textured viscose washcloth. It was long and narrow like a scarf or sour gummy ribbons and had a sporty-looking black stripe down one side. "Italy towels," as I later learned they're called, are a staple in many Asian households. I don't know what's so Italian about scrubbing yourself in the shower as if you're trying to erase the sin from your skin, but *mamma mia* was that a regular torment! I'd squirm away and splash around, making it so much harder for my mother to bathe her finicky child, but it instilled in me a very early idea that all things hygiene- and grooming-related required suffering. Imagine how pissed I was when I grew up and learned that it only gets worse from there.

Beauty has evolved and innovated so far as to be able to vanquish nearly every perceivable blemish and flaw now, but the tech often favors the results over the experience. Just trying to achieve clear, blemish-free skin can involve any level of implement, including needles, blades, lasers (yeah, freakin' *lasers*), and more. Even before skincare gave us twenty-five different products to use every morning and evening, achieving "good," clear skin was a frustrating mystery that often required small doses of violence. And it was *already* painful, given that my mother has the eyes of a hawk when it comes to any facial blemishes. A detectable pimple was an urgent matter to be evicted before it enacted squatter's rights. I did not have aggressive acne in my teens, but I had clogged pores here and there, and at certain times when she was feeling up for it, my mother would go to town pricking and squeezing every last one of them out, as I squirmed against the bathroom wall. It was incredibly unpleasant, not wholly effective, and probably a source of trauma between us that I've long since disassociated. I would absolutely wail, which would annoy her even more, and then by the time we were both so emotionally worked up, it would have to end. It didn't occur to me to just run away for maybe the same psychological reasons most people walk solemnly to their own doom at the beckoning of their creators. My tormentor only wanted the best for me. It's amazing how much good intentions can traumatize a person.

When I was older, she'd take me to her Korean spa in Flushing, Queens, where a professional aesthetician would cheerfully, relentlessly, and efficiently obliterate every last pore on my face—even in my ears! She'd extract things I didn't even realize were there. And I'd emerge an hour and a half later looking like I stuck my face in a wasp's nest. "I hope you don't have plans after this," she said to me the first round. I would be in the worst mood afterward, having depleted all my adrenals just clenching my fists through the discomfort. And then in two days, the tiny scabs and marks would flake off and my skin would be like new, and my mother would say, "See, wasn't that worth it?" She was already at the wise age where she could endure such torture and deem it worth it by the measurable means of "I went in with blemishes, I came out without them."

The fact that I can go for a facial with a full round of extractions today and fall asleep on the table maybe speaks to how low my threshold for discomfort was back then. Or perhaps that I just have way fewer clogged pores now. I might be a bit too bold now when it comes to auto-extractions, as an adult woman with the time and tools to fuck up her own face, spelunking into a comedone that should be left alone. You read it in all the skincare tabloids: *Don't pick at your face! It'll leave a scar! It'll infect the surrounding pores and make it worse!* And they're right. But that has yet to stop me from going full Lady Macbeth on my spots. It's a harrowing paradox, a blood sacrifice made for a flawless complexion that is immediately compromised by my very efforts.

Most grooming is uncomfortable and painful when it's left unattended for too long. When you keep it up, at a certain point there's a coasting level where your pain tolerance gets stronger. To invest in beauty is to invest in pain; you're going to have to get comfortable around needles and the idea of them in you, repeatedly, sometimes with heat. The kind of beauty that requires numbing cream is often the kind that yields much more dramatic results. At least, that is what I was told the first time I did microneedling. That's a type of facial where an aesthetician takes a tool that's like a tiny Iron Maiden in the form of a gun filled with micro-sized needles and it's pressed into your skin to create tiny injuries, which then kick your skin cells in gear to heal themselves, producing collagen and all sorts of plumping, wrinkle-filling juice. Imagine getting staple-gunned in the face over and over while a big machine attached to the gun sings friendly R2-D2 beeps throughout its progress, mainlining infrared LED and radio frequency into your dermis. It feels like a wasp sting, even with the numbing cream, and you emerge looking accordingly. Sometimes you can even see the grid of pricks in certain tender areas.

I visited one of those modern med spa franchises on offer (meaning, they offered the treatment to me, a member of the press, gratis) during which a medical aesthetician around my age cheerfully went about zapping Beauty™ into my skin with this mini nail gun device. After about an hour—the perfect increment of time to make a brief visit to the threshold of my sanity—she was done. I looked like store-bought beef carpaccio, pink and puffy. Radio frequency microneedling is an expensive treatment, about $1,200 a pop in New York City, and the best results are seen after about three sessions. I never went back for more, and I can't remember if I felt or saw a noticeable *improvement* in my own face. Then again, this kind of treatment is as extreme an intervention you can do to thwart gravity's effects on your face. The most dramatic before-and-afters are usually people who are at an age when they become most susceptible to gravity's will. My curiosity for preventive skin-bolstering treatments as well as my gullibility of taking advantage of gratis four-figure beauty treatments had led me to this fate, which, having now undergone it, I am going to have to assume that anyone willing to commit to the three-session package is beyond any level of torture.

Yet! That's not even the first time I've had someone put needles in my face for cosmetic reasons. The only tattoos I have are on my face, right on my forehead. They're very precise, delicate strokes of ink that mimic brow hairs. I don't have any others, so I cannot gauge the average amount of pain getting a tattoo usually causes—probably more than microneedling on account of the fact that the latter allows for topical numbing cream? But either not enough lidocaine or maybe just the perseverance of a buzzing tattoo pen will do you in. Microblading requires a very fine blade or tattoo needle to open the finest line into your skin and deposit pigment—enough to look like a hair stroke but not enough to look like you drew them on (even though that's exactly what's happening). It's billed as a semipermanent treatment but I'm on year four now and these micro blades are going strong. They've faded a bit but they're still noticeable.

Having a buzzing tattoo pen on your face, right above your eyes, is an alarming sensation. On the one hand you can hear the buzzing but you can also feel it across your forehead, bouncing on your skull. And at first that vibration is all you feel, your forehead a dumb slab of dampened nerve endings cushioning the ouchies. And then as the session went on (my microblader was very precise), the lidocaine gradually faded and the buzzing started feeling like a stinging. It felt like the one time I was stung by a jellyfish, a sharp burning sensation, like too much static electricity voltage concentrated in one area.

As she went on and the numbing cream faded even further, the stinging persisted—maybe it was more intense or maybe prolonged pain becomes a cumulative sensation rather than something you just get used to. I was just reaching the moment when I had to tap out, at which point she took a step back to check her work. Thank fuck. "They're fine, they're great!" I said, hastily. I mean, they were. They were nicely defined, neat, each hairline stroke *stroking*, but my entire forehead throbbed in discomfort as if to say, *Haven't your brows browed enough? How much browier can they be??* For about two hours of crescendoing discomfort, you too can have perfectly precise eyebrows that you never have to touch for upward of two-ish years. That's the bargain you trade; you can't alter your physical vessel in any permanent or semipermanent ways without incurring the wrath of its nervous system, which is probably wondering what part of the manual it missed in keeping you alive. After all, to leave an indelible mark it often takes fire, blood, or blade.

Pain may be a barrier to beauty, but pain is also extremely subjective. There are way more factors than just physical stimulation (like ripping off a strip of wax or lasering your freckles away) that contribute to one's pain perception. While it remains a bit of a scientific mystery, a few studies suggest that one's tolerance for and perception of pain are determined by much more than just physical sensation. The experience of pain has two distinct neural stages or pathways. The first is just noticing it; pain stimuli zip to parts of the brain associated with its perception,* like when you accidentally burn the roof of your mouth on a piping hot coffee or slather on a chemical exfoliant with a way-too-high alpha hydroxy acid percentage. But the feeling of pain and its intensity comes from a second neural pathway, which is determined by the activity in the medial prefrontal cortex and nucleus accumbens, two regions of the brain conventionally associated with motivation and emotion. Basically, your brain is able to bargain with pain, determining how *worth it* the pain is, weighed against intent, context, and experience. You can manipulate yourself away from feeling pain with things like meditation, distraction, and visualization.

I remember when I was an adolescent, reading some blurb in a teen magazine about how thinking about kissing your crush or the smell of them has an analgesic effect, like your own personal painkiller. And that's not entirely untrue (although maybe not necessarily correlated to any specific person). So next time you're wincing through laser hair removal, you can play Usher's slowest jams and visualize boning your partner (or just someone very boneable) to make it slightly more bearable.

Other principles of pain determine how much one is able to tough out all the lasers', extractions', and epilations' worst ouchies. Your sense of personal judgment on your own capabilities to handle a situation (self-efficacy) and the degree of confidence you have in your control of an event's outcomes as opposed to external forces beyond your

---

* The anterior cingulate cortex, which also handles a lot of other cognitive behavior that determines just how much you want to flip out when met with specific distress.

locus of control can both shape your foundation of pain perception. Also, a person's involvement in how they adhere to the specifically patterned social role of being sick (like Munchausen syndrome) and their skepticism of placebo effects can also determine their anticipation and therefore perception of pain. Pain is indeed in your mind, literally, which means you can manipulate it as well as you are able to manipulate your mind in other ways. Pain and beauty share subjectivity in common.

Suffering is a surefire method for parsing the worth of anything that requires it. Most of us are lucky to never have to learn the limits of our own thresholds (the closest I've ever gotten was at the Bumble and Bumble salon when I nearly burned my entire scalp off in pursuit of platinum-blond hair). Throughout history and folklore, transformations are not easy, quick, or comfortable. Back in the olden times, the kind of beauty that secured a good life (aka rich husband bait) often involved some form of physical transfiguration with no xannies or anesthetics for the ride.

At least today, you can undergo beauty's sacrifices with as much comfort as you can afford. As uncomfortably constricting as shapewear is today, in the Victorian era, when they took the hourglass figure quite literally, the ladies of the court laced themselves into organ-squelching whalebone and starched silk that pulverized their insides in pursuit of that king-trapping, heir-birthing silhouette. All that feminine fainting was because they were gradually bleeding internally from crushed organs and hyperventilating from squeezed lungs, not necessarily because they were particularly moved by anything going on around them. But what a great way to get out of doing boring things like state dinners or whatever.

Going farther south down the body, foot binding became a big deal in tenth-century China allegedly after one imperial hottie had such delicate, petite feet that the emperor at the time (definitely a foot guy) expressed his admiration of her tiny feet after seeing her dance barefoot, ultimately inspiring Chinese women to bind their feet and the feet of their daughters to make sure they stayed delicate and not very walky (being ornamental and useless was a sign of status, which I guess hasn't *entirely* changed today). The toes would be folded under and bound so tightly that after time, these girls could only hobble around on their extremely painful bound feet that would eventually become permanently disfigured. The Brothers Grimm no doubt took inspo from this little historical bit in their Tarantino'ed retelling of "Cinderella," in which the stepsisters cut off parts of their feet to try and fit into the prince's slipper after being told by their mother that they wouldn't be needing such plebian things as toes or heels when they're queens. Grim, indeed.

The double edge of vanity glints between self-care and self-mutilation. At least in the scriptures of beauty's foundational culture where purity—or at least the impression of it—is the beauty benchmark. Conversely, having a slowly uglifying portrait conveniently hidden in your attic isn't such a bad trade for immortal youth and beauty. Funny how in the canon of "beauty will ruin your life" morality tales, the only figure to be spared self-mutilation in the narrative is a dude.[*] As much as the stakes for beauty have risen and shifted in modern day, what with the Kardashian and social media effect of glamorizing plastic surgery, we can achieve almost any appearance we wish, given we can afford it and then endure it.

The pursuit of perfection has people chasing whatever extreme measures they deem necessary to achieve their goals, no matter the cost (and sometimes at perilously low discounts). Hundreds of

---

[*] Stabbing your own cursed portrait does not count.

thousands of people get injections, tucks, tweaks, augmentations, and implants each day, but you only ever *really* hear about it when it goes wrong, often to great dramatic effect. Like the women who contracted HIV from a plasma facial by an unlicensed aesthetician. Like the victim of cement, tire sealant, and caulk BBL injections from a fake doctor. Like supermodel Linda Evangelista's CoolSculpting lawsuit after the fat-freezing treatment led to paradoxical adipose hyperplasia, an adverse reaction in which the procedure had the opposite effect of creating hardened masses in places that were targeted for fat dissolving, leaving her body "brutally disfigured" (she shared in an Instagram post, explaining her absence from the public eye).

Beauty gone wrong becomes a ghastly horror story, and one we cannot look away from, heralded as some ominous fable when one dares to beauty too close to the sun. To defy your lot in life by indulging vanity's ultimate imperatives corrupts beauty into an express pain train. Our morbid curiosity turns it into perverse entertainment—seven seasons, actually, of the popular reality show *Botched*. We love a juicy plastic-surgery-gone-wrong story. I think it's because it touches upon our own anxieties and insecurities about our appearance, validating the overarching moral parables about the consequences when people succumb to their own vanity. Or perhaps it allows us a smug sense of ill-conceived justice to learn that even the rich and famous are not immune to insecurities, and all that money can't guarantee perfection. It gives us a reason to pity those who otherwise lead more privileged lives, and suddenly we don't feel so badly about our own. Or perhaps being confronted with the living artificiality of it gives us the heebie-jeebies. Body horror has universal appeal.

Botched cosmetic procedures offer up an easy target to blame because these victims could've avoided their tragic fate altogether if they had just been content with their appearance and learned self-love instead, putting that energy toward other more socially valuable endeavors (like fulfilling the many thankless nurturing roles that are expected of women). Instead of blaming con artists, malpractice, or the medical experts we pay handsomely to trust with our greatest vulnerabilities, the original fault is always one's own vanity. It's a kind of cultural critical voyeurism that mirrors our obsession with true crime—another tragic narrative that exploits the suburban fears of those living in relative comfort. The real and possible danger of being assaulted or murdered is something that happens all the time, usually to vast indifference, but it's glamorized in blood by romanticizing a perfect murder victim.[*] Whether someone potentially puts themselves in harm's way via elective procedures or perhaps just marries the wrong homicidal boyfriend, they are trusting those things with their lives regardless. Plastic surgery shouldn't maim or kill you and neither should your husband, and yet both things happen sometimes. Our sympathies don't tend to agree on which is more deserving of its fate, I suppose, because indulging vanity's aspirations doesn't possess the same virtue as fulfilling our society's expectations of being some guy's wife. Victim-blaming is very much so going out of style now that we've been able to (kind of) come to the nuanced acknowledgment that blaming someone for the harm that befalls them does not translate to self-protection. A blade can bring beauty or it can bring death, depending on who wields it.

Beauty is pain predates the more annoying mantra: *What doesn't kill you makes you stronger.* Similar but not quite the same. It's a modern sentiment to validate your trauma, reframing it as a catalyst for progress and growth, and calling it a triumph of the human spirit. It's

---

[*] Usually always young, pretty, white, middle-to-upper-class women, under no influence of substances and doing something innocuous and mundane, something you probably do every day.

almost like a pathological optimism.[*] We cling to narratives that champion individuals overcoming hardship and place them as a benchmark for how adversity is to be dealt with as a culture. The pursuit of beauty may be uncomfortable and unpleasant at times, but pain is simply a universal currency one can pay toward beauty, an investment even. It is deemed acceptable, gratifying even, when it leads to the desired outcome, if it does at all. Sometimes it doesn't. And in those cases, what doesn't kill you might make you want to die.

In my favorite movie about beauty, *Death Becomes Her*, a campy 1992 horror-comedy, two glamorous frenemies played by Meryl Streep and Goldie Hawn take an immortal youth potion that grants them bodies forever in their most glorious prime—but with the caveat of an inability to heal, as well as an inability to die, no matter what injury. Throughout their competitive scraps, diabolical scheming, and husband-stealing, they suffer bone breaks, 180-degree neck twists, tumbling down grand staircases, shotgun wounds through the belly, and flesh-peeling lacerations, all to be repaired and maintained by their ex-surgeon paramour, played by Bruce Willis with a mustache (very different from Bruce Willis without a mustache). Despite what should be fatal injuries, they don't seem to feel pain, which is the nudge in the dividing line that makes the film a graphically cartoonish comedy, rather than a straight-up body horror if they did. The two women's antagonistic obsession with each other weaponizes beauty to their own destruction.

After Willis's character has aged and passed away, they're left only with each other to navigate immortality, endlessly bickering and crudely patching up each other's many flesh wounds with acrylic spray paint and morgue-grade cosmetics. How much can one corrupt the body in the name of beauty, and at what point does it take a turn

---

[*]   Not surprising considering how resistant we are to grieving.

for the grotesque? The movie ends on an inconclusive note, as both women fall down church steps, taking each other down, their limbs popping off their bodies to a scattered mess below, like broken dolls. I guess one could gather that their insatiable commitment to beauty led to their demise, but considering how death isn't an option in this plotline, we are left to wonder what the worth of beauty is when vanity turns into irreparable violence. What is the limit of beauty that pain is able to grant?

I've had my entire scalp chemically scorched and resurfaced dozens of times now. I've had my face tattooed (twice). I've burned myself with a curling iron countless times to the point where I honestly wonder who thought it would be a totally sound idea to put a 425-degree branding iron in the hands of civilians.[*] I don't even wince when waxing now. Needles barely register. I think about how much whining I covered in my childhood, my nerve endings on the fritz as soon as I had to get my hair brushed, anticipating an overly vigorous tug through a knot, or the aching throbs that caused my whole body to tense up and sweat when getting my face picked apart. I've woven an intricate web of disassociation in my mind channeling my thoughts and feelings away from pain or discomfort and toward anything else. Sometimes a sexy little love fantasy can be a sufficient balm—I'd say that takes intermediate-to-advanced level discipline to effectively accomplish (without embarrassing yourself) in an actively distressing situation, or if you don't happen to have a crush of any sort at the time to focus on. That's why it's important to always have a crush—could be a matter of life or death. Most of the time, I just remind myself that this unpleasant feeling is temporary, that I'm in good hands, and *Hey, what's the worst that can happen?*

Not all of beauty's torment is an episodic event, punctuating our

---

[*] One time on my boob—wouldn't recommend that.

routine grooming and maintenance schedules. Sometimes it's a long, drawn-out process of self-torment in pursuit of a kind of beauty ideal that rarely comes naturally. Sometimes it involves denying oneself pleasure and nourishment at the behest of negative self-talk and criticism. Sometimes pain becomes the benchmark to hold oneself to when you believe you live in a body worthy of punishment—not an entirely unbelievable idea considering we absorb so much messaging about how we can never be thin, pert, or youthful enough. The danger in that is when you stop noticing what pain is and just accept it as the baseline of existing, as a scaffolding of discipline to give structure to your life. I think about Kate Moss's notorious quote, "Nothing tastes as good as skinny feels," now and I wonder how, with that logic, one can corrupt pleasure in favor of beauty (or just one narrow view of it). And what is corrupted beauty if not pain embodied on display? By those ideals, how are we meant to survive beauty? Does how much we live for it outweigh how much we die for it?

The arduous rituals of fitting into the kinds of fit (read: petite, feminine) beauty standards have us exalting bodies with less than 3 percent body fat, taut midsections, and perky breasts and butts. It's the kind of body sculpted by rigorous workouts and restrictive diets. It's easy to see how women in positions of beauty, when their appearance is paramount to their public image, can often pathologize nourishing their bodies with danger. Food holds social and cultural meaning as much as it is simply fuel for our bodies to live; stripped of its social and cultural significance, it becomes data or a prescriptive chore in maintenance. That kind of void of suffering is masked with glamour because it grants access to the kind of adoration that valorizes thinness as beauty's inherent value. The punishment for indulging a craving threatens a slip of status, slowly turning one invisible the bigger they allow themselves to become. The pain of this type of beauty is often an unseen pathology that is normalized and celebrated by society, locked into a value system that colonizes the mind with obsessive dietary protocol and bodily discretion. Some people do have naturally thin bodies. And some people who don't have those bodies engage in a slow disintegration of health for the sake of lost inches, that when done efficiently enough inevitably leads to an early death. For the living, we parse the pros and cons of fad dieting, trying on lifestyles that promise so much they're destined to fail; and when they do, we feel like it was us who couldn't live up to its promises rather than that the idea of solely eating one kind of food or cutting out entire food groups can make us "healthy" in our own warped external perception of what health looks like and what we want it to look like.

Self-discipline is something I struggle with in most areas of life, especially when it involves denial of pleasure. It's a different kind of pain, but it's hard for me to justify unnecessary suffering in my one precious life. And yet physical pain is perhaps the one thing I am able to focus on for a prolonged amount of time (a talent for hypochondriacs of all levels), which makes me a champion for the kind of beauty that requires it. Every time I think about cutting calories for the sake of reaping the visual benefits of all those Pilates core workouts, a static fugue invades my brain like a looming frowny-faced cloud, presenting the question *To what end though?* and I cannot muster any motivation or ambition. But. It doesn't make me wish I had a vertical belly button any less. It doesn't make me any less aggrieved with my LEGO-shaped face, wishing it was more chiseled and angular. But it does make me resentful of my lack of discipline—framing self-discipline as the one barrier to an ideal figure. Never mind that my dissatisfaction with my perfectly fine and healthy midsection was not of my own making, but it's easier to control one's own impulses than change the entire script of beauty standards that everyone seems to corroborate (there goes that locus on control). Somehow, illogically, it is possible to reject beauty standards and still feel resentful that I don't live up to them. Weird how that's allowed to occur.

No one needs to be born with beauty when you can be *reborn* into it (as I was when I first bleached my hair and nearly lost my goddamned mind). It's like how diamonds, swords, and other mythical weapons get made—they're forged through fire, pressure, sweat, blood, and tears. Their significance is imbued by the extreme forces that made it. Beauty, too, can be achieved through pain, grit, and gore, endorsed by your dedication to its demands.

It's easy for the mentality of "beauty is pain" to prevail when you feel like you're not good enough. Because even when you don't feel good, you can still feel some sense of satisfaction on the way to good. Does anyone trust anything that comes too easily? How else is beauty made, if not from one's own will? How much can we subject ourselves to the brutality of idealized images?[*]

Making oneself palatable for consumption is infrequently a palatable act (if you've ever dressed a turkey for a holiday meal, you're well aware). Its minor horrors are an exercise in mortal exploration through our timid measures of discomfort. In fact, "discomfort" is often the word of choice to describe beauty's unpleasantries (or routine gynecological exams). *You may experience mild discomfort.* After a while you just get used to it. What we choose to acclimate to is indicative of perhaps what we believe we deserve; at some point it's difficult to know what we think we deserve more: pain, or the beauty that comes from it.

Anyone who desires to be desired is subject to vanity's scrutiny and its machinations, so I can only suggest taking it as seriously as your pain threshold is. Vanity is not for the faint of heart. It nestles silently

---

[*]   Which are usually mythological by origin, by the way.

in your daily routines, your diet, your exercise, it performs itself at you on your screens, day in and day out. You can meet it at the salon, under the knife, or whatever bootcamp-themed workout class is popular these days. You can also give it a rest when it's not useful or relevant for you; I'm a big fan of taking breaks from vanity every once in a while, to just be a person and remind myself that pleasure can be just as potent as pain. At a certain point, there's only so much one can gain from pain anyway. There are no perfect victims when it comes to beauty.

Well Enough Alone

As a hypochondriac, I'm a perfect candidate for Wellness™. Every time I have a sniffle, an itch, or just feel a bit out of it, I consult Google, which tells me all the ways I may have symptoms of a terminal illness, autoimmune disease, or parasitic infiltration. Is it possibly just a cold? Maybe, but that would be too easy. Why settle for such a plebian diagnosis when a search engine can convince me of far more harrowing and intriguing possibilities? My browser history is filled with inane questions like: "Why do I keep getting Charlie horses in my foot?" "Why is my ear making crackling sounds?" "What does celery juice do?" And "Why pain in left lower abdomen?" It turns out, I just wasn't being active enough, my sinus infection has extended to my ear canal, no one knows for sure, and it was just gas (not diverticulitis). Over time, my Google searches have extended to the names of supplements, amino acid compounds, and plant medicine. My herbal vocabulary greatly exceeds my understanding of what they do beyond vague assertions of "boosting" and "supporting" my overall well-being.

Wellness (as a product category) was always a kind of a cousin to beauty and fitness—one of those estranged relatives who you see maybe once a year, at which point they regale you with stories about their silent meditation retreats, their singing bowl collection, how quitting refined sugar changed their life, and why you should consider arranging your schedule according to the moon cycles. Conversing about your new wellness lifestyle used to be oddball behavior, and now I overhear these kinds of conversations everywhere. But rather than scanning for the nearest exit, everyone is paying rapt attention and taking notes.

As far as I can recall, at least in media years, wellness (as we know it now) became a lifestyle interest around the 2010s, really gaining speed within that decade to the point where "wellness editor" is a common role at many media brands now. Wellness really got a relevance boost from YouTube and social media content where a surprising amount of people of varying levels of self-appointed expertise can teach you how to optimize your well-being in varying degrees of invasiveness. $4.4 *trillion* dollars later, people are desperately trying to delve deeper—and chasing total well-being has spawned a booming wellness industry.

All these alternative methods for improving our functionality—whether that's sleeping, working, libido—suddenly felt way more doable. Those methods actually started to feel easier than all of the traditional advice being put up there, especially since they came through messengers who look and seem like they have it all together. And now the early adopters of wellness, once dismissed for their spirituality-driven, woo-woo approach and disbelief in Western medicine, have gradually become their own class of millionaire entrepreneurs who've made mindfulness, self-care, and spirituality into what's known as Wellness™ today.

For a lot of the modern Western world, their intro to Big Wellness came from Goop, a celebrity-driven lifestyle brand whose founder represents the epitome of traditional beauty goals[*]: thin, white, blond, and of course, rich. My intro to wellness actually came from a chia pudding. Early in my career, I attended a beauty event hosted by a brand of supplemental powders containing gut-healing, skin-clearing, and blood . . . bloodening (activating maybe? I don't know, it claimed to do something refreshing to your blood) actives that would return you to your most revitalized, energized, and potent self. The brand's founder

---

[*] Well, the goals of women belonging to the class with money to burn.

was a beautiful white woman whose looks belied her age (a major te-
net of successful wellness entrepreneurs: looking far more youthful than
those of your age). The breakfast at the event was dosed with these
beauty powders and they were delicious, so much so that I ate probably
three of those tiny chia pudding cups, mainlining their gloopy health
benefits.

Health can be taken for granted, considered mostly when whatever routine checkups are scheduled (or when we are feeling decidedly
ill). But Wellness is *aspirational*. It's rarely better illustrated than by
moments like this. When there is a professional chef preparing a luxu-
riously healthy snack for you, it's not the same as you at home dumping
a powder into your store-bought yogurt. Still, I diligently went through
the tub of this magic potion in the coming days and weeks—which
promised to repopulate my gut bacteria, clear my skin, promote better sleep and focus, only to discover that . . . nothing happened. The
promises made at the event didn't come true. I looked the same, I felt
the same, and I was just as tired, distracted, and bloated. *Hmm, maybe
that wasn't enough wellness*, was my first thought. *Perhaps I need a
surplus of wellness to make up for so many years of consuming casually toxic materials.* Instead of discouraging me, it made me curious to
delve deeper, trying whatever was at my disposal to bio-hack my way
to inner beauty.

The industry goes way beyond the standard tenets of maintaining health and living well. Wellness™ has come to represent the commercial culture spawned from our desire to chase a health beyond
health, an ultra-optimized body-mind-spirit connection that borders
on superhuman. At the height of human development and advance-
ment, it seems that the last frontier of human experience we have left to
conquer is mortality (and maybe those low vibrational energies I keep
hearing about). Wellness has a way of convincing us that that's possible, even though we are all vaguely aware that at some point, life ends.

Even with the awareness of mortality's inevitability, chasing Wellness™ dangles a tantalizing enough promise of control to most people. Some of it is legit, but a lot of it borders on delusional. It feels like every day there's another article about how to detox your organs, cleanse your system, juice up your focus, and maximize your ability to *do it all*. The amount of scientific research (and in lieu of scientific research, pseudo-science) that goes toward learning how to optimize the body in the most granular ways is staggering today. But before the words "bio" and "hacking" joined in holy hyphenation, and before we attempted to herd bacteria into regulating our digestive systems with probiotics, the external body was the only way to project health and beauty, usually achieved through diet and exercise. Diet culture walked so Wellness™ could run. They both valorize a certain body ideal; the methods may be different, but the aesthetic goals are similar. Diet culture championed thinness as its overall goal. It gamified food into points systems, villainized entire food groups, and smashed the words "jazz" and "exercise" together to create a form of dance cardio. I don't think the reputation of carbs has fully recovered from the early 2000s. The enemy to health was fat, so weight loss results often trumped inner health.

Wellness™ as the sequel to diet culture goes deeper, diet-ier, and in many ways is more demoralizing. It's the link that binds diet culture more closely to beauty culture today. But on a more practical level, wellness's popularity is evidence of the failings of our social care systems. Wellness culture thrives in the gray area where many of us are unfamiliar, overwhelmed, or skeptical of Western medicine. It fills in as a step-figure to where crucial needs are not being met by our government and our healthcare systems. It also offers a holistic approach to improving our own well-being and appearance while masking any underlying intentions of vanity.

Diet culture has a moralistic framework, one which requires a choice be present for opting for "good" foods versus "bad" ones. It's even adopted a sort of loyalty prejudice, projecting the sin of adultery upon eating something you enjoy. As someone who counts carbs as a confidant, and desserts as a lifeline, my raison d'être (and the reason I know French), if I don't have a little treat every single day, I will plummet into an existential ennui. I don't remember agreeing to see broccoli and quinoa exclusively. Diets aren't monogamous; they're simply what you eat. Those who cannot afford to have as many food choices eat what they can to survive, and that may not include "whole foods," which are hard to find in food desert neighborhoods or are sometimes priced at a premium. (I mean, have you seen how expensive vitamins are?) Poverty is plenty stigmatized enough without then villainizing some people's most accessible food source. Processed foods may be proven to be unhealthy, but unhealthy food is better than no food.

Wellness and diet culture share the same old body hang-ups with new philosophies. Healing your gut, colonics, de-bloating, lymphatic drainage massages—they are practices with theoretical roots in benefiting your overall health while *conveniently* helping you to be thinner and feel better for it. Without the binary right or wrong food choices of diet culture, what wellness offers is a scattered variety of options to achieve *optimization*. The framing tweak feels novel but can be just as confounding. Some people do have real issues with food fucking up their insides. And it's often a nightmare to try and figure out who the culprit is. I've read some truly out-of-pocket things about ingredients that could be labeled as character assassination—the notorious PR for gluten, for instance, goes way beyond a digestive intolerance, scapegoating it as the reason you're bloated, can't lose weight, or have constant brain fog. Maybe it happened to a couple people, but the way it wears a scarlet letter would make it seem like gluten should be avoided at all costs. Labeling foods as "bad" or "good" reinforces the denial of pleasure that food becomes an unwitting agent for (even though, yes, some of those delicious things on the bad list, like hyper-processed foods, are not great for you). It makes it easy to reframe disordered eating as "clean" eating, intermittent fasting, and other forms of extreme dieting, because of the moral implication associated with the choice.

Moralizing food and health have done way more for promoting nutrition than science has. Converting our preferences to moral principles furthers the idea that food and what we consume generally defines our identities (rings even truer when you consider how these describe the person, not the food—"*I'm* a vegan," not "*my diet* is vegan"). If you recall, there is a long-standing history of food's relationship to virtue, going way back to Eve and that apple. Some religions avoid pork or shellfish, others eschew meat altogether, while fasts are built into certain observances of faith (not to say that has anything to do with our current cultural climate of orthorexia, but that the history of religious observance involving food gives it moral precedence). We may not be so driven by religion now, but purity culture is still broadly found in our cultural practices and behaviors; you can usually tell because they're the ones that inspire the same feelings that soured people away from religion in the first place (righteousness, judgment, holier-than-thou smugness—admit it, someone you know just popped into your head right now). Preference aside, categorizing food as "clean" also then implies the unclean foods are pollutants and poisons.

The tenets of wellness culture go deeper than diet alone—wellness is an inside job, after all. Fitness covers a lot of the more external and visual bases, but to prolong the ideal body requires a software upgrade focused on what's *within*. Most people unburdened by chronic health issues have perfectly functioning organs that effectively sift through whatever they consume to keep things running smoothly. With the arsenal of Wellness™ at one's disposal, the idea is that your organs could be doing more, even though that is not how organs work. But a human body is a vessel that has one broad trajectory throughout its life span—mature, then decline. There is only so much that can be done to prolong that decline, but eventually no tidal wave of green juice will get in between you and it. Well-being and living well feel more estranged than ever.

We need all the coping mechanisms we can get in these "unprecedented times" (war, bad economy, social inequity, our reproductive rights being taken away, the earth always being on fire, global pandemics, being too online). For at least four-to-five hours a day (according to my screentime metrics), I'm mainlining climate crises, social injustice, and political upheaval juxtaposed with hot people performing meditation mantras, fitness hacks, and twenty different ways to abolish belly fat, as well as hack my brain. How are all these people glowing up in times so unprecedented? We are living in the least chill era, and unchill times call for unchill measures.

✹

WELLNESS FOUND A CONVENIENT ENTRANCE INTO BEAUTY THROUGH THE MAINSTREAM clean beauty movement around the mid-2000s and early 2010s. Both advocated with a purity-driven campaign of chemical-free, toxin-free subtractive marketing. Beauty marketing took on a "made without" mantra, boasting what a product didn't contain more than what it did, sometimes to redundancy* or fear-mongering synthetics like preservatives† without context. And it loves the word "natural." "Natural" doesn't make something safe (poison ivy is natural and we all know we should stay the fuck away from it), despite the optimism that nature inspires. The return to nature makes for a feel-good narrative and in the case of some products (like so many natural deodorants) it sacrifices efficacy for the idea that it's "better" for you. I'd argue that in certain

---

* Meaning, the list of excluded ingredients included harmful substances that would never be found in a cosmetic product anyway.
† Preservatives are used to prevent mold and bacteria growth in products, and in appropriate doses have not been found to be harmful.

cases, no product would be best if you're so determined to live a natural lifestyle. All the greenwashing and sustainability claims can be just as false as conventional beauty's promises. After all what's more sustainable than *not* making more products? But planet-friendly language and do-good mantras really do go far when consumer choice only has other products to compare them to, rather than relevant context and scientific research.

Many clean beauty companies were founded as a reaction to bodily dysfunction, hormonal imbalance, and infertility issues, offering an alternative to "toxic" products under the assumptions that our beauty products are primarily responsible for the chemicals we introduce to our bodies (environment and diet do a lot of the heavy lifting with that). The most prevalent marketing copy seems to lack understanding of what chemicals are, as it describes an unregulated space. Water is a chemical, humans are made up of chemicals, and chemicals make up the air you breathe and food you eat. Any product that claims to be "chemical-free" better be made of pure energy or heat if it expects to be believed. But it *sounds* comforting, and that's where what's harmful versus what's helpful tends to get fuzzy.

Almost every clean beauty brand founder I met with as a beauty editor had a very well-rehearsed origin story of how a health issue (cancer diagnosis, fertility issues, hair loss, bad rash, et cetera) inspired them to start their own clean beauty brand. Positioning beauty products as a leading cause of health issues has always been low-hanging fruit—vanity has always been a convenient scapegoat for many perceived social ills (and not for nothing, historically speaking, beauty products were laden with poisons like lead and mercury before regulatory groups were formed for consumer safety). It's a very successful marketing strategy, leveraging fear the same way the beauty industry traditionally has leveraged insecurity. The earliest days of "clean" beauty were handmade products in unpolished, cardboard packaging, using household items for various beauty applications (coconut oil, essential oils, and shea butter got a *lot* of lip service). To appeal to the growing market of interested parties, the products have evolved to look and feel just as luxurious as any other "unclean" products, including the price tag.

Not soon after beauty shelves became inundated with clean products, marketing shifted to an educational, ingredients-focused approach, especially in skincare. Stores like the Detox Market and Credo (launched in 2010 and 2014, respectively), which stocked only "clean" beauty brands, popped up to cater to a growing market, and Sephora created its Clean at Sephora seal in 2018, bestowed to brands and products that follow guidelines excluding a list of "unwanted" ingredients.

Given that there's no regulation for the term, it's difficult to say how clean is clean enough. But if you had the choice of something whose packaging seemed safer than its alternatives, why wouldn't you choose it? This kind of storytelling and vetting is meant to instill trust with consumers, but the terms are only as sound as the science. And with global companies like Sephora, at a certain point it becomes contradictory to reserve a section for "safe" products while still selling "unsafe" products. And in late 2022, Sephora was sued[*] for misleading claims about its Clean at Sephora products, namely that some products on the list do allegedly contain harmful ingredients.

In some cases, chemophobia is totally warranted. Certain common household products like baby powder, for example, were found to be the cause of ovarian cancer and mesothelioma for thousands of

---

[*] Priya Rao, "Sephora Responds to Claim Its Beauty Programme Is Anything But," Business of Fashion, February 2, 2023, https://www.businessoffashion.com/articles/beauty/sephora-defends-clean-beauty-programme/.

people, most of whom are women. Trace amounts of asbestos in John-son & Johnson's talc-based products like baby powder were linked to tens of thousands of cancer cases, beginning in 1999.[*] Twenty years later, internal J&J documents revealed that the company was aware that its talc was laced with asbestos as far back as the 1950s, and it had also made significant lobbying campaigns to tamp down evidence suggesting that talc-mining was harmful. (Talc by itself isn't known to be harmful, but the way it's mined makes it high risk for contamination by carcinogens.) The company had even filed lawsuits against the doc-tors who published studies linking talc-based personal care products to cancer in 2023.

The depth of the Johnson & Johnson scandal did a number on consumer trust in personal care companies, which was never solid to begin with. Big Beauty's ability to infiltrate and lobby the bodies of government meant to ensure our safety is enough to inspire para-noia in the entire industry, eroding our trust in our government as well as inspiring fear in what lurks within our products. I'm not sure that the hero that presents itself, however, is necessarily the one we need. More stringent regulation and testing of substances for potential harm seems like it'd be a much more wholesale way to address the mystery of what potentially harmful ingredients are lurking in our personal care products. "Clean" beauty succeeds where regulation has so far re-mained silent. It offers us a way to keep up our beauty routines without having to think too deeply about the disturbing practices of the beauty industry at large.

I often think about how wellness's cultural relevancy feeds upon itself. The more we're reminded of our own deficiencies and mortal-

---

[*] Lisa Girion, "Johnson & Johnson Knew for Decades that Asbestos Lurked in Its Baby Powder," Reuters, December 14, 2018, https://www.reuters.com/investigates/special-report/johnsonandjohnson-cancer/.

ity, the less well we actually feel. It's made me hyperaware of being in a body (as if that was easy to forget) and how that body could be better performing. It provides product-based solutions to culture-created problems. It pulls whimsical narratives from ancient indigenous practices to leverage some form of cultural resonance and authority in co-opted practices, ingredients, or treatments. And it doesn't help that Wellness has an irritating way of infiltrating participants' behaviors and becoming personalities. There's a whole new set of toxic positivity vocabulary attached to the lifestyle that can feel a bit like adult baby talk to sell it to you (including so many cringe names for vaginas). It's a lot of "good vibes only" and "elevate your vibration."

Natural, earth-friendly beauty brands have always been around (usually found at co-ops, Whole Foods, or local mom-and-pop shops, wearing the kind of crunchy-looking compostable packaging that fulfills the sustainability- and naturally-derived tenets that wellness-heads are after). I mean, just look at Dr. Bronner's. That clean, sustainable, vegan, and natural products didn't become in demand and aspirational to mainstream culture until they gained a luxury rebrand and a premium markup should tip you off to who this is all for.

*

COMMERCIAL PURSUITS OF WELLNESS™ SO OFTEN FALL UNDER THE UMBRELLA TERM "self-care." Self-care was originally a medical term coined in the 1950s; it was a practice to help medical patients bolster their own sense of self-worth by actively participating in their own recovery and well-being. The idea was that through the act of caring for oneself, they would physically heal and also learn to appreciate all that their body is capable of. Not long after the term's invention, it was propagated by the Civil Rights Movement as a necessary component of resilience when engaging in activist work. The most prevalent tenets of self-care stemmed from the work of the Black Panthers, who promoted the importance in taking care of one's own mental and emotional well-being in the face of sociopolitical inequity.

More recently, self-care has become a balm for the consequences of hustle culture, most often as a practice of pampering (think sheet masks, bubble baths, and massages). The language of value and worth in beauty is used a suspicious amount for campaigns that bank upon your self-improvement: *Because you're worth it. You deserve it. Self-love.* I've seen self-care invoked in the name of Botox injections, blowouts, manicures, facials, and any number of beauty treatments. And obviously, there's nothing wrong with taking in beauty practices that make you feel more relaxed and attractive. The girlbosses need rest and relaxation. But the communal aspect of self-care—taking care of yourself so you can continue showing up for your community—has been pushed to the side, downplayed by the commercialization of our own well-being and self-optimization. Self-care now has become literal; it's not so much a pit stop to engage in communal agendas, so much as it is so you can keep up with your own. I suppose at best it means indulging in pampering as a means of self-soothing, and at worst (most cynically) it's come to mean anything that cushions the fear of mortality or worse—letting yourself go.

That fear of mortality is easily harnessed by Wellness™ and its disciples. It's a nice idea that you could revert your body back to its optimal version, or that issues can be solved holistically. And I am not even asking for much: just a tummy with the digestive productivity of my youth; the ability to feel rested after I've slept; and for my back and neck to not hurt all the time. These are all little cumulative aches and struggles I didn't start to really feel until I surpassed my thirty-year warranty. When you're not of the 1 percent who can afford wellness treatments at spa resorts with sound baths, flotation therapy, herbal remedies, vitamin IV drips, LED saunas, ayahuasca retreats, and food grown in its purest state, you have to rely on the more rudimentary elements of well-being.

As a beauty editor, I have somewhat of a loophole, at least from the "things I can 'buy' to make it go away" perspective. Beauty editors know *all* about product-based solutions. I am constantly inundated with products promising better digestion, clearer focus, glowing skin, thicker hair, and generally a more optimized body. It's easy to see why people are jazzed about it; anything that appeals to your well-being makes you feel better when you believe you're doing something good for your body. Just look at that emperor with his new clothes; he was totally feeling himself, jazzed about his new outfit, until some court urchin outed him as a naked fool. Sometimes the ritual is just as much the cure as it promises to be. Even if the effects aren't what you hoped, the feeling of control over aging seems like a win.

Among the things I've tried in the name of wellness: the probiotic smoothie powder supplements made me bloated and constipated for days; the vitamin IV drip didn't give me any more energy (but it did make my pee neon); and the botanical facial I got at a chic, luxury beauty apothecary caused me to break out in hives. I've tried jump-starting my mental focus with nootropics and adaptogens; healing my gut with probiotics; and lobbing a combination of amino acids, ashwagandha, and valerian root at depression and anxiety. None of these worked as advertised. There were also sound baths and energy realignment sessions that, while pleasant, didn't actually make me feel much different; LED saunas that made me sweaty and tired; and a variety of meal prep kits and supplemental additives that as far as I could tell were so expensive just so you could eat *less* food. And in the end, I was no more well than I had started out in the beginning. Instead, I'd have to return to tried-and-true methods of exercise, balanced diet, getting enough sleep, stress management habits—all things that do not come delivered in liposomal encapsulated form.

That's not to say that any of this is without merit or validity. I did discover that weed is very effective for insomnia, and that acupuncture was legitimately helpful. Perhaps my bias toward being a hater put me at a wellness deficit to begin with, despite how I long to be revitalized and more well. I know plenty of people who swear by saunas and cold therapy and meditation. I'm happy for them, if not slightly unconvinced (because it's never just *one* thing, is it?). But the mass commercialization of wellness has diluted the meaning and the efficacy of how so many of these supplements, herbs, routines, and practices are able to benefit us. It keeps me coming back to the "one thing," and how when one doesn't work, we're trained to move on to the next. And then the next, and then the next . . . and then it doesn't end until we do.

Wellness thrives for a reason, though. I mean, we had to do something about the stress of *the economy* and *the world today* and the total overwhelm of being a person in this current social climate. Our poor acclimation to the culture of *everything, everywhere, all the time* that we've created for ourselves needed a stress release valve, and wellness was more than primed to step up. I have to routinely remind myself I'm not underperforming, it's that most people aren't mentally and emotionally built to field the incessant news cycle, social media's endless doom scrolling, and economic chaos of our techno-reliant culture. Supplements are much more convenient fixes than opting out of a culture we've become reliant on for our lifestyles of convenience—and sometimes they even come in tasty gummy form.

Wellness™'s wholesale body dysmorphism is one of its foundational platforms. It offers a more wholesome pathway toward achieving our existing beauty standards, as well as the evolving ones that extend to our lifestyles as well as our appearance. It posits holistic well-being as the answer to beauty's demands, both of which end up looking similar when done well enough—the exception being that it often feels doubly like a moral failure if they don't. Most women are reminded how perception of their personhood extends to the appearance of our bodies throughout our lifetimes, as we are routinely psychically (and physically) compressed into smaller and curvier figures, like we are new macaroni shapes being invented at the pasta factory. The self-care, mindfulness, and "wellness" we sought as relief from chasing beauty's ideals lassoed us into a similar rodeo that champions the same ideals (just with organic hemp rope).

If injectable beauty and surgical intervention are considered on the extreme side of beauty's efforts, wellness's dubious health claims and expensive accoutrement are on the other side of that blade. And in reality, it's not really one or the other—it's usually a bit of both. I am perplexed by the number of people I meet who only eat the "purest" foods and buy into clean beauty's agenda, while also regularly getting neurotoxin injections. It tells me that wellness is more supplemental to beauty than it is an alternative, and it reinforces my belief that any aesthetic that becomes a commercial lifestyle aspiration warrants scrutiny. Both may be opposing beauty methodologies, but when used in tandem, they tighten the tension between the illusion of beauty's morality and the class-driven glamour of aesthetic treatments. Wellness raises the stakes of beauty by valorizing the kind of *effortlessness* that wealth and privilege afford, suggesting how you too can live like that with the right products and practices; all of it serves to pathologize superficial flaws, visible illness, and disability as symptoms of a certain class.

What you stand to gain by buying into commodified Wellness™ is often more in conceit than a body that absolves you of the flaws you find most deficient in yourself. But it is most successfully endorsed by a body that looks the part—thin, radiant, supple, younger than one's years. I think the greatest irony is that we'd probably be way more well if we weren't so fixated on the performance of our bodies. I didn't know I possessed most of the alleged deficiencies I had were it not for wellness making me aware of them (and it has yet to deliver on solving). I mean, I possess the type of neurosis that can think its way into a hives breakout (one time it did!). But I haven't found a way for solving that through Wellness™.

Wellness gives beauty meaning and significance beyond superficial gains, its work-around being that beauty is the result of your healthy discipline rather than your commitment to vanity. It can bypass a lot of the stigma or shame around vanity because it wears health like a Trojan horse—even though the truth is that there's a lot of overlap between wellness culture and vanity's agenda. Med spa franchises are becoming as common as fast-food chains in some major cities (there are currently three in my neighborhood), as quickly as wellness treatment centers and spas are cropping up as well. They even share a similar pleasantly anesthetized branding facade that's come to redefine modern luxury—muted, earth-toned colors, aesthetically raw or undone finishes, and tactile textures that invite touch and imply richness.

Maybe wellness wouldn't have taken off the way it did if we had adequate trust in our healthcare systems and government and didn't feel the need to grasp at any means of personal control to make up for that lack. Or maybe it was an inevitable alternative to the pressures of beauty standards, a way to seek meaning from vanity. Wellness can be just as harmful as the beauty industry it claims to protect you from, which is why a second thought (and maybe a third or fourth) is a good idea to decipher if your needs are a product of your fundamental well-being or a detriment that was introduced to you. It seems like working toward repairing the systemic issues and cultural burnout that led to such a great need for wellness is the way forward—for everyone, not just billionaires who can swap blood with their grandchildren. Whether pure or polluted, bodies all share the same fate. I don't think we can truly separate vanity from mortality, but I think when we separate what true well-being feels like from what we think it is meant to look like, we can create a clearer path to living well.

Even E-Girls Get the Blues

I n my early twenties, I dated someone who would go on about how he much he preferred long hair on girls.* At the time I had thick, voluminous waves of black hair past my shoulders, grazing my boobs. This proclamation might've seemed flattering to some women who have normal reactions to compliments, but *something* about it bypassed whatever part of my brain that stores verbal affirmations and instead lobbed it straight at my antagonism triggers.

Not that the idea wasn't *already* circulating around my mind, but the perceived dare inspired me to get a very on-trend bob at the time— one of those shoulder-length, flippy ones that all the It Girls at the time had. I brought photos of the models Lou Doillon and Alexa Chung to my hairdresser, desperate for that wavy, flippy, messy-but-not-too-messy coif. My natural hair texture had its own interpretations of what this meant, but after the chop, I did indeed feel lighter, freer, and chicly tousled. When I showed up to that boyfriend's apartment that night, he frowned at me. We broke up about a month later. Not because of the hair (but not *not* because of the hair, I suspect). Perhaps cutting your hair *at* someone is not the indicator of a totally healthy dynamic, you know? Breakup haircuts are a fairly common ritual, but considering our mounting incompatibility, I was perhaps giving myself a head start.

Having long, luscious hair is considered the apex of femininity, and we've fully internalized this idea that beauty is found in cascades, ringlets, and waves of hair. There's a massive global market to prove it. If

---

* Just their heads, though.

you're on social media, you've probably been targeted by ads for hair extensions, hair-growth products, and hair-thickening treatments and supplements.

The haircare industry is incredibly profitable, considering how much of our identities we imbue our hair with. If you really think about it, hair is technically just dead keratin that grows out your body, pushing itself farther and farther away from you. Yet, by modern standards, it's a formidable part of your identity.[*] Great hair—and by great, I mean healthy-looking and abundant—is a sign of fertility, sexual desirability, femininity, and of course, power. People really respond to a woman in her feminine power. And when it comes to signaling idealized femininity as far as it can be realized from the top of your head, the reference often looks like one particular kind of hair: blond.

I don't know if people still care whether blondes have more fun, but I can tell you what they do have more of: the audacity. Specifically, bottle blondes—platinum blondes or what the pros may call oyster blond, pearl blond, baby blond, and otherwise all variations of creamy and crystalline paleness. I think everyone should try being blond at least once, if for no reason than to just notice how differently you're perceived by the world. Being perceived is a specialty of blond hair. It reflects light, creating a shimmering halo blinding all those who look upon you. But in the absence of genetics, there is always chemistry.

For those of us born with darker hair, the process of going blond requires bleach, which is a mixture of potassium persulfate salt powder and a peroxide. Together they strip the hair of its natural pigment to the pale, buttery shade of natural keratin within.[†] Your melanin is still there, the molecules are simply rendered transparent. It's the most naked your hair will ever be, devoid of whatever shade of genetics you

---

[*] Other mammals don't grow so much hair out of one concentrated part of their bodies; it must look ridiculous to them how bald most of our bodies are in comparison. Leave it to human nature to romanticize nonbiological imperatives.

[†] I guess it's technically true then, that we're all blondes deep within.

were born with. If you weren't born with naturally light hair, this process takes time—several hours, sometimes. Bleach respects no one's schedule. Bleach is a mercenary that saps the pigment from the melanin molecules in your hair after busting open the cuticle protecting the hair strand. It eats keratin for breakfast and spits out what's left. If you don't neutralize it, it will continue eviscerating protein bonds until your chewed-up hair feels like overcooked spaghetti before melting off your head.

No one told me any of this before I decided to go platinum blond.

I did not imagine I'd be shutting down the uptown Bumble and Bumble, one of the trendiest, celebrity-driven hair salons uptown, until nearly midnight (my appointment was at two in the afternoon) while my scalp throbbed with chemical burns of sizzling open sores oozing with serosanguineous drainage (a clear-ish, pinkish mixture of blood and blood serum) as I mentally and emotionally orbited the outer circles of hell, courting a uniquely sensational pain. It's the kind of pain that inspires a novel sense of dread, the kind of dread that prompts you to ask yourself: *Hmm, is this what dying feels like?* When does all the fun that blondes allegedly have begin?

I cried all the way home as the chunks of hair that remained on my head, once silky and verdant, now felt like the end of a witch's broom; the roots crystallized into scabby mounds. Have you ever had a leaky scalp, and felt a mysterious dripping snaking its way down to the nape of your neck, only to wipe it away and find a pinky blood liquid smeared on your hands that looks maybe like pus but isn't? I have. It still sends chills down my spine. My hair, once long past my shoulders, withered in my hand, shedding with each brush stroke, floating to the ground like cotton candy strands. I had dipped my head into the liquid flames of hell and lived to tell the tale, though my scalp looked like a Cronenberg film. I'd find chunks of scabs in my hair for weeks afterward as it healed (just in time for my first touch-up).

This makes it sound like it was a disaster. It wasn't. It went as successfully as it could have, and I looked hotter than I ever had. No, I *felt* hotter than I ever had. And I don't just mean because my head was throbbing from inflammation (but it was). And I am not just saying that because the suffering was so great as to psychologically influence me to deem it "worth it" by any measure of denial. No, it had exceeded all my expectations of how I would look as a blonde, which until then in my brain was some foggy depiction of Debbie Harry but Asian. And all it took was nine hours in a hair salon and the willpower of a Greek myth where a humble peasant dared to defy the gods' will of having dark hair. I imagine this is how the Joker became The Joker™—swan-diving into these kinds of chemicals will absolutely change your DNA. I felt fundamentally changed, and that was only just the tip, proportionally speaking.

I've always had thick, jet-black hair that grows at an accelerated rate that would out-Rapunzel Rapunzel. I was told my whole young life how beautiful, luscious, and formidable my hair was. And as much as a sucker for flattery that I am,[*] people who give compliments about people's "virgin" hair usually follow it with some useless suggestion like "Never cut it!" or "You look so good with your hair down." People love to give unsolicited advice in the form of compliments about people's appearance.

There is a reason characters and perps are described first by their hair color—it's right on top of your head, the part of your body that people recognize first in a crowd. Changing your head is a big deal. It's probably the easiest thing you can do to change your appearance the most drastically. That's why haircuts cost so much—hairstylists are reconstructing your identity, externally and in many ways internally. If

---

[*] The Achilles' heel of all those born with Leo in their Venus placement.

you've ever shed tears over a discrepancy of how long an inch is, you know exactly what I mean.

If hair is the first flag to one's visual identity, I've always vied to harness its expressive capabilities to form my own, especially in my adolescence. At least that's what I thought the first time I colored my hair. I was in high school and naively believed that a box of L'Oréal Féria Cherry Crush would show up on my black hair without bleaching first. (All those box dye model photos are photoshopped, which should be a crime.) The havoc those box dyes have unleashed on every impressionable woman's psyche! There should be warnings, or at least someone manning the aisle, holding a key to the plastic barrier case containing all the hair dye, who can steer you away from a color that absolutely will not work on your current hair color (or current emotional state, should that be the inspiration). But I digress. Box dyes may very well be a ploy to keep professional hair colorists well compensated, considering all the botched jobs they are paid to fix after one ambitious night with a semipermanent cocktail (my colorist can attest to *many*). Control of one's own image is always a matter of urgency or expense—sometimes both, when executed in that order.

Cherry Crush ended up leaving a faint reddish sheen on my black hair, not enough to be immediately noticeable but noticeable enough to get me in trouble for coloring my hair, which I was not allowed to do at the tender age of something-teen. I ended up covering it up with another box of Féria in Bright Black, which had a blue tint to it, like a comic book character. The end result was a completely redundant exercise in passive-aggressive beauty rebellion.

I'd attempt coloring my hair again in a college dorm bathroom my freshman year. Streaky raspberry-orange chunks with a store-brought highlighting kit, complete with a little brush to more expressly ruin yourself in targeted sections. But I would not encounter bleach again until that fateful year (2014), armed with beauty press credentials that allowed me to self-immolate for the low, low price of my innocence and naiveté. Sometimes there really is no more satisfying masochism as beauty. I never imagined I'd be negotiating my own mortality in one of New York's trendiest hair salons on a winter weeknight. But what doesn't kill you sometimes allows you to be reborn. And I was a born-again blonde, so help me.

Blond has always been a shade of hair that comes with a mythical reputation, its paleness a banner for purity or divinity, according to Western culture.* And it has the added baggage of carrying with it an implication of race and status—to be called "a blonde" has meaning beyond just hair color. People don't generally go around saying they're better for being blond (but some will become defensive at the denial of their blondness, even after their natural hair color darkened over the years), but they are protective of the social status that it carries. It's an implied preference that goes without interrogation most of the time. Everyone wants status, but nobody wants to reckon with the consequences of that status once they acquire it, sociologist and professor Tressie McMillan Cottom wrote in a *New York Times* op-ed: "They can also help us make sense of why so many women in conservative media are also blondes."† The label itself, used to describe who is *a blonde*, implies someone the likes of Gwyneth Paltrow or Taylor Swift—not Beyoncé, who has been honey blond for most of her career, or for that matter me, even when I was splashed all over Google's image search results for "blond Asian hair."‡

Why was becoming a blonde the first thing I was so intent on ex-

---

* Which also deems it an indicator of vapidity and bimbo-ism in more recent times, so that bears consideration as to how seriously you want to take it.

† Tressie McMillan Cottom, "The Enduring, Invisible Power of Blond," *New York Times*, January 19, 2023, https://www.nytimes.com/2023/01/19/opinion/the-enduring-invisible -power-of-blond.html.

‡ My colorist attests this is true by the sheer number of subsequent clients who brandished my images as color references when seeing her.

ploring once I had access to the professional resources who could do the job? It's one part "grass is always greener" curiosity, and one part subverting the specific kind of racialized beauty I was typecast into. To escape the pressures of being one kind of beautiful, I opted for another—one with a verified track record of mainstream appeal. I wasn't fooling myself or anyone—blond would by no means appear natural on me. But that wasn't the point. Its clear and apparent fakeness on me challenged the preconceptions of what a blonde is meant to look like while also claiming its inferred social status. Blond's enduring and sought-after manufactured aesthetic is so well established, its legitimacy no longer requires authenticity.

It is tricky when you ask what type of person can be a blonde, especially now that with chemical assistance, anyone can be. Beauty is, after all, also a performance of class. But even "bottle blondes" are expensive to attain and maintain, requiring its own proximity to privilege. I would love to say that my entire life changed, and I soared into my most potent era after going blond. There were some incremental perks—being blond certainly opened a lot of doors for me, professionally (see page 39).[*] But my platinum period was granted by my profession just as much as it benefited it; I never could have afforded the process had I paid these New York City hair salon prices. My status as a beauty editor granted me that privilege entirely.

And the price tag also didn't account for the *labor* required for upkeep. Maintaining a platinum-blond head is a bit like having an expensive show pony growing out of it. It needs special shampoo, but it can't be shampooed too often. It needs so many conditioners and oils to remain looking like human hair. It requires special pillowcases (silk only) to curtail friction. You cannot brush it too fervently. You can't blow-dry it too frequently. And it takes a full day to air-dry. That's no

---

[*] I was even featured in one of those uplifting Dove campaigns about doing a temporary wash-out blue hair dye.

exaggeration. When hair is that porous, it hoards water and never lets it go until you separate them by heat styling, which is a gamble because every time you blow-dry, flat-iron, or curl your hair you're damaging it even more (yes, even though hair is already dead). The grooming schedule alone is like beauty jail. If you have a finicky dog, or a newborn, or perhaps a rare exotic night-blooming orchid you need looked after, ask your platinum-blond friend. They would understand.

After several months of root touch-ups every five-to-seven weeks wherein I would clear my schedule for the day to sit in the salon for upward of five hours as my scalp got another chemical licking,[*] I did a very stupid thing. I thought—I really thought—I could take a little vacation into L'Oréal land once more with Colorista #BLUE600, a temporary direct dye. I blue myself, expecting to return to blond in four-to-eight shampoos, as promised.

It did not wash out. Ever.

Those blue pigments squatted in my hair until a professional had to evict them (thank you, Elizabeth), forcibly and chemically. Something else to know about bleached hair: it absorbs everything—smells, dyes, bad habits—sometimes for good. I had no one to blame but myself for this, and while I wasn't upset, I was not prepared for a life so blue. Any makeup beyond that no-makeup makeup aesthetic suddenly looked garish and costumey on me. I felt like a cartoon character. I couldn't wear anything red or else I'd feel like I was in some Americana cosplay. If I wore blue, I felt like Violet from *Charlie and the Chocolate Factory.* All sartorial and aesthetic decisions stemmed from or in contrast to my very vividly blue head.

However—*plot twist*—blue hair turned out to be my power color. Whoever is saying that blondes have more fun is wrong. They don't. They're at home, marinating their heads in Olaplex twice a week and

---

[*] The first cut is the deepest; believe it or not, you somehow acclimate to the sensation, but not the scabs.

washing their silk pillowcases. No, it's the blues, the pinks, the uni-corn rainbows, the moody violets, the crimsons, and the punk greens who are out there *blue-ing around*, having the time of their little blue lives.[*] Possessing hair of a color not found in nature tends to project personality. *The girl with blue hair.* It's memorable, it's mysterious, it's intriguing.

My blue was somewhere between cerulean and denim blue—not too Manic Panic vibrant, it was a little bit smoky and would fade into aquamarine after a few washes. I wore it shoulder length for a while until the chemical breakage forced me to snip it into a bob. I imagine I looked a bit like a young Marge Simpson (in the flashback episodes where she had a seventies, flowy kind of shag). Strangers would stop me on the street to talk to me about my hair. My selfies were shared (without permission) and distributed throughout hair Instagram. Sometimes people would tag me in photos that strangers took of me on the street (Also without permission! Don't do that, it's creepy!). Babies smiled at me. Everyone was up in my business. I'd never been so flush with matches as when I was mermaiden-haired.

What is it about blue hair that made me Player One in the game of life? I've polled this with others who have also had a period of blue hair, and the anecdotal evidence would suggest that, in a bizarro turn of events, gentlemen (and everyone else) do indeed prefer blues. In all my previ-ous knowledge of what woos the male gaze, typically a low-maintenance (or just a low maintenance–appearing) kind of conventional beauty ap-proach does the job plenty well. A woman's hair is often seen as some default seducer of men, especially when worn long and "feminine," its abundance suggesting fertility and perhaps that it's full of mysteries and secrets. Disney princesses, fairy-tale heroines, all the classic Botticellian babes—hair well past their asses. None of them were blue, though.

---

[*]   Not in the cop sense.

One spring morning I was rushing to see my colorist for a touch-up, sprint-walking to the subway as usual. As I waited for the Manhattan-bound L train, a handsome dude was sitting on a nearby bench reading. "Handsome" is a slight understatement. This man was astonishingly attractive. He was doing too much, honestly. No one needs to be giving an excessive amount of face on public transport, where plebes and gremlins like me get around in the relative solace of anonymity and solidarity that half of us don't know how to drive and the other half don't own a car.

He looked up at me from his book as I walked past him and we made eye contact, as you invariably do with strangers sometimes. And then he had to take it further by *smiling*. At me. With his whole handsome face. There were teeth in it. I saw them. I wasn't expecting to be accosted by such a face and thus, forgot how to act. Mentally and emotionally unprepared to be flirted with first thing in the morning, my brain-to-facial expression synapses short-circuited, leaving my faculties with but one default face—the kind of face you make when you see a waiter passing your table holding someone else's order that looks delicious and suddenly makes you doubt your order before it's even arrived. It's the kind of whiplash response you make when you say "you too" to the airline concierge who says "enjoy your flight."

The L train approached to take me and my dumbstruck-looking face to my appointment. I squeezed myself onto a packed car (the L is never not packed), looking back at him through the window because I'm somehow only bold enough to reciprocate a flirty glance when there are physical barriers in between me and any anonymous hottie. He waved as the train left the station, and I exhaled in relief, thinking, *Phew, that was close! What an innocuously sexy New York moment, he-he!* One can only remain in a fight-or-flight state of mind for so long without completely depleting their adrenal glands.

Well, New York City is a much smaller city than anyone can imagine, and not even a week later, in a completely different neighborhood, as I was waiting to meet up with a friend for dinner on some sidewalk in the Lower East Side, who should walk by but this stressfully hot man. He smiled warmly and approached me, saying, "Well, that hair is hard to miss, isn't it?"

I mean, come *ON*. By all meet-cute laws, we should have boned happily ever after, right? I'd love to be able to say that we fell in love and had lots of hot blue-haired babies, but as the saying goes, God doesn't give with both hands. It would upset some universal balance of social equity if he was that professionally good-looking (yes, he was a *male model*; I was correct) and charming, smart, kind, and not a serial killer or a narcissist. We went on a couple dates, where I enjoyed looking at his face and he enjoyed looking at my hair. It turns out that mutual attraction was the extent of our compatibility. *Quelle dommage.* But he would not be the last man to be absolutely blue-struck by my azure-colored head. For the rest of that year everyone I dated, seriously and not so seriously, expressed a fascination with the color of my hair, to the point that I was beginning to wonder if there was perhaps some kind of blue-hair fetish I wasn't aware of. I've had pink, green, blond, copper, red, silver, and even those chunky striped face-framing panels on hair, and blue was the most head-turning out of all of them combined.

When I think of blue in nature, it's the color of the sky, of water. It represents calm and serenity, and baby-boy things in the binary gender spectrum. If you want to get psychological about it, it often represents peace and orderliness, mostly by conditioned associations with government and healthcare staff uniforms and buildings, and blue light is thought to even have a preventive effect on suicide in certain areas.[*] My hypothesis is that blue hair diverts the color's preconceived notions by being on a person's head, which then communicates a kind

---

[*] https://www.psychologytoday.com/us/blog/your-personal-renaissance/201810/surprising-research-the-color-blue

of familiar mystery that beckons more than it intimidates. I'm just riffing on what I've read about the color blue in that context, but otherwise, this is not a conclusion I could've drawn by any other way than firsthand experience.

Years later, long after I'd experimented with many more hair colors away from blue and toward shades that some people are actually born with, I attended a press event for a professional hair extension brand. I sat in a salon chair as a hairstylist chose a twenty-six-inch set of clip-in hair wefts in a near-perfect match to my actual hair, which was an ashy, mid-toned brown at the time.[*] The wefts being attached to my head had lighter balayage highlights striped throughout for that added hot girl effect. There must've been some hot girl summit where all the Victoria's Secret models concluded that balayage was *the look*, and it set everyone off to chase that manufactured sun-streaked effect that adds something visually synonymous with dimension and depth to their hair. It's a trick of the light, playing with color contour to suggest hair that is more abundantly faceted than hair to become Hair™.

After some sectioning, teasing, styling, and some snips to blend the processed ribbons of someone else's hair into mine, I suddenly had shimmering waves down past my boobs, bouncing along as I walked. I left the event with a much fluffier head and walked down Sixth Avenue in Chelsea to an unexpected streetside fanfare. The two and a half blocks I walked to the subway, I was enthusiastically ogled by no less than five strange men (three of whom vocally lauded how pretty I looked, one of whom tried to get in my face about it); a small child said "wowwwww" at me; and one street photographer got in my face with a lens as I crossed the avenue to descend into the Twenty-Third Street station like it was some sidewalk safari. I was wearing a nice dress, walking around, having my own *Pretty Woman* moment, and never have I

---

[*]   A shade that would fall under the "mushroom brown" micro trend of the early 2020s.

received these kinds of public reactions with hair just above my shoulders, which is about as close to a scientific control for this kind of unintended experiment I can name.

And yeah, *I know*, you don't need a scientist (or sociologist) to tell you that men love hollering at unaccompanied women on the street, the volume and intensity of such holleration increasing exponentially the more inches she has dangling from her head. The power and influence of even a casual hair flip remains timeless; it's a gesture of femininity in motion, like the modern flick of a fan. I don't make the rules, I just flip the hair.

The canon of long hair is backed by centuries of mythology. It barely requires the kind of marketing of trends like The Rachel or whatever bob, lob, or pob is in season. Every time Victoria Beckham gets a different haircut, scores of women march to their hairdressers to follow suit, craving the kind of life her chic minimalist style emulates. But a long, flowing, Siren-like mane possesses the kind of power that launches ships and sends sailors to their watery graves—and that's the kind of shit that *never* goes out of style.* But possessing this knowledge and experiencing that visceral reaction in first person is the difference between apples and GMO apples. As much as I love fanfare for simply existing, it's never *not* jarring to dodge the sweaty eyeballs of Manhattan's most unabashedly vociferous men when they encounter a pleasing woman. Catcalling is still a social casualty programmed into a generation that grew up consuming a hammerheaded kind of masculinity. What a prison of the mind to have to make a comment every time a woman walks by, like a Pavlovian response or a real-life Captcha.† (I usually walk around with music blasting in my ears because I'm not trying to hear all that.)

---

* By this logic, Samara from *The Ring* would absolutely eat it up in these streets if she wasn't so hell-bent on mangling the faces of anyone who watches her DVDs rather than trimming her split ends.
† *Select all images with women in them.*

The hair extensions were clip-ins and so they released me from their command over the male gaze come bedtime. Wearing someone else's hair always feels a bit like I'm in some Hannah Montana disguise. There's just so much of it to throw around. It feels like some kind of experimental art performance, snatching strands that blow awkwardly into my mouth as I'm loosely aware that I am eating someone else's hair. It took someone else's hair to meld with mine to pump some nitrous into the engine of my perceived femininity, so that I could feel like a princess for a day (or a Transformer—the girl one). But truthfully, it's a relief to unclip those babies at the end of the day, massaging my tired scalp, which is not accustomed to upholding all this added weight of surplus femininity. Heavy is the head that wears the weave.

Hair makeovers are always the most gratifying and life-altering kinds of changes. Whenever I get a haircut, it's usually twenty-four to forty-eight hours after I've decided that I want a haircut. I think nothing of shearing off several inches of something that took me several months to grow. Armed with a mantra that serves to self-soothe as well as enable (*It's just hair; hair grows*), I have managed to delude myself into many hairstyles that have absolutely no business being on my head. Even with good haircuts, there is always a period right when it's done that you gush to your stylist how much you love it, and then walk out of the salon, spook yourself with your own reflection in a store window, and have an absolute existential *Oh God what have I done?* panic. Thank God more hair salons aren't walk-in serviceable because someone needs to save me from myself. I'm too easily suckered in by a professionally styled hair photo that scrolls my way on Instagram—the source of all my beauty temptations—as I envision myself as *that girl*, whoever she is. Sometimes it's a carefree Parisian blogger with the perfect lived-in shag (the kind of living that's done to these styles is very subjective), a punk with a chopped-up Chelsea cut, a Japanese street style account with a perfectly uniform, wavy bob, and mostly it's always hairstyles that I am dimly aware will be a struggle with my coarse, dense, stubborn hair texture.

And I should know better; I know there are hairstylists behind these immaculate images, who whip every single flyaway in its place with gobs of styling products and heat styling, all painstakingly done to look as if no effort at all was applied. And, of course, there's Photoshop. But does that stop me? Obviously not. Do I learn? I refuse to! Life is kept consistently interesting by the kind of mounting tension that can only be found sitting in a hairstylist's chair.

While for me a haircut is usually something I decide to do on a whim, when it comes to models, or anyone who profits off their appearance, a haircut actually *does* mean a lot. Watching the early seasons of *America's Next Top Model*, there were always one or two contestants who got their heads shaved or completely cropped, without pushing back until the final look, at which point they're completely in tears. One test shoot later they realize that the pixie cut Tyra chose for them really does bring out their smize, while also securing a place in the competition for at least two more episodes. The worst thing you can be as a modeling competition contestant is ungrateful.

Who among us hasn't experimented with a pixie cut, anticipating freedom and empowerment? I am sure many people with huge doll-like eyes, cheekbones that could cut glass, and a tiny jawline can attest to that. My round, childish face, however, received a head full of cowlicks and an identity crisis. Look, I know the whole face shape haircut chart theory is largely prescriptive bullshit and incredibly subjective—*Cosmo* told me my face is heart-shaped, while *InStyle* insisted my face was square, and *Seventeen* told me I was round-faced. All of them agreed that long, swoopy, side-swept bangs were a flattering choice, however. This was the kind of beauty scripture I obeyed unfailingly in my teens.

How to make your face look less like your face with a haircut is the kind of information we absorbed without much question whether we actually wanted long, swoopy, side-swept bangs.

Nothing will make you think *Maybe they were onto something with those haircut geometry theories* like being confronted with your own head upholstered in a haircut of essentially high-pile carpeting. To my credit, I never read that a pixie cut was strictly off-limits for any face shape, including mine. The nuance was lacking though. When I was seventeen, after watching Mandy Moore in the 2003 romantic comedy *How to Deal*, I felt compelled to cut my long hair into her feisty, grown-out pixie cut. At that age, I fancied myself as some unique, not-like-the-other-girls, manic-pixie-wannabe and felt that the one thing holding me back from realizing my full Riot grrrl potential was an edgy haircut. What I should've done was pick up an instrument, but that's not how this story went.

I went to the one Chinatown hair salon on Pell Street that I'd been going to since I was a kid; at the time they always charged twenty-six dollars for a cut, shampoo, and blow-dry. I showed my hairdresser, Susannah, a photo of Mandy Moore from the 2002 Teen Choice Awards, and she looked at it for a long time silently, as her brow furrowed deeper into her forehead. After that contemplative pause, she just said, "Okay!" and went to town on my head. To her credit and my horror, she gave me exactly what I asked for. It looked JUST like the picture . . . without taking into account that Mandy Moore and I do not share many facial feature similarities, let alone head shapes. Was it the edgy and rebellious departure from basic I was hoping it'd be? Sure. However, I realized that perhaps I am not so edgy after all to wear it with the confidence to embody whatever I was going for at the time. (My junior prom photos feature me in these consequences, looking cute but incredibly awkward.)

The first time you chop off all your hair (apropos of no significant life events), it will become a significant life event all its own if you don't have the confidence to live your choices. I was glad hair accessories like butterfly clips and barrettes were cool in the early aughts because my whole head was a strategic pin cushion for them. I think my peers were used to me going gently and inoffensively against the grain as far as trends went, so it wasn't a surprise that the try-hard alt girl chopped off all her hair. There's something about a face unencumbered by so much hair that's refreshing and inviting. For other people, though. Not for me.

Our poor hair often becomes the first casualty in a moment of emotional turmoil or crisis. Sometimes when you're under an intolerable amount of stress,[*] your hair just might decide to leave of its own volition. As the keeper of our confidence, insecurities, secrets, comfort, and our (entirely too outsized) sense of control, our hair is made the unfortunate martyr of an impulsive bid for regaining control. The fact that a haircut can indeed be life-changing for the better only compounds that idea. The most memorable hair makeovers in cinema can attest to this (Mia Thermopolis in *The Princess Diaries*, Fern Mayo in *Jawbreaker*, Laney Boggs in *She's All That*, it goes on). Control is sometimes sought after in the most chaotic ways when you let outsized emotions take the wheel. That's why there are so many scenes in movies where girls hack off some crooked bangs over a bathroom sink to indicate a personal crisis, or in other cases, going so far as shaving their heads completely (See: *Empire Records*, *G.I. Jane*, the first season of *Heartbreak High*). It's a symbolic shedding of the self, a visceral point of no return. It's become a cinematic trope, separating a woman from who she is now from who she's leaving behind. Shaving your head is one of the most visceral ways to shed an identity wholesale. We get a cinematic front-row seat to watching a woman manage her emotions with clippers.

---

[*]   I can always track my stress levels by the size of the hair nests in the shower drain.

Not just identity, hair also holds lots of cultural meaning as well. Korean superstition says you shouldn't wash your hair on New Year's Day because it will wash away luck. And some indigenous American tribes view their hair as ties to their cultural identity, an extension of one's thoughts, a symbol of power, and connection to the earth.

In 2013, a member of Japanese pop group AKB48, Minami Minegishi, shaved her head on YouTube to express remorse for her crime of . . . having a boyfriend. J-pop idols are forbidden from romantic relationships by the record companies that create these groups to uphold the fantasy of accessibility for fans, and she was photographed leaving her boyfriend's[*] house at a time that implied something irrefutably saucy, no doubt. Nobody *forced* her to do it, but to express her deepest and most sincere apology for disappointing their fans, Minegishi resorted to an extreme gesture of contrition in Japanese culture—shaving her head. The video was removed from YouTube on account of how much it bummed everybody out.[†] With a hastily sheared, uneven buzz cut, Minegishi tearfully begged for forgiveness to the public and to be allowed to remain in the group, after she was demoted to a trainee for her transgressions. What I saw was a girl who robbed herself of one very visible part of her personhood containing her confidence and identity as an idol. The act of self-flagellation was far more extreme compared to the "crime."

Of course, you cannot discuss public buzz cuts without mentioning Britney Spears, who famously gave herself a buzz cut in 2007 at a random salon while seventy paparazzi photographed the event. Spears told a tattoo artist, who she hit up right after the buzz cut, "I'm sick of people touching my hair." The buzz cut didn't separate her from the extreme fame that came along with being Britney Spears as perhaps she'd hoped; it just exacerbated it. Spears's public rebellion was chum for ruthless

---

[*]   Another J-pop group member, who didn't shave anything as far as I know.
[†]   https://www.bbc.com/news/world-asia-21299324

paparazzi and a juicy scandal the media was thrilled to deliver, the re-runs of which we look back on now with the unease of retrospect—how publicly we all sensationalized a woman in despair with no immediate outlet but self-sabotage. The paparazzi photos reportedly sold for half a million dollars.[*]

The photos of her battering an SUV with an umbrella, enraged and bald, looked photoshopped to me at the time. It seemed unthinkable to me that someone so glamorously famous would shave her own head, a form of self-sabotage that bordered on mutilation given the stakes of her celebrity. Pop stars are meant to charm and titillate, often with their appearance as much as, if not more than, with their talents. (Their looks are carefully constructed, sometimes focus-grouped, and very much so integral to their mainstream success. Also, many of them are all wearing some form of a weave to toss around onstage for visual effect.) Celebrities are people with the same emotional thresholds as civilians, but without the tolerance of their audience to express the things we flip out about daily, at least not without consequences to their livelihood. A hasty haircut could mean a career's end—and in the case of Keri Russell in *Felicity*, the end of a show.

Our hair is often the creative outlet for our misdirected anguish and anxiety. I think the idea is that in order to feel changed, we must change physically—by subtraction or negative sculpture, an outer shedding, a fresh start, an emancipation from all sorts of things much more difficult to release otherwise. That's why breakup haircuts are such a thing. You think a different hairstyle can separate you from your identity in that relationship, that your codependency symptoms can be so easily removed as your hair. Personally, I have a codependent relationship with my hair. Many people do! Our mood can change depending on whether

---

[*] https://www.mtv.com/news/1580191/britney-spears-economy-brings-in-millions-for-magazines-label-paparazzi/#:~:text=In%202007%20alone%2C%20X17%20sold,the%20singer's%20head%2Dshaving%20incident

we like our hair that day or not. A bad hair day can have devastating effects on our confidence, and we spend way too much time fussing with it every time we pass in front of a mirror. We cry every time we get a bad haircut (and maybe even when we get a regular haircut) because it's just so distressing to have to reconcile your self-image with how you hoped you'd feel after a change.

When I like how my hair looks, I feel grounded, confident, and like I can just walk around life like a charming little game where charming little things happen to me. Good hair days give me very main character energy. Perhaps too much. Stupid-looking hair days—or when I catch a glimpse of myself in a store window to see that Mother Nature has decided to style my ill-begotten bangs into looking like one of those tiny shih tzu dogs—have the ability to significantly trip up my confidence.

"Hair is everything. We wish it wasn't, so we could actually think of something else occasionally, but it is! It's the difference between a good day and a bad day. We're meant to think of it as a symbol of power, that it's a symbol of fertility; some people are exploited for it, and it pays your fucking bills. Hair is everything." That's from *Fleabag*, a monologue Phoebe Waller-Bridge's character asserts at her hairdresser after he gives her sister the exact haircut she asks for, to her great and immediate regret.

The way we interpret and appraise our own hair relies so much on how the world interprets us based on our hair—some of which is not all within our individual control, and a lot of which is based on how "normal" hair is defined on a spectrum of Eurocentric standards. It seems to me that many people who presume to fall under the normal hair category don't have to think too much about the state of their hair anyway, probably because it's never come into question beyond what a wash and cut can do every once in a while. "Normal" hair flows silkily down one's back. Normal hair reflects light off its naturally smooth cuticle and has probably never once broken the teeth off a comb. Normal hair comes in colors like brunette (sometimes dark brunette), auburn, and all variations of blond. Normal hair doesn't require protective styling or even all that much grooming beyond a preference of length. When your hair does require more consideration and even more labor to "tame" it into these behaviors, it's normal to resent what *normal* represents. Access to power and status almost always requires looking the part to demonstrate how much you deserve to be there (and that goes beyond hair, but hair is a common place to start). "Good" hair days cost more for others—particularly Black women, whose natural hair texture is routinely politicized. And the effort, capital, and time it takes to groom oneself into this manicured standard may sometimes be deemed worth the inconvenience when it grants acceptance into spaces of power and status where one's natural hair is considered something that requires *managing*.

The reality that so many hairstylists aren't trained to work with Black hair textures and the haircare products made for them are often kept in separate store aisles or sometimes specialty beauty stores altogether is a stark indication of the racialized connection between hair and status. In the beauty industry, hair is a canvas, a plaything that can be manipulated to suit your mood or occasion, and a fun form of grooming that often belies the historical tension between what's considered appropriate and what's considered grounds for dismissal. Otherwise, why would it stress us out so much? There are unlimited ways to poison yourself in pursuit of good hair, which most of us happily participate in even though no one should ever be made to feel that they have to.

A healthy move would probably be learning to manage our emotional turbulence without reaching for the shears (as well as de-villainizing frizz). There is nothing wrong with changing your appearance when it's something you really want for yourself, rather than a misguided reaction to something that has nothing to do with it. (I've since dispensed with antagonistic bobs.) But if there is one thing that's for certain, our sense of self is not so easily reclaimed by shedding what we think defines it. And perhaps our hair has been carrying that burden of definition for too long. As time goes on, buzz cuts become pixies, bobs become lobs, and bangs become . . . curtain bangs. The meaning of it all changes slowly, probably as long as it takes hair to grow.

"If you want to change your life, change your life. It's not going to happen in here," the hairdresser says back to Fleabag. It's something to consider if you find yourself at the bathroom sink late at night with a pair of shears aimed at your forehead. Or you could always just dye your hair blue. It's just hair. Hair grows, right?

Smoother Operations

P opular opinion would likely credit the onset of menstruation as the time when a girl becomes a woman.* However, before first blood, the rite of passage toward maturity in my experience seemed largely determined by who had fur to shave and who didn't. I remember it like this: one day, I was swapping puffy stickers with friends in our laminated Sanrio sticker books and then one day I was holding my newly fuzzy armpits hostage with one of my brother's disposable Bic razors, trying not to nick myself.

Razor commercials seemed to be on the TV every fifteen minutes when I was in between getting my period (age thirteen, at a friend's birthday party) and getting to pick out my very grown-up, glittery, plastic razor. Those slim, tanned, hairless calves sashaying across a sandy beach on my television screen taunted me like that cartoon candy dancing to the concession stand on-screen before the previews play in the movie theater. TV sold me on the luxury of shaving, depicting women in voluminous bubble baths with an impossibly long limb extended skyward as they gracefully glided a razor across their (already hairless) shins. Quite different from the rushed reality of shaving with one foot up on the side of the tub using a bar of soap, as I witnessed most of my friends and college dorm mates do.

Those razor commercials played nonstop. *I'm your Venus, I'm your fire . . .*† Also on the shaving playlist was Jewel's 2003 hit, "Intuition,"‡

---

* Can anyone really be a Woman™ at age nine?
† I still don't fully believe that was not a commercially created jingle, but it was actually a song written in 1968 by the band Shocking Blue.
‡ Ironically, the song was an indictment of the culture of self-commercialization and Jewel was criticized for selling out by going pop despite what was clearly sonic satire.

which served as the soundtrack to Schick's Intuition razor with "intuitive" moisturizing pads, a main competitor to Gillette. I will never *not* associate those songs with CGI-smoothed legs. In retrospect, the peach fuzz under my adolescent arms didn't warrant the lawn mower treatment, but because all my junior high school friends were fully on the Gillette agenda, I felt that I ought to be as well. Body hair, while mysterious and private, very much felt like a platform for womanhood considering how its removal was considered one of femininity's chief duties. There's a time at the beginning of any development before you're introduced to critical thought and when the newness feels exciting before it becomes a chore. While the main narrative for hair removal spoke of smooth, feminine limbs, the inverse was a lot more stigmatized. Armpit hair? Unacceptable. Leg hair? Shudder-inducing. Even eyebrows fell victim to the fuzz-phobic sentiment of the late nineties and early aughts (little did we know how much that attitude would change in two decades). Pubic hair was weirdly affirming at first the same way I guess periods are, implying sexual maturation, before very quickly becoming something that must also be meticulously groomed and reined in. Beauty's scope was flexible enough to celebrate individuality and uniqueness, but it has yet to loosen its grip about body hair. I remember one girl I went to high school with being nicknamed "Werewolf" because of her visible arm hair. And then she was teased for shaving her arms after she found out. You really can't win.

Coming of age in a very body-hair-intolerant culture that considered bullying a very normal occurrence made me hypervigilant of my own. Being as sensitive as I was (almost as sensitive as my underarm skin, which immediately broke out in red rashes after shaving) I was exceptionally neurotic about not giving anybody anything to make a fuss over. My shins, which were still so bare save for a few fine, downy hairs, were subjected to the blade. Their mere presence was an aberration that could only be ameliorated by a bright orange triple-bladed Gillette Venus. It seems ludicrous now, thinking back on it, but we were *obsessed* with the ritual of shaving. "We" being my teenage peers, who spent grades seven through twelve marinating in Skintimate shaving cream and Nair. In the pre–smart phone and pre-streaming era we had little to distract ourselves, so what else were we supposed to do in our leisurely evenings but routinely epilate ourselves as we daydreamed about what clueless lacrosse player we'd try to seduce with these gleaming gams while running track.

My household was strictly a no-shave zone, my parents issuing the authoritative decree of "You don't need to be doing all that." Did I do it anyway? Yes. My poor pits suffered such razor burn, probably not helped by the fact that I was reusing the same disposable razor for *way* too long. It wouldn't be until much later, after years of subjecting my underarms to dull, disposable razors, I had the novel thought to try something different: waxing. Now, waxing requires that there generally be a grabbable length of hair (about a quarter of an inch) for the goop to successfully harvest it wholesale, so in my early twenties I allowed my harassed pits to finally chill for a bit while the hair grew out enough to meet its untimely reaping. Maybe it's because I'm hopeless at gauging measurements by sight, or maybe I just forgot about it, but after the hair had grown long enough to taper off (about a half inch), part of me was curious as to what would happen if I just let it keep going. It turns out, not a whole lot!

This is how you end up as that girl who doesn't shave her armpits. It was around the time I started beauty writing, the early 2010s, and armpit hair would have yet to become trendy (again) for another nine or ten years. Whenever there would be a shot of me from the bust up in any of my beauty articles and even one little hair peeked out from under my arms, the commenters would zero in on it swiftly:

"I'm sorry, I just can't with unshaven pits 😥"
"Umm, I think you missed a spot with your razor 😂"
"Sorry, but that armpit hair is so distracting, it ruins the whole look"*

People will always find something about your appearance to insult behind their screens. And apparently, armpit hair makes for a very easy target—on women, specifically. Throughout the twentieth century, mainstream imagery of women in media was devoid of body hair, so our minds have all collectively normalized a lack of visible body hair. It's so default that even gritty Hollywood depictions of a postapocalyptic, zombie-ridden world will feature nomadic survivors roaming what's left of civilization for months—who we're to assume conveniently completed all their sessions of underarm laser hair removal before society crumbled and they had to form collectives to rebuild society and fight zombies. Or maybe they all just happened to stash some razors in a pack to shave their pits off-screen in a tree or a cave while danger lurks around the corner at any given moment. A heroine can be covered in mud, blood, and shit, but her armpits will remain hairless throughout.

It's not like this is a new fixation either. Humans have been messing with their body hair since the beginning of civilization, using seashells and other weird detritus to pluck their stuff. And trends of how people wore their body hair (or didn't) shifted time and time again—there was even a time during the Middle Ages where women would remove hair from their foreheads to scoot their hairlines backward because five-heads were in, and Elizabeth I made the no-brow look a big thing when she was queen of England in the mid-1500s (she had her own era named after her, so clearly she was very influential).

---

*   (The look being completely unrelated to anything below my neck.)

Body hair removal became not only a matter of feminine duty, but also vital to the perception of one's hygiene, after Charles Darwin's whole natural selection theory in the late 1800s associated body hair as a connection to our more primitive selves, and opined that hairlessness was a sign of being more evolved and *sexier* (his words, not mine). Suspiciously, those ideas fell mostly on women to follow, as a means of gendered and heteronormative socializing. With women gaining greater social influence, something had to be done to keep them in their place—and shaming this one element of mammalian biology was it.[*]

Scientific and medical experts at the time promoted the idea of hairiness being an indication of criminality, mental illness, disease, and sexual perversion, which set the whole stigmatization of body hair in place. And then in the early twentieth century, upper- and middle-class Americans aligned the imagery of a smooth, hairless bod with the idea of femininity as well as separation from the lower class, poor people (and immigrants). As fashions for women slowly showed more leg, more arm, more everything throughout the twentieth century, hair removal became compulsory to wear sleeveless dresses, shorter skirts, and bikinis without offending onlookers with their body hair.

In 1999, at the *Notting Hill* movie premiere in London, Julia Roberts revealed her very fuzzy pits when waving to fans on the red carpet. Roberts, who was the reigning queen of rom-coms and Hollywood royalty, became tabloid chum when she was photographed, arms up mid-wave, revealing pits with some robust growth. Tabloids made conjecture that it was some feminist statement, and that her boyfriend at the time preferred his women unshaved and stinky (I do not know where the odor component came from). Tom Loxley, a journalist for *The Independent*, wrote a bizarre debate article about Ms. Roberts's personal grooming habits: "Northern European men would prefer not

---

[*] Maybe they figured women would have way less time to overthrow the patriarchy if they're constantly worrying about leg stubble.

to discover too much fuzz on a woman's legs or under her arms. Again it's to do with celebrating the difference between the sexes. Hairy women will most likely remind us of, well, hairy men."

The affirmative counterpoint from an Andrew Male (har, har) argued that it's the overly airbrushed, plasticized, and vacantly preened ideal of feminine beauty that should be criticized, and if Julia Roberts's boyfriend preferred his women smelly and unshaven, then bully for him and for men who love *natural women* everywhere. Both dudes fully based their perspectives on the preferences of the woman in question's romantic partner, offering not even any ill-conceived assumptions of what Roberts herself might have intended (or not) with her rogue armpittery.

Loxley's argument goes so far as to imagine the consequence of such growth: "Nature, after all, can be a pretty brutish thing. From under-groomed armpits it is a short step to growing cabbage in the ears, spinach in the teeth and nits in the hair."[*] Did he really believe that women rewild into vegetable gardens after ditching their razors?

But pit hair specifically has come a long way since then. Progressive attitudes about androgyny and the disassembling of gender made it less objectionable in more recent times, but no less of a statement. While ten to twenty years ago, pit hair was repulsive, now it's an edgy, rebellious move—something that challenges old-timey femininity's somewhat pedophiliac agenda of a hairless desirability. I suppose when the aspirational female form is one that never appears to age, body hair is just another affronting reminder of maturity—sexual and otherwise. Even as anti-ageism and *adulting* is newly celebrated, we still have a tricky time separating youth from sexiness when it comes to women. I don't know how punk something is once it's on the cover of American *Vogue* (Emma Corrin's pit hair specifically in the August 2022 issue),

---

[*]   I don't know what a nit is and I refuse to look it up.

but it's a cultural turning point for sure that indicates that pit hair is not only allowed but being normalized (at least on people who already hit most of the marks of conventional beauty). Even Emily Ratajkowski, twenty-first-century sex symbol, has been photographed with fuzzy pits and quoted in *Harper's Bazaar* as saying that sometimes growing out her body hair makes her feel sexy.

Armpits in general are a fairly inconsiderable part of the body—it's a crease under your shoulder, something that largely remains hidden until you spread your wingspan. Whatever is in there is generally less offensive than what might come out of it. Legs, on the other hand, are formidable appendages in the arsenal of seduction. And you *never* see fuzzy legs on women in any context denoting aspiration or elegance. The day I see a woman's hairy legs on the cover of *Vogue*, we can talk about body hair normalization.

Body hair, as we allow it, is one of the main visual components involved in gendering a person, so anything that defies one clear expression tends to confuse folks; and confused folks very easily become annoyed. And we're still not accustomed to seeing visible body hair, so it does come as a shock to some. I suppose hairlessness and smoothness are one and the same when it comes to what's considered alluring. Many body products promote smooth, touchable skin as the main effect. Soft, smooth, silky, velvety are all adjectives to describe lovely skin, but "touchable" implies what all this work is for. Women are encouraged to be a pleasurable experience, to be touched, seen, felt, smelled— *consumable* in as many sensorial ways.

This way of conforming to femininity involves a gauntlet of hot wax, razors, lasers (all things within the selection of torture devices from an Indiana Jones or Bond film). Body hair is mostly politicized to affirm heteronormative gendering; its removal is so tied to femininity that men who remove their body hair are also subject to emasculating stigmas. The emotional connection of body hair to its relationship with femininity—from peach fuzz to rebellious stubble—remained mostly packed up and unquestioned until nowish.

The global hair removal industry was valued at $4.01 billion in 2019 and is projected to be at $4.94 billion come 2027 (unless there's another pandemic). I don't think *all* of that money is thrown begrudgingly at Big Razor—there is pleasure to be derived from self-smoothing as well. There are few treats of living in a body quite like stroking your own very smooth skin and feeling it as soft and silky as when you were born—whether this was a sentiment that Big Razor just happened to successfully capitalize on, or if it's a result of our widespread hairlessness boners, it's hard to say for sure. Not to get all Buffalo Bill on you, but it's very femmebot-core. There's nothing like that post–body scrub smooth, when you feel so slick, so aero- (and hydro-) dynamic. It's a personal indulgence, kind of like a tactile ASMR—just a weird little thing you can do with yourself that comforts and soothes. There is no shortage of ways to smooth your hairless hide, including gritty scrub bars, exfoliating washcloths, alpha- and beta-hydroxy acid body washes and lotions, body scrubs, and even outsourcing the chore to the pros.

Nothing will get you as smooth as inhumanely possible (and more acquainted with body hairstyles) like going to a Korean spa. Not like any spa, Korean spas (aka *jjimjilbang*) are an entirely different concept than what many Americans consider a spa to be. One of my favorite treatments is the full body scrub experience, in which a matronly figure[*] splashes you with buckets of warm water over your body like you're a beached whale in between going to absolute *town* on every crevice and inch of your body with nylon, scrubby exfoliating towels. I've scrubbed myself in the shower with these same exfoliating cloths and I do NOT get the same results as I get at the Korean spa, which are big, fat, gray eraser dust rolls pilling off my body—years of dead skin being

---

[*] In my experiences, it's always someone who looks like my grandmother wearing a black one-piece swimsuit, with superhuman upper-body strength.

sloughed from my body. It is as repulsive as it is cathartic. You'll be lying there, your limbs rearranged periodically like a mannequin, for a good forty-five minutes. You emerge an entirely new person, reborn from the keratin casing that your microbiome has been hoarding for years. This is how cats must feel in a patch of sunlight, I'm sure of it. When you're hanging out in the spa, pre-scrub, everyone around you is fully naked. The spa was the first place where I was able to witness pubic hair trends in real time and I was surprised to find that I was among the most *styled* with slight grow-out from a neatly waxed mons pubis. Everyone else was either full bush or semi-full. No one was bare and no one seemed to give a shit. I felt somehow even more naked than everyone else, and simultaneously fascinated and relieved that no one seemed to follow the implicit assignment of grooming your pubic area like hedges—neat, squared-off, trim. It's not like *only real women go full bush* or anything; of course, even *Sports Illustrated* models and porn stars are "real women." They just happen to be a small subsect of real live humans who are able to write off laser hair removal on their taxes.

Pubic hair seems to bear the brunt of cultural assumptions about expressions of natural sexuality the most. I guess the fact that we fuss over pubic hair so much is because hairiness implies uncleanliness, the same way hairy armpits imply smelliness—neither are necessarily correct. You can't escape being in a body by de-fuzzing it from the neck down, though that is often how it feels to stigmatize any traces of visible body hair—like you're trying to distance yourself from your body and its insistence on rewilding itself despite your repeat efforts to de-forest it. But however you choose to landscape your mons pubis, one thing I'd recommend is don't shave your crotch. There are too many folds! Your poor labia are way too vulnerable to an errant nick, and you do *not* want to be lacerating those bits. Also: ingrowns. One time, in college, I went to the student health center, thinking I had a genital wart or something and the nurse just asked, "Do you shave down there?" I nodded, hesitantly. "Yeah, that's just an ingrown hair. You really don't have to do that, you know. You're *supposed* to have hair there," she said, exasperatedly, as if she'd examined hundreds of neurotic girls' crotches with sus-looking ingrowns before.

Big Razor's days are fraught, however, as body hair becomes not only less objectionable, but a statement of self-expression. And I suppose in a culture that has long villainized body hair, it is. People are still going to be epilating and removing body hair, of course. It's a personal preference for some, thoroughly ingrained into our minds. Our culture's relaxing attitudes toward body hair and emphasis on body positivity are making it trickier for the brands hawking hair-removal products to know how to market them successfully. So far, they have pivoted to marketing the path of least offense: choice. It leaves the guesswork of why we're meant to be shaving up to us.

The few unicorn brands that have made a boon from direct-to-consumer shaving equipment find themselves in a bit of a marketing bind, eating their own words and spitting them back out, in an attempt to avoid body-shaming while encouraging people to be themselves, take pride in their natural bodies, but also to buy their razor (just in case that whole individual expression thing doesn't work out). Even the design is different from old-school razor brands, made rounder, more sensual, less threatening. Choice-based marketing is a convenient loophole to gesture an acquiescence of power to the individual while conveniently ignoring all the historical context and cultural hang-ups of why this is an issue in the first place. The personal choice becomes more about brand aesthetic than participation in the age-old practice.

Growing hair, like many of the body's natural functions, has been thoroughly stigmatized to the point where choice has less to do with a solution as removing the shame associated with body hair in the first place would be. Enjoying your own silky-smooth skin is one thing, but feeling inherent shame about anything that grows out of it makes being in that body a self-defeating existence. There are much kinder ways to be in a body without being constantly aggrieved of its business as usual.

The first time I tried sugaring*—an allegedly more merciful alternative to waxing—was at a beauty event. A few coworkers and I had been invited to a cocktail-waxing hour by a hair removal studio that had a newly opened salon, and they were offering complimentary treatments. We munched on charcuterie while the salon owners explained sugaring's superiority over waxing to us (something about it being less irritating to the skin).

One by one, we disappeared into the numbered treatment rooms. And when it was my turn, the woman who would be sugaring my pubes turned to me, bare-assed on an oversized baby-changing table, and perfunctorily asked, "Upper lip too?" (I said yes.) Few things make me blush but the shocking intimacy of having a stranger epilating your genitals, a violent service done gently, made me entirely too self-conscious about my bits. She chatted with me, bubbly and enthusiastic, talking me through the process. First things first, she took some clippers to my upper-most bush, trimming everything to a rippable length (is that a normal step for a professional bikini wax?). Nothing like the buzz of clippers grazing your nether region to make you immediately start stress-sweating. I don't know how someone so sweet and petite managed to be so absolutely vicious on the pull, but this woman yanked that wax (sorry, no—*sugar*) strip away from my body with the kind of professional ruthlessness of a priest performing an exorcism, or as if she'd just gone through her husband's phone, read all his texts, and discovered we were having an affair. I'm sorry, but sugaring's reputation eludes me. It is simply rebranded brutality, and as I'd learn in the next three weeks, makes you just as prone to ingrown hairs as well. I don't know how to describe the sensation of a newly shorn vulva other than

---

* The epilation treatment, not the hypergamic practice.

rare. I walked cowboy-style out of that salon and into the night with my newly smoothed coworkers, as we waddled off to our respective subway stations.

Having a bald crotch did nothing in terms of making me feel sexually more dynamic or anything, even though I felt like maybe it was supposed to? One memorable plot point on *Sex and the City,*[*] plus lip service from the most influential celebrities at the time (Gwyneth Paltrow, Naomi Campbell) gave Brazilians their glamorous appeal. This was not long after seven Brazilian sisters (The J Sisters—all their names started with J) opened their eponymous waxing salon in New York City's Midtown in the late eighties, bringing a bit of South American flair to our pubic grooming (and other places too, I'm sure). As pop culture became raunchier and more sexually explicit in the late nineties through the start of the new millennium, that area below the belt and above your actual genitals became a point of style and intrigue. Bikinis became skimpier and low-rise jeans were so scandalously low as if to imply the fact that one was fully waxed without flaunting it. That Brazilian culture is very comfortable with showing lots of skin and body-ody-ody gave the service a sexualized reputation.

Hair removal and its connections to sexuality are where the Venn diagram of beauty and shame overlap most broadly. It's also ironically where the *naturalness* we traditionally demand of innate beauty is rejected in favor of strict grooming. Nobody aside from yourself knows your intimate landscaping until intimate things are happening, so there's little to be self-conscious of until such an event occurs. I've always been aware that there's an expectation for women to be groomed, slicked bare, or nearly bare to present a manicured depiction of sexuality. No man has ever explicitly said to me that he expects me to be landscaped—but I've heard it often from other women who impressed

---

[*] "She took everything I got!"

upon me the importance of palatability, and how anything resembling a bush downstairs will potentially repulse our sexual partners.* Expectations for a specific sexual aesthetic somehow evade the shame that plagues sex itself, which should tip you off as to where that beauty belief stems from. It is so ingrained into us that we don't need to be told to discipline ourselves; we keep ourselves in line. I don't know how women's pubic hair gained such an unhygienic reputation that men's pubic hair seems to avoid, but this is the boneheaded misinformation we find ourselves fielding in pursuit of love (or lust). Luckily, anyone who has had the privilege of witnessing my personal grooming choices, or lack thereof, has had the good manners to never say anything disparaging of them. But a handful of my girlfriends have experienced this, which makes me believe that perhaps in some instances we need to bring back bullying some men.

Skin-to-skin contact is one of humanity's most primitive pleasures and comforts. Body hair can be a buffer or a textural indulgence, according to your tastes, which is perhaps the most innocuous way it can be viewed, removed from hygiene and cultural standards. But it's never innocuous. Body hair's reputation is determined by its presence. It bears the burden of expected gendered expressions, of being both feminist and anti-feminine; it's an indicator of masculinity in men and a rejection of femininity in women. It's an inherently political symbol of bodily autonomy and rejection of patriarchy; meanwhile it says a lot less about women themselves than our prevailing attitudes toward women and how we allow them to exist. And in the context of editorial coverage, the presence of body hair is especially confusing—it's rebellion against beauty standards by beauty's most conventional platforms. It always has to mean *something*.

Based on the outsized reactions my innocent little fuzzy pits still

---

* Also, something to consider: anyone who's grossed out by pubic hair, in general, will most likely be miserable at sex. Grow up!

elicit to this day, body hair remains triggering for most people. The idea that you can just *not* is very unsettling to anyone who's internalized Big Razor marketing as the truth about femininity. The fact that my armpit hair prompts vocal comments remains perplexing to me. I guess anyone opting to forego a socially obliged, hygienically perceived grooming habit (even though body hair is not any more unhygienic than the rest of your unwashed bod) reads as a refusal to conform to the gender role that's been assigned to you. And the world generally runs on everyone performing their assigned roles. (Although, this particular form of rebellion has an esteemed club with the likes of Sophia Loren, Madonna, Lisa Bonet, Grace Jones, Drew Barrymore, Miley Cyrus, Juliette Lewis, and Janelle Monáe as members at some point.)

There are so many objectionable behaviors of the human body (most of them olfactory-related, some fluid-related). That half the population (well, a little more than half) is tasked with fastidiously keeping themselves fuzz-free is bizarre, don't you think? Social trends come and go, but body-shaming is one of those funny things that can bear the brunt of criticism while still sticking around. Negotiating the contradictory rules of what is acceptable for women's bodies remains a timeless pursuit, I suppose. Everyone can rally behind reproductive rights and bodily autonomy while still grimacing at visible leg hair.

Let's say that leg hair became an in-fashion trend. Let's say the Kardashians (or celebrities of equally outsized influence) started sporting some upholstered shins. Let's say some people actually think leg hair on women is sexy, the same way some people find chest hair on men sexy. Would it then become something we were encouraged to groom and style, like the hair on your head—making sure it was soft, sleek, and evenly cut? It's not an unrealistic thing to wonder, considering how beauty trends evolve so quickly now (usually with their own caveats and quirks that may stray from one ideal while in possession of several others).

I have yet to wax my pit hair, as was originally intended with the grow-out ten years ago. My armpit hair isn't a statement, it's just a forgotten curiosity, one as taboo as the hair itself. It felt perverse to me at first because of what happens when you allow a part of yourself to grow out, unrestrained and uninhibited—a part that represents something so tied to femininity. I also gave up shaving my legs altogether after some adolescent trial runs—mostly because it turns out my legs just don't really grow that much hair.[*] Their downy fuzz is mostly detectable if you pet my shins backward. Whether you hate it or come to love it, body hair will always come back again; at some point it is worthwhile to get familiar with it.

Since I stopped routinely shaving it, I barely ever think about my armpit hair. But if someone else wants to, have at it; I'm not going to tell anyone how to waste their own time. Few people have ever commented personally, *to my face*, about my visible body hair (cowards!). Some people have said rude things on the internet or social media, and some people have said that seeing my armpit hair had caused them to grow out theirs just to see what would happen—and then they too realized they would not become a social pariah upon lifting their arms, and that by and large, nothing would change except their own relationships to their own bodies (and with razors). Shame and stigma are funny that way; there isn't always fire where there's smoke. Sometimes, when you separate yourself from shame-driven behavior and see stigmas for the lame, scaredy-cat bullshit they often are, you're rewarded with a kind of fearlessness and peace that cultivates confidence and poise—you know, all the stuff that Beauty™ encourages you to possess anyway.

---

[*] I might feel differently if they did, who knows?

EPILOGUE

Age Against the Machine

When it comes to saving face, beauty is so often our chosen savior as well as our adversary. I grew up being taught that beauty is something some people possess and some people don't, and those who dare to acquire any beauty greater than what they've been genetically dealt are vain, self-centered people who are not to be trusted, and are not very nice or probably very smart (well, those last bits are always more implied than explicitly stated, but folks love to talk their shit, don't they?). Seems . . . *a bit much*, yeah? Almost enough to make me wonder, why can't we get it together about beauty?

Vanity and beauty are at constant odds with one another by these terms. It took entirely too long for me to realize that a) that's not how beauty works, and b) what a total bummer to go through life in that binary. Vanity's stigma seems to be the most reinforced by people who live in constant negotiation of how their appearance determines their self-worth; it forms a barrier of shame and resentment between them and beauty. I will never get back all the time I've spent being self-conscious or discontent about the way I look, or the ways in which I *think* I need to optimize. Sometimes I think about all the things I might have accomplished in life by now were it not for vanity's time-sucking tentacles entwined around my cognitive function (even though I am aware of the irony that I've made a career out of it).

The Narcissus myth has never been more relevant; we're all swimming in our own reflections in the beauty fun house. It's far too easy to be drowned by the riptide of beauty culture's endless demands when you mistake any of it for a lifeline. What's Hot today is not guaranteed to be hot tomorrow. We've never tried to collectively evolve as a global culture in history because it's never actually been possible before. We've never had the same resources all at once before. We're reconciling so many incongruous interpretations of attitudes about beauty at once. And it's impossible for beauty to evolve without confronting its most uncomfortable truths about the status quo and standards that benefit some people while harming others. Not everyone's going to rally at once (wouldn't count on the ones on top). Have you ever tried to get a room of people to even agree on a place to eat? Impossible. Plus, nobody knows what's best and most meaningful for everyone—not even me.

Throughout the whole process of writing this book and my editorial career as well, the question that continuously swirls around my head is: *What is beauty for?* Exploring beauty's meaning is the only way I've been able to constructively engage with it. And that's definitely become more confusing to do with every new technological innovation, culture-sweeping trend, and aesthetic shift that makes beauty doubly as daunting as it may be exciting. I had my own personal stigmas to wrestle with, and a certain amount of indulgence was required to turn my theoretical ideas about beauty into actual lived experiences to reform them. And funnily enough, the closer I got to grasping my manicured mitts around some form of beauty ideal, the more I felt a bit removed from myself—someone hotter maybe, but it instilled in me a parallel kind of anxiety that my appearance would speak a bit too loudly for me and perhaps even misrepresent me. Not that it diminished any joy of transformation or evolution, but it also put them into perspective for me. The language of beauty is highly malleable; we communicate in it more than we think we do. But we also rely on its visual incarnation in ways that limit its full expression. Beauty is fun for brief spells but exhausting in ways that I often do not have the stamina to keep up with—not without a point of view. Hotness for hotness's sake is a bureaucratic engine, one that doesn't necessarily communicate who you are, or even anything resembling beauty, so much as it signifies a level of status, or at least an appearance of it.

Beauty culture's dystopian dilemma is that as we innovate wellness hacks and medical aesthetics, we are working to remove the barriers to a beauty culture that evades investigation into its side effects or even into the true underlying desires beneath it. Soon there will be no need to endure the social barnacles of a lacking appearance. Skincare products are getting more affordable, injectables more accessible, and the fat more easily shed with medicated discipline in the form of pharmaceutical workarounds. Beauty culture's trajectory appears to be hurtling toward a non-invasive homogeny, aesthetics without personal context. A beauty-pilled society doesn't have to reckon with the widening equality gap between the pretty and the so-called plain when we have more resources to build a bridge to the other side. Now we can all be gorgeous sociopaths.

I have to routinely remind myself to zoom out from Big Beauty's tractor beam every once in a while. When I clear my beauty cache, zero-out my inbox full of hundreds of daily PR emails announcing new beauty products, treatments, and trends I haven't even heard of yet, and log off from whatever whiplash trend that currently has beauty by the throat . . . I remember that none of this is permanent. You're not going to look this way forever, just like you're not going to feel this way forever—in fact, your feelings are liable to change way more frequently and faster than some hastily cut bangs will. The world is so much bigger and more complex than my feelings about my body. But the existing definitions of beauty standards can't be ignored—we all live by them, or despite them. And even now, we can examine them to a fault, pin down every treacherous angle, debunk all the false promises, reclaim our own dignity from the inherent shame-based principles, and *still* feel compelled to achieve them. Cognitive dissonance is a bitch.

Vanity comes for us all eventually (ominous) and that is how you can explore its limitations. You don't have to unravel beauty's complicated history to understand how it makes you feel. I've no doubt that everyone has similar stories of their past selves' iffy haircuts, frustrating trend experiments, and self-conscious conformity that went against your true desires (or perhaps eluded them). And when you look back on those photos, as I do mine, you may not recognize those people because you're not the same person you were back when overplucked eyebrows or a penchant for ponytail Bumpits were in. (It's hard to take beauty seriously when your false lashes flap away on a strong gust of wind.)

I think about beauty differently than I did in my teens and twenties, when I could function on four hours of sleep the night before and still have the kind of energy of a canned beverage in the morning. I took skin elasticity for granted and had yet to spot a gray hair (which are now gradually taking up residence around my temples). Now as I'm much closer to forty than I am to my twenties, my physical appearance might still betray my years in ways many people would consider advantageous, yet I notice changes all the time—changes that can only be the hallmark of time and gravity. They don't freak me out yet, but I suppose that is where a lot of my own preoccupations with deconstructing beauty culture come from—call it preventative care. My appearance may be very much the product of many occupational perks, but even they have their limits.

I put a lot of my optimism in how beauty's most redeeming feature is like art—at its core it eludes institutionalism, any singular cohesive interpretation, and as we've seen time and again, expectation. Just when you think you've got it figured out, it can still, and it will, surprise you. Beauty can be a tool for control just as much as it is an engine for liberation (or anarchy). There will always be those who use beauty for rebellion. Real beauty is always some organic amalgamation of unique imperfections shaped by lived experiences; it suggests a wealth of stories and personality. It has its own energy. Beauty's magnetism is a form of energy that is hard to describe but you know it when you feel it.

True beauty is hard to define, and I think it should stay that way. I mean, defining beauty so uniformly is how we got in this mess in the first place. So the only consistent beauty advice I can recommend is to mind your own business. Minding your own business is the most effective way to block the noise of everyone telling you how much better you could look, how to glow up, and what new thing you need for some reason. I mean, how many times have you totally been fine in relative ignorance until you learned all the intricate ways that you're not good enough? It's lies. Minding your own business frees you from the tyranny of *should*s. People who mind their own business and stay in their lane can find peace in embodying the choices they make for themselves—whether that involves even fucking around with beauty at all. Maybe it doesn't! Go with what excites, intrigues, and maybe even scares you—go with whatever makes you feel the most alive in the right now. Ephemerality is beauty's specialty, after all.

Beauty isn't the kind of thing that requires permission to access, nor is it something you owe to anyone. In fact, dispensing with the idea that your worth as a person is defined by any measure of beauty is a great relief. Even body positivity feels a bit too beauty-coded sometimes. *All bodies are beautiful* maintains that bodies still be defined by beauty—the thing that's causing all this angst about it to begin with. Beauty's darkest influence relies on our acquiescence to it, after all. Its methods shift to appeal to whatever is relevant in the moment, and this will go on until our economy picks another system that's a bit more chill about profits, or until we finally gain shape-shifting mutations, like in that *Outer Limits* episode where that dude grows jellyfish stingers and gills and stuff. Personally, I would love to have chromatophores that give me iridescent skin, or to be able to echolocate (how fun would it be to scream your way through the dark like some vocal GPS).

Reckoning our relationship to beauty, vanity, and the stigmas attached to both is an uncomfortable process. It's tedious as hell. There is nearly equal individual pressure to conform to new beauty ideals as there is judgment for resisting them. But consistent, incremental shifts in thought patterns lead to bigger social shifts when enough people do it. Thoughts like: Acknowledging someone else's beauty does not diminish your own. Comparison is the thief of joy. Nobody is truly symmetrical. "Flawless" is an unstable concept and likely fake news. Authenticity isn't found on an app. Wellness is not the same thing as health. And true empowerment cannot be injected, slathered on, or bought.

Vanity is only as useful as what it can reveal about yourself, behind the mirror. The fingerprints of your desires and your impulses are often written all over your body—makeup, scars, marks, and all. Vanity is a bit of a self-perpetuation myth. It's not like as soon as you're in the 1 percent of hotness, everything in life works out for you. Being hot does not offer immunity toward failure, illness, poor treatment, or poor self-esteem—but it can often grant second chances. Being hot won't stop your partner from cheating on you, but it might give you a bevy of rebound options. Being hot won't stop you from losing your job, but it may have opened lots of doors for you in the first place and will hereafter. Even for its perks and privileges, the benefits of hotness are capped—being hot won't stop you from dying.

Aging may be daunting, but not as daunting as a lot of the lengths people will go to resist it. Empowering oneself through beauty is a double-edged sword because beauty work is never-ending (the reward for good work is usually more work). The more that beauty stakes rise, the more we innovate ways to meet them—you can wear a full beat of face-"blurring" makeup to avoid the artifice of filters or get "preventive" Botox to delay the use of antiaging creams, but these semantics don't alleviate the pressures so much as they further invest in them. You'll never be done striving to fulfill beauty ideals that diminish the longer you live. You either jump ship at some point you decide or go down with it.

We're currently in beauty's most progressive evolution, one that promotes inclusivity, diversity, and a championing of individualism. It bears some celebration but with a bit of skepticism as well. "Empowerment" is one of those words that's been co-opted by marketing, trading in actual empowerment for the option to buy-in. If you're not intentional about it, the buy-in grants you access to the same prescriptive standards. After all, empowerment can't be bought or sold—true empowerment entails freedom from systems that rely on the oppression of some people to uplift others. Selling us products to help us become our authentic selves is a kind of wholesale "fake it till you make it." But it's never that easy, and not everyone makes it because not everyone feels empowered to be who they are, removed from beauty's ideals.

Acknowledging modern beauty's paradox does not make it any less thorny to know where to begin in disentangling ourselves from the doctrine of beauty—I mean, from a personal angle. The more rigidly we define beauty, the more it's degraded and limited. Beauty's subjectivity is too easily removed of context, especially because context complicates how we're able to access power through beauty. Power doesn't really benefit from context, and it makes everyone a lot less likely to extricate themselves from the systems they may be benefiting from. But if we're ever going to be collectively empowered or healed, that would involve an overhaul of how we engage in beauty wholesale. Beauty isn't a solution to the problems we've created; we are. That goes for lookism, the aesthetic pressures that exacerbate comparison and its self-defeating misery, our gendered socialization that make a woman's appearance her primary value, and the misinformation rife in our healthcare and wellness systems. It's a big task. Collective power is so rarely cultivated unless things are *dire* (and we're getting there). Just look at every major revolution in history—folks have got to be properly fed *up* before things get serious. And then it's guillotine time.

On the individual level, we can all start where we are—interrogating what we do and don't like about our appearance and where we learned that from, taking inventory of how much pleasure beauty brings us compared to how much misery, and recognizing what keeps drawing us back to it. Embodying your authentic self requires a sense of personal resilience and commitment to owning your life on your own terms (and taking the concept of "authenticity" with a grain of salt). You need a thick skin against the machinations of a beauty culture that would much prefer you volunteer your flesh for its gains.

Any time I talk to women who are significantly older than me, it's a totally different conversation from the kinds I have with peers. They're at ease with themselves in ways I suspect only time and maturity can grant. Most of them express how relieved they are to gain each subsequent decade. Beauty's commercial promises have less sway, probably because they've figured out that most of it is a scam, or probably because the abundance of life's years have given them so much more to live for. They know themselves better, they know how to mind their own business and stay in their lane, and they don't worry as much about what other people think about them.[*] It seems that in filling their lives with things they love doing, solid friendships and partnerships, as well as the accumulation of mundane errands that tends to creep up when busy living life, beauty doesn't feel as daunting as it may have in

---

[*] It's always a good idea to have friends younger and much older than you, I think; keeps the whole life span thing in perspective.

the past when we thought having it was the difference between living well and living without. It turns out there may very well be a statute of limitations on vanity's grip over your sense of self.

There's already so much cool stuff I've learned about myself the older I get—perhaps most useful the realization that "beauty rules" I thought applied to me don't actually apply to anyone. But even if they did, what are they gonna do about it, huh? There is no beauty police. (I told you shoplifting is a gateway to adopting a mentality of justified criminality.) Having visible wrinkles, crooked teeth, or those little chubby bits around your armpits that hang out over a tube top can only take up so much mental anguish in my mind before they just get boring to think about in the same way. Removing them or changing them doesn't make you think about them any differently—it's mostly proof of a concept that a flaw can disappear in one of those ways: from your body or from your mind. Embracing the impossibility and futility of perfection gives you more room to determine beauty on your own terms.

Working in the beauty industry seems like something that would have fundamentally altered me; honestly, given the resources I have access to, I should've had a whole new head and body by now. But I found that the more I explored the connections between beauty and vanity, the more I felt emboldened to explore different aspects of myself. It made me brave enough to dye my hair all different colors, to try treatments on a whim, to find a style that really feels like *me* (whoever that was at the time).

In the end, beauty brought me full circle back to a place not too dissimilar from how I was before I entered its matrix, but now I have a much broader perspective on how beauty is constructed and propagated. I've witnessed the puppet strings of marketing behind industry hype and wondered where all the money comes from (venture capitalists and generational wealth, most often). I've fallen for the hype and lived to *meh* another day. I've swatch-tested all manner of countless (truly infinite) products on my appendages, and that never gets old, but they are by and large a lot of the times the same.

It's helped steered me clear of its more toxic iterations, fortunately, and allowed me to probe what beauty does for me. I like having colorful, stripy hair. It makes me happy to see it in the mirror every day. I like wearing eyeliner far away from my actual eyes sometimes, and feral-looking eyebrows most of the time. I like decorating my face with those little pimple stickers that look like stars. I like leaving lipstick prints on coffee mugs and people's faces. I even like my chipped tooth now. And even though my adolescence was a challenging time for me with deodorant, now I love radiating scent (intentionally) far and wide. There is no inherent shame in taking pride in your appearance or wanting to look good, just as there's no shame in coming just as you are. That's something I was able to better shake off once I got clear on how I liked to present myself, without trying to fit into someone else's idea of what looks good or trying to conceal evidence of my own mortality. One of my favorite things is connecting with other people via beauty, whether that's fielding beauty-related questions or offloading the obscene amount of product samples I'm sent for my job onto appreciative friends who are so stoked to get to try all these fancy things that I'm all but burnt-out on. But I'm not done learning about beauty—or myself—yet.

So much about living revolves around being in a body and what it looks like. Being a person often gets confused for being a body. But you are not your body. Your body is simply an electrified meat vessel that houses your individual spirit—quirks, charms, neuroses, and all. It's resilient in many ways and vulnerable in so many others. But until we have the technology to transfer consciousness, treat it well because it's the only one you've got. To borrow a sentiment from philosopher and writer Gillian Rose, *There is no democracy in any love relation: only mercy.** I like to look at beauty this way as well (or self-love if that suits you better). Mercy and vengeance are two sides of a coin you can toss again and again. Where you cash it in is up to you.

---

*   Gillian Rose, *Love's Work* (New York: NYRB Classics, 2011).

Acknowledgments

First of all, I'd like to thank ME for doing the work. *Haha*, psyche, absolutely not—I'd like to apologize to me for writing this book, because this process just about melted my brain, which wasn't entirely solid to begin with. But this part isn't about me. This is about all the people who have had a part in making this book come into the world. (For more about me, turn to page 1.) Okay, time to get mushy.

Big, big thanks to my agent, Kate Childs, who works at a major fancy agency and took a chance on a total stranger over Zoom; thank you for believing in me and shepherding me into the big wide world of publishing. You have no idea what this has done for my ego. And, of course, huge thanks to Jenny Xu for introducing us. Yours is, to date, my favorite cold email I've ever received, and I'd be lucky to work with you again one day. Major gratitude to my editors Kate Napolitano and Anna Montague. Kate, from the moment we Zoomed, I could tell *she's the one!* You have a rare spirit that's able to harness chaos and make it sing bars, and I'm honored to be in your illustrious author net. And Anna, thank you for taking said chaos (my initial manuscript) and finessing it into what it is today—a marketable masterpiece (hopefully)!

My eggs: Alle, Kara, Marci, Rachel, Tynan—our friendship is the best thing I've ever received from writing on the internet. I cannot imagine better company with which to navigate this digital/analog world or a car accident (real or imagined). I look forward to the day we all live together Golden Girls–style in a big house with a pool and a sauna (we *will* use it, it's *not* too much work, it's worth it, trust me).

Thank you to Adrian, Dara, Jared, Lorenzo, Devon, Brett, and Scott for your continuous support, inspiring creativity, and friendship all these years (even though I'm bad at reaching out first, sorry!). Noah, thanks for always being my hype-man; I can only hope to live up to yours.

Thanks to Michelle Lee and Phillip Picardi who offered me a job without making me do an edit test, and my Condé Nast coworkers throughout the years—you guys were the best part of working in an increasingly ominous corporate environment. Thank you to all the editors I've worked with throughout my career who paid me on time. That's important.

Grace, my spirit guide, thanks to you, I look at the world in such expansive ways that most people would have to take a lot of drugs for, but I'm lucky that I have you to hold my hand through this lifetime. Mom and Dad, thanks for always buying me books, encouraging my creativity and art, and making sure that education would always be available. And my brother, Geoff, I'm so happy we've grown together, grown apart, and then together again, each time richer than the last. You'll always be my first and last friend (and bully and protector and foil and zombie apocalypse partner).

Thank you to all the cafes and restaurants that provided the coffee and pastries that fueled my brain with sugar to write. You are my lifeblood. And thank you to all the kind, smart, silly weirdos who give me optimism about not just beauty but everything else as well. And to everyone who subscribes to and reads my work—your support keeps me doing it, even though if I did not do it, I don't think you'd mind that either, which is totally fair but unfortunately will not stop me ;)

About the Author

Sable Yong is a person and writer from New York. She has written for the *New York Times, GQ, Vogue* (*Teen* and regular), *Elle, The Cut, Harper's Bazaar,* and more (you can google it) in between a stint as beauty editor at *Allure.* She is often mistaken for Sable Young (different person, not sure if they're a writer), so just, you know, maybe watch out for that.